Mirror for Magistrates

𝔐irror for 𝔐agistrates.

EDITED BY

JOSEPH HASLEWOOD.

VOLUME II. PART II.

LONDON:

PRINTED FOR

LACKINGTON, ALLEN, AND CO. FINSBURY SQUARE;

AND

LONGMAN, HURST, REES, ORME, AND BROWN, PATERNOSTER ROW.

1815.

[THE

Mirrour for Magistrates,

AS] A

WINTER

NIGHT'S

VISION:

Being an addition of svch Princes especially
famous, who were exempted in the
former Historie.

PART IV.

By RICHARD NICCOLS,

Oxon. Mag. Hall.

From the edition imprinted by Felix
Kyngston, 1610.

TO THE RIGHT HONO-

rable, *the Lord Charles Howard,*

Earle of Notingham, Baron of Ef-

fingham, Knight of the noble Order

of the Garter, Lord high Admirall of

England, Ireland and Wales, &c.

one of his Maiestie's most

Honorable priuie

Counsell.

As once that doue (true honor's aged lord)
Houering with wearied wings about your arke,
When Cadiz towers did fal beneath your sword,
To rest her selfe did single out that barke :
  So my meeke muse, from all that conquering rout,
Conducted through the sea's wilde wildernes
By your great selfe, to graue their names about
Th'Iberian pillars of Joue's Hercules :
  Most humblie craues your lordly lions aid
Gainst monster enuie, while she tels her storie
Of Britaine princes, and that royall maid,
In whose chaste hymne her *Clio* sings your glorie :
  Which if (great lord) you grant, my muse shall frame
Mirrours more worthie your renowned name.

> Your Honor's euer most hum-
> blie deuoted,
> RICHARD NICOLS.

TO THE READER.

CVRTEOVS Reader, before I enter into the discourse of what I haue written, I will acquaint you with the causes why I haue written. Hauing spent some truant houres in the study of this art, and willing to imploy my pen to the benefit of mine owne studies, and the profit and pleasure of others, I chanced in reading that worthy work, intituled, *The Mirrour for Magistrates,* to coniecture, if I should vndertake that imperfect historie, that not only experience, the mother of prudence, would furnish my priuate studies with better iudgement; but also that I could not better benefit others, by offering them a taste of the vnsauourie fruits of my labours; then by giuing them paternes to shun vice and follow vertue: in this coniecture my voluntarie will, not to do nothing, did set such edge vpon my desire, and the presidents of diuers learned, yea, some noble personages, pen-men of that worke, gaue me such encouragement, that though I wanted not iudgement to know, that I should want skill to compasse it; yet that want of skil, being supplied with good wil to do wel, I haue collected the liues of ten famous princes, worthie mirrours, omitted in the former part of this worke: which I present not in their proper places, as I did purpose, but as a part of themselues with dependancie vpon an Induction, that the reader may obserue that method of arguments before euery life, which I did intend to haue continued through the whole worke, if time and mine owne affaires would haue suffered me to proceed, but being called away by other employments, I must of force leaue it either vnto those, whose good opinion of so worthie an historie, may induce their endeuors towards the perfecting of the same, or vntil I shal find occasion hereafter to continue that, now almost finished, which I haue left vnaccomplished; of those ten, which I haue penned, the last, though it were written before in the former part, yet for that the matter and stile thereof were generally disliked of M. *Ferrers*, M. *Baldwine*, and others: and also for that many principall occurrents in the same were exempted, I haue written againe, placing it in his order, being the last of the ten. In the handling of which, not taking a poeticall licence to fashion all things after mine owne fancie, but limiting my selfe within the bounds of an historicall writer, I haue followed those authors, who in the censure of our best iudgements are the most authenticall. For the verse, I haue chosen the fourth proportion, which is the stanza of seuen, preferring it before the fift, which is the staffe of eight, because it is chiefly vsed of our ancient and best historicall poets; and though I confesse that of eight to hold better band, yet is it more tedious to a writer, being it binds him to the band of two foures intertangled, which if he obserue not, it is no huitaine or staffe of eight, but fals into the first proportion, making two qua-dreins. To the learned I only write, in whom is my chiefest hope, for that they be learned, a cause sufficient not to doubt any enuious construction, being a vice not proper to their good education: whom if I haue pleasured, I craue but their good word for my good will; if otherwise, their pardon for my paines. Farewell.

THE INDVCTION.

My muse, that mongst meane birds whilome, did waue her flaggie
    wing,
And cuckow-like of *Castœ's* wrongs, in rustick tunes did sing,
Now with the morne's cloud climing lark must mount a pitch more
    hie,
And like Ioue's bird with stedfast lookes outbraue the sunne's bright
    eie:
Yea she, that whilome begger-like her beggers ape did sing,
Which iniur'd by the guilt of time to light she durst not bring:
In stately-stile tragedian-like with sacred furie fed,
Must now record the tragicke deeds of great *Heroes* dead,
Vouchsafe then thou great king of heau'n, the heau'nly drops t'infuse
Of sacred iuyce into my pen, giue strength vnto my muse
To mount aloft with powerfull wings, and let her voice be strong,
That she may smite the golden starres with sound of her great song:
When Ioue-borne Phœbus fierie steeds about the world had bin,
And wearied with their yearely taske, had taken vp their inne
Farre in the south, when cold had nipt the hawthorne's rugged rinde,
And liuely sap of summer sweet, from blast of blustring winde
Had sunken downe into the roote, whose thornie browes besprent
With frostie dew, did hang their heads, and summer's losse lament;
My limbes benumb'd with vnkind cold, my life-blood waxing chill,
As was my wont I walked forth to ease me of such ill:
But when I came in fields abroad, and view'd the wastefull spight
Of wrathfull winter, grieu'd I was to see so sad a sight:
The shadie woods, in which the birds to build their neasts were seene,
Whose wauing heads in aire shot vp were crown'd with youthfull
    greene:

Now clad in coate of motlie hue did maske in poore array,
Rough Boreas with his blustering blasts had blowen their leaues away :
In stead of blossomes on the boughes, the spring whilome begun,
Which through the leaues did seeme to laugh vpon the summer's
    sunne,
Now nought but hoarie frost was seene, each branch teares downe
    did send,
Whose dewie drops on ysiccles vpon each bough depend :
The mistresse of the woods quaint quire, the warbling Philomele,
That wont to rauish with delight, th'inhabitants, that dwell
About the greene wood side, forgot the layes she sung before,
For griefe of summer's golden losse she now could sing no more :
And all the quire that wont with her to beare a part and sing
Concordant discords in sweet straine for welcome of the spring,
Sate silent on the frostie bow, and shuddering all for cold,
Did shroud the head beneath the wing, the day was waxed old,
None but the red-brest and the wren did sing the euen away,
And that in notes of sad record for summer's late decay :
The field, which whilome *Ceres* crown'd with golden eares of corne,
And all the pasture-springing meades, which *Pales* did adorne,
Lookt pale for woe, the winterie snow had couered all their greene,
Nought else vpon the grasselesse ground, but winter's waste was
    seene :
The shepheard's feeble flocke pent vp within the bounded fold,
So faint for food, that scarce their feete their bodies could vphold,
Did hang the head with heauie cheare, as they would learne to
    mourne
The thrall in which they now did liue, by shepheard left forlorne :
All sweet delight of summer past, cold winter's breath had blasted,
The sunne in heau'n shone pale on earth to see her wombe so wasted :
All which, as I grieu'd at such sight, the fields alone did range,
Did teach me know all things on earth were subiect vnto change :
How fond (me thought) were mortall men, the trustlesse stay to trust,
Of things on earth, since heere on earth all things returne to dust?

Who so in youth doth boast of strength, me thought the loftie oake
Would teach him that his strength must vade, when age begins to
      yoke
His youthfull necke, euen by it selfe, his leauie lockes being shed,
And branched armes shrunke vp with frost, as if they had been dead:
The louely lillie, that faire flower for beautie past compare,
Whom winter's cold keene breath had kill'd, and blasted all her
      faire,
Might teach the fairest vnder heau'n, that beautie's freshest greene
When spring of youth is spent, will vade, as it had neuer been;
The barren fields, which whilome flower'd as they would neuer fade,
Inricht with summer's golden gifts, which now been all decay'd,
Did shew in state there was no trust, in wealth no certaine stay,
One stormie blast of frowning chance could blow them all away;
Out of the yeares alternate course this lesson I did con,
In things on earth of most auaile assurance there was none:
But fancie feeding on these thoughts, as I alone did wend,
The clocke did strike, whose chime did tell the day was at an end;
The golden sunne, daies guide, was gone, and in his purple bed
Had laid him downe, the heau'ns about their azure curtaines spread,
And all the tapers lighted were, as t'were the watch to keepe,
Lest past her houre night should vsurpe, while he secure did sleepe:
Then clad in cloake of mistie fogges the darke night vp did come,
And with grim grislie looke did seeme to bid me get me home;
Home was I led, not as before with solace from the field,
The wofull waste of summer past had all my pleasure spill'd:
When home I came, nipt with sharpe cold of Boreas bitter aire,
After repast to my warme bed forthwith I made repaire,
Where, for the nights were tedious growen, and I disturb'd in mind·
With thoughts of that daies obiect scene, not vnto sleepe inclin'd,
I vp did sit, my backe behind the pillow soft did stay,
And call'd for light, with booke in hand to passe the time away;
Of which each line which I did reade, in nature did agree
With that true vse of things which I the day before did see

A Mírrour hight for Magistrates, for title it did beare,
In which by painfull pens, the fals of princes written were:
There, as in glasse, I did behold, what day before did show,
That beautie, strength, wealth, world's vaine pompe, and all to dust
      do go:
There did I see triumphant death beneath his feet tread downe
The state of kings, the purple robe, the scepter and the crowne:
Without respect with deadly dart all princes he did strike,
The vertuous and the vicious prince to him been both alike:
Nought else they leaue vntoucht of death except a vertuous name,
Which dies, if that the sacred nine eternize not the same :
Why then (ye thrice three borne of Ioue) why then be ye despis'd ?
Is vertue dead? hath daintie ease in her soft armes surpris'd
The manhood of the elder world ? hath rust of time deuour'd
Th'*Heröe's* stocke that on your heads such golden blessings showr'd ?
This silent night, when all things lie in lap of sweet repose,
Ye only wake, the powres of sleepe your eyes do neuer close,
To shew the sempiternitie, to which their names ye raise
On wings of your immortall verse that truly merit praise :
But where's the due of your desert, or where your learning's meed ?
Not only now the baser sprite, whom dunghill dust doth breed,
But they that boast themselues to be in honor's bosome borne,
Disdaine your wisdome, and do hold your sectaries in scorne :
No maruell then, me thought, it was, that in this booke I read,
So many a prince I found exempt, as if their names been dead,
Who for desert amongst the best a place might iustly claime :
But who can put on any spirit to memorize the name
Of any dead, whose thanklesse race t'whom learning shapes the leg
In humble wise, yet in contempt bids learned wits go beg ?
As thus in bed with booke in hand I sate contemplating,
The humorous night was waxed olde, still silence husht each thing,
The clocke chim'd twelue, to which as I with listning eares at-
      tend,
As signes of fraile mortalitie all things I apprehend;

The daylight past, as life I deeme, the night as death to come,
The clocke that chim'd, death's fatall knell, that call'd me to my
    doome,
Still silence rest from worldly cares, my bed the graue I thinke,
In which, with heart to heau'n vp-lift, at length I downe did sinke:
Where after still repose when as thin vapors had restrain'd
The mouing powers of common sense, and sleepe each sense enchain'd,
Whether the watchfull fantasie did now in sleepe restore
The species of things sensible, which I had seene before:
And so some dreame it only was, which I intend to tell,
Or vision sent I'le not discusse, to me it thus befell:
A sudden sound of trumpe I heard, whose blast so loud was blowne,
That in a trance I senselesse lay, fraile mortall there was none
That heard such sound, could sense retaine: my chamber wals did
    shake,
Vp flew the doores, a voice I heard, which thus distinctly spake:
"Awake from sleepe, lift vp thy head, and be no whit dismai'd,
I serue the deities of heau'n, their hests must be obei'd,
And now am sent from her that keepes the store-house of the mind:
The mother of the muses nine, for thee she hath assign'd
For her designe, the night to come in sleepe thou must not spend:
Prepare thy selfe, that gainst she come, her will thou maist attend."
As to these words I listning lay, and had resumed spright,
I boldly looked round about, and loe, there stood in sight
True fame, the trumpeter of heau'n, that doth desire inflame
To glorious deeds, and by her power eternifies the name:
A golden trumpe her right hand held, which when she list to sound,
Can smite the starres of heau'n, and bring the dead from vnder
    ground:
Vpon her head a chaplet stood of neuer vading greene,
Which honor gaue, to giue to them that fauour'd of her been:
Her wings were white as snow, with which she compast heau'n and
    earth
With names of such, whom honor did renowne for deeds of worth;

As I beheld her princely port, yet trembling alt for feare,
A sound of heau'nly harmony did pierce my pleased eare,
In rapture of whose sweet delight, as I did rauisht lie,
The goddesse dread whom fame forespoke did stand before mine eie,
The ladie of mount Helicon, the great Pierian dame,
From whom the learned sisters nine deriue their birth and name,
In golden garments clad she was, which time can neuer weare,
Nor fretting moth consume the same, which did embroydered beare
The acts of old *Heröes* dead, set downe in stately verse,
Which sitting by the horse-foot spring, Ioue's daughters did
    rehearse:
Fiue damsels did attend on her, who with such wondrous skill
Do in their seuerall functions worke, to serue their ladie's will,
That what she seekes on earth, to see, to heare, smell, taste or touch,
They can present the same with speed, their power and skill are
    such:
As in amazement at such sight I in my bed did lie,
She thus bespake: " I am," quoth she, " the ladie Memorie,
Ioue's welbelou'd Mnemosyne, that keepes the wealthie store
Of time's rich treasure, where the deeds that haue been done of yore
I do record, and when in bookes I chance to find the fame
Of any after death decai'd, I do reuiue the same:
Turning the volume large of late, in which my *Clio* sings
The deeds of worthie Britaines dead, I find that many kings
Exempted are, whose noble acts deserue eternitie,
And mongst our Mirrours challenge place for all posteritie:
For which, my station I haue left, and now am come to thee,
This night thou must abandon sleepe, my pen-man thou must bee."
To this said I: " O goddesse great, the taske thou dost impose
Exceeds the compasse of my skill, t'is fitter farre for those,
Whose pens sweet nectar do distill, to whom the power is giuen
Vpon their winged verse to rap their readers vp to heau'n:
The pinions of my humble muse be all too weake to flie
So large a flight; theirs be this taske that loue to soare on high:

But how can they such taske vp-take, that in a stately straine
Haue rais'd the dead out of the dust; yet after all their paine, ¹
When their sweet muse in vertue's praise hath powred out their
　　store,
Are still despis'd and doom'd for aye with vertue to be poore."
To this, "alas," quoth Memorie, "it grieucs me to behold
The learned wits left all forlorne, t'whom whilome it was told
Mæcenas was reuiu'd againe: yet grieue I more to see
The loathed lozell to prophane that sacred mysterie:
Each vulgar wit, that what it is, could neuer yet define,
In ragged rimes with lips profane, will call the learned nine
To helpe him vtter forth the spawne of his vnfruitfull braine,
Which makes our peerelesse poesie to be in such disdaine,
That now it skils not whether Pan do pipe, or Phœbus play,
Tom Tinkar makes best harmonie to passe the time away:
For this I grieue, for this the seed of Ioue are held in scorne,
Yet not for this our worthies dead are to be left forlorne:
For so no future age should know the truth of things forepast,
The names of their forefathers dead would in the dust be cast:
Then do not thou thy helpe denie, I will conduct thy pen,
And fame shall summon vp the ghosts of all those worthie men,
That mongst our Mirrours are not found, that each one orderly
May come to thee, to tell the truth of his sad tragedie."
Thus hauing said, she tooke the booke from vnderneath my head,
And turning ore the leaues, at last, she thus began to reade.

THE FAMOVS LIFE AND

Death of King Arthvr.

THE ARGUMENT.

THE first I find exempted in our storie
Is noble *Arthur*, Albion's ancient glorie,
Who heere at home subdues the Saxon kings:
Then forren nations in subiection brings,
The Roman host with *Lucius* for their guide
To his victorious sword do stoope their pride:
But home-bred broiles call backe the conquering king,
Warres thunder 'bout the Britaine coasts doth ring,
Gawin's firme loyaltie at his last breath,
Arthur's last conquest, wounds and timelesse death,
The truth of which, that we may heare, let fame
Summon his ghost to come and tell the same.

ANOTHER ARGUMENT.

Fame sounds her trumpe, king *Arthur* doth ascend
Tels *Mordred's* treason, death, and his owne end.

1.

No age hath bin, since nature first began
To worke Ioue's wonders, but hath left behind
Some deeds of praise for Mirrours vnto man,
Which more then threatful lawes in men inclind,
To tread the paths of praise excites the mind,
 Mirrours tie thoughts to vertues due respects,
 Examples hasten deeds to good effects.

2.

'Mongst whom, that I my storie so renown'd
May for a Mirrour to the world commend,
Summon'd the first by fame's shrill trumpets sound:
Loe, 1 am come on earth to find a friend,
Who his assistance vnto me may lend,
 And with his pen paint out my historie
 A perfect Mirrour of true maiestie.

3.

In which the truth of my corrupted storie,
Defac'd by fleeting time's inconstant pen
I will declare, nor to aduance my glorie
Will I present vnto the view of men
Ought, but the scope of what the truth hath ben:
  Meane time thou pen-man of Mnemosynie,
  Giue heedfull eare vnto my tragedie.

4.

As from aire-threatning tops of cedars tall
The leaues, that whilome were so fresh and greene,
In healthlesse autumne to the ground do fall,
And others in their roomes at spring are seene:
So proudest states amongst the states of men
  Now mount the loftie top of fortune's wheele,
  Now fall againe, now firmely stand, now reele.

5.

Foure times the state of this same noble Ile
Hath changed been by froward fate's decree,
And on foure nations fortune's front did smile,
Graciug thir high attempts with victorie
Ouer this empire of Great Britanie:
  Yet none but one the scepter long did sway,
  Whose conquering name endures vntill this day.

6.

First the proud Roman *Cæsar* did oppresse
This land with tributarie seruitude:
Next those two Saxon brethren heauen did blesse,
Who in our Brittish blood their blades imbru'd,
And to their lordly will this land subdu'd:
  Thirdly the Dane did heere long time remaine,
  And lastly Normans ouer vs did raigne.

7.

Thus seest thou fortune's vnimpeached force,
And what it hath been in our Britaine state:
By this thou seest her wheeles inconstant course,
And how on earth nor prince, nor potentate,
Can long withstand her ruine-thirsting hate,
    Which my true storie's sad catastrophe
    Vnto the sonnes of men can testifie.

8.

I am that *Arthur*, who on honor's wing
Did mount fame's palace 'mongst the worthies nine
Fourth from false *Vortigerne* th'vsurping king:
Who, that he might with strong allies combine
His shaken state, which then began decline,
    Wretch that he was into this land did bring
    The Saxons with hight *Hengist* their false king.

9.

The sonne I was of *Vter* that stout knight,
Pendragon called for his policie,
Not in ignoble birth brought forth to light,
Though foes false imputation vilifie
My royall birth with taint of bastardie:
    But in true wedlocke's bands a noble dame
    Bore me, the fruit of loue without defame.

10.

Whose former husband *Goilen*, that proud duke,
At Duuilioc in fight my sire strooke dead:
And 'mongst his spoiles *Igren* the faire he tooke,
With whom he did ascend loue's amorous bed
And lest the fruit of his delight new bred
    The time might turne to shame in lawlesse birth,
    He took the dame to wife, who brought me forth.

11.

By peeres consent 1 in my youth began
Vpon the throne the supreame sway to beare :
And at that time against the boldest man,
That breath'd on earth my spirit did not feare,
In single fight the combatant t'appeare,
  Skilfull I was in knowledge of all fights,
  That then was vsed amongst martiall knights.

12.

And at that time my close-neere fighting men,
The frame of euery bloodie fight to know,
In martiall feates, haue exercised been,
And euery one would 'gainst the forren foe,
With emulation striue their deeds to show,
  In courts where kings, adore *Bellonae's* shrine,
  There the bright blaze of chiualrie will shine.

13.

Vpon the mind, whose glorie-thirsting heart,
By deedes of armes did at true honor aime,
Such edge I set, that from each forren part,
The brood of Mars to Britaine's *Arthur* came,
Of him to purchase the reward of fame :
  And take that order, that I then did found,
  Which till this day men call the table round.

14.

Vpon this table's superficiall part
Statutes ingrauen were by my decree,
Vnto the which each man of valiant hart,
That of this famous fellowship would bee
At Camelot by oath did first agree,
  And call'd they were amongst our chiualrie
  Armes, seuen religious deeds of charitie.

15.

But where is now this honor'd dignitie,
That wont to be the care of noble kind?
Or is it dead, or will nobilitie
Let that, which only was to it assign'd,
 Be now polluted by the baser mind?
    Alas the while, that once the best reward
    To vertuous deeds is now of no regard.

16.

No golden churle, no elbow-vanting Iacke,
No peasant base, nor borne of dunghill mould,
Could find such treasure in his pedler's packe
To purchase that, which fame on high did hold
For true desart, aboue the reach of gold:
    This order then dame vertue kept in store
    For such, as did her sacred selfe adore.

17.

In this new flourish of my flowring spring,
When honor's hopefull buds appear'd in mee,
And promis'd goodly fruit in time to bring,
My forward thoughts being set on fier, to free
My natiue land from Saxon tyrannie:
    With phantasie still working 'gainst the foe,
    In sleepe this spectacle to me did show.

18.

As I (me thought) did sit on royall throne
With peeres about me set, a ladie faire
In presence came and making pitious mone,
Tearing the tresses of her golden haire,
And wringing both her hands, as if despaire
    Had her bereft of hope her griefe to show,
    With teares did vtter forth these words of woe

19.

" Behold," quoth she, " behold me wretched wight,
The forlorne ladie of this noble Ile,
From towring state cast downe by foes despight,
And of an empresse, which I was ere while,
Of Saxon yoke now made a subiect vile :
 What bootes it what I was, sith now I am
 The scorne of fortune and the Briton's shame ?

2

O, noble prince, vnsheath thy conquering blade
And saue that little, which is left to mee,
Left not for aye my antient glorie vade,
Nor let me subiect liue, as thus you see,
To pride of barbarous foes, but set me free :"
 Thus ended she her plaint, and in sad plight
 With piteous lookes departed from my sight.

21.

The phantasie presenting euerie howre
Th'apperance of such thoughts did so excite
My furie 'gainst the foe, that all my powre
I muster'd for the field, and *Howel,* hight
Of litle Brittaine prince, a valiant knight,
 Allide to me by blood, did crosse the maine
 To purchase honor with his martiall traine.

22.

Here could I sing the deeds of warre to thee,
Whereby my famous conquests thou should know,
How beauen did grace me with such victorie,
That in twelue battailes I did ouerthrow
The mightie forces of my warlike foe :
 And by my valor, how I did expell
 Those Saxon foes, which here long time did dwell.

23.

Hight *Colgrim* greatest amongst Saxon kings
I first subdu'd with honour'd victorie,
But happie he vpon the wind-like wings
Of hastie speed to saue himselfe did flie
Ouer the seas broad backe to Germanie:
 Yet could he not escape vntimely death,
 But here in Britaine breath'd he his last breath.

24.

Vnto his friends, when he in safetie came,
He could not shun th'edict of destinie:
But backt by them he proudly did proclame
T'inferre swift vengeance on our Britannie,
If he were not restor'd to dignitie:
 Which I disdain'd and did prepare for fight:
 Because to that he claim'd he had no right.

25.

And in a faire field by those bathes apart,
Which *Bladud* sometimes king of Britanie
Had founded by the depth of powerfull art,
My tents I pight: for there did fates decree,
That great king *Colgrim's* ouerthrow should bee:
 Whose mightie force my folke at first did dread,
 Which by three kings was in Battalia led.

26.

For first did *Bladulf* brother to this king,
Conduct the vaunt gard for this valiancie,
Next *Chelderick* vnto the field did bring
His Germaine powers, the strokes of death to trie,
Who was a mightie prince in Germanie,
 And in the rereward *Colgrim's* selfe did lead
 The Picts to fight, a people full of dread.

27.

The battailes ioin'd, each aduerse part opposde
Their strength to strength, the aire with dreadfull sound
Of souldier's shouts did echo as they closde,
And each one equallie gaue wound for wound ,
Till with the foes fresh strength, which did abound,
  My men opprest to flight began to fall,
  Whom thus with mouing words I did recall.

28.

" Yee emptie harted sonnes of *Brute*," quoth I,
" Not worthie valiant *Brutus* farre-spred name,
What great defame of your big formes will flie
Throughout this world's whole round, if this great shame
Of shamefull flight, yee doe not streight reclaime ?
  Where will ye boldly fight and scorne recoile,
  If not in fight for your owne natiue soyle ?

29.

Are these th'effects of those same glorious words,
With which of late your tongues did oft abound,
Saying one hundred with their powerfull swords
A thousand hartlesse foemen should confound,
To your owne shame, alas, this shall redown'd,
  Vnlesse with speed ye turne couragious hed,
  And make them flie from whom yee lately fled."

30.

All th'host applauding my high valiancie
With deepe impression of my words being driuen,
Did break into the midst of th'enemie,
Where cuffe for cuffe on either side was giuen,
The noise of which flew ecchoing vp to heauen,
  And with the thunder claps of clashing armes
  Made aire to sigh with sound of humane armes.

31.

The skirmish burn'd, both parts did equall beare
Their heads aloft in this daye's bloodie fight,
All stood it out, none stoopt to seruile feare,
Their swords made mutuall wounds, and in their sight
Their friends each where in field lay reft of light:
   The earth made drunke with blood did then abound,
   With fruites of death thick strow'd vpon the ground.

32.

But when the trampling steedes of heauen's bright sun
Fell to the seas and left Olympus steepe,
And when the king of flames began to run
His golden head into the wauie deep,
When out of east bright Venus gan to peep,
   Our strength increast, which conquest did diuine,
   Our foes shrunke back, their valor did decline.

33.

For when king *Colgrim* by my launce strook dead,
And *Bladuff* by my power cast downe as low,
With their gigantike bulkes the earth did spread,
The foes with one consent their backes did show,
To saue each other in that common woe:
   With whom hight *Cheldrike* fled, who for the spoile
   Of this our land had left his natiue soile.

34.

Who being shrouded with the night's black wing,
Trusting that she would his designements hide,
Tooke towards the marrin strand, in hope to bring
His folk disperst, in darknesse vndescride,
Vnto his ships, which then at shore did ride:
   But death betwixt them and their nauie stood,
   Our natiue earth drunk vp their stranger blood.

35.

The stout duke *Cador*, that illustrate knight,
Pursu'd the flier till the rising sun
Descride the foes, who turning from their flight,
Both parts stood firme, the fight afresh begun :
But *Cheldrik* lost, the conquest *Cador* wonne,
   Whose spoilfull sword did spare no foes in death,
   For *Cheldrick's* self did there expire his breath.

36.

Meane time to rescue that bold Britaine king,
Prince *Howell*, king of little Britanie,
Who ore the gulfie flood his folke did bring,
T'assist vs gainst our common enemie :
Towards Scotland's bounds wee marched speedilie,
   Where gainst the barbarous Picts he was the barre,
   While gainst the Saxon we did wage the warre.

37.

But he vnable to sustaine their force,
Which th'Irish *Guillamore*, th'assistant king,
In person did support with foote and horse,
Of whose alarmes the countrie round did ring,
Did send to vs requiring vs to bring
   Our powers, with expedition to suppresse
   The foe's haut pride, and succour his distresse.

38.

Of which when I did heare, as from the skie
A tempest stooping on the deepe's profound,
Hurles waues on waues in heapes, and makes them flie
Before his rage, so with the horrid sound
Of dreadfull warre into the Pictish bound
   I entred with my host, and in the way
   For fire and sword made all the passage pray.

39.

The foe's stout pride we did in field subdue,
And *Gwillamore*, that did escape the fight,
To his owne kingdome's bounds we did pursue,
Where we did bring him to his heart's despight,
Vpon his knees by warre's impulsiue might,
 Forcing him yeeld obedience to our crowne,
 By golden tribute yearely paid vs downe.

40.

After this good successe, perceiuing well,
That heauen with sunshine lookes grac'd our affaires,
My hopefull heart with glorie gan to swell,
Bidding me seeke by fame in forren warres,
To fixe my name amongst the golden starres,
 And leaue a name on earth to liue for aye,
 When rapt in mould my limbes forgotten lay.

41.

This stout suggestion of my mightie mind,
Made me despise foule ease and pleasures light,
Which softens th'heart, strikes strong desier blind,
Drownes all eternitie in depth of night,
And leaues reproch for prise of such delight :
 For fame liues not, except for vertue's merit,
 Deeds of delite on earth no place inherit.

42.

A king, that only liues a king in name,
That dull'd with ease and drown'd in fancie's lust,
Can stile his title with no deed of fame,
Being dead, his name iron-eating time shall rust
And in the end obscure it in the dust,
 When he, though meane, that vertue's race doth runne,
 Doth liue eterniz'd like th'immortall sunne.

43.

This was the winde that set my ships on saile,
In forren shoares true honor to obtaine,
This was the prize, for which with prosperous gaile,
I plow'd my passage through the liquid maine
Vnto the Arctike pole, where *Charles* his waine
  Fixt fast in heauen, his station there doth keepe
  With other starres neare diuing to the deepe.

44.

And there in that cold iland Island call'd,
Whose mountaines with high heads did heauen aspire,
Which white with snow as if they had been bald
Did yet breath forth blacke smoakes and burning fire,
A wonder strange for humaine sense t'admire,
  I with my Britaines bold bore to the Strand
  And vncontrol'd march't vp into the land.

45.

Whose people rude and liuing in their kind,
As beasts that wander in the desert field,
The rationall and best part of the mind
In vse of heauenly things not being skill'd
Against blind ignorance the soule to shield,
  We did in fight subdue, and by strong hand
  Did them enforce to stoope to our command.

46.

Their king *Maluasius* noting well the oddes
Twixt vs and them in feats of martiall skill,
And finding, that no place of safe abodes
Was left to him, in feare of future ill
Did soone submit himselfe vnto our will,
  And from that time vnto my name's renowne
  Did yeeld obedience to the Britaine crowne.

47.

The fame of this exploit being set on wing,
And through the iles adiacent taking flight,
Doldauius of the Gotland nation king,
And great *Gunfacius* king of Orkney hight
Despairing to oppose our force in fight,
　　Did yeeld to hold their crownes and dignitie
　　By tribute to the Britaine emperie.

48.

But should I vnto light assay to bring
Each fight then fought and euery deed of worth,
Had I the strength of thousand tongues to sing,
Or the shrill trumpe of fame to echo forth
My conquests, in those ilands of the north,
　　Yet would the glasse of time be quite outrun
　　Before that true report her part had done.

49.

Should I relate the many a field I fought
Against *Aschillius* that bold Danish king,
And 'gainst proud *Lot* the Norway king so stout,
Whom after thousand soules being set on wing,
We at the length did in subiection bring :
　　Scarce would the eares of fraile mortalitie
　　Giue credit to our noble historie.

50.

Yet thinke, what dread of death and dangerous wounds
We in those trauels then might vndergoe,
From Albion's rockes vnto the Russian bounds,
And our great conquest 'gainst the northren foe,
The fame of our admir'd exploits will show :
　　For to the Lap-land kingdome's vtmost end,
　　Our Britaine empire's bounds I did extend.

51.

In deeds of fame, thus did I spend the prime
Of goden youth, which lul'd in pleasure's bed,
Flies fast away vpon the wings of time,
And scarce is knowne t'haue bin, when th'hoarie hed
With white of wintrie age is ouerspred :
   For age with shame of youth's fond deeds strooke blind,
   Doth oft abhorre to beare the same in mind.

52.

Who doth to sloth his yonger daies ingage
For fond delight, he clips the wings of fame :
For sloth the canker-worme of honor's badge.
Fame's fethered wings doth fret, burying the name
Of vertue's worth in dust of dunghill shame,
   Whom action out of dust to light doth bring
   And makes her mount to heauen with golden wing.

53.

After my high atchieuements in the north
I being returned to my natiue land,
Fame through the world did so renowne the worth
Of these deeds done by my victorious hand,
That greatest kings did in amazement stand,
   Strooke blind in looking at the sunshine blaze
   Of my great worth, yet enuying at my praise.

54.

For when true vertue's glorious excellence,
Mounts vp aloft, and like the sun in skies,
Breakes through the clouds of darkesome ignorance,
Then enuie rous'd from her darke den doth rise,
And dazel'd with the golden shine, that flies
   From vertue's splendor, seekes t'obscure the same,
   And muffle it in her blacke clouds of shame.

55.

That enuious beast of twice fiue hornes of might,
Who ore the world did long time tyrannize,
From Rome's high towres viewing the golden light
Of my great fame, which dazled her weake eies,
Selfe swolne with haughtie pride, rows'd vp did rise,
   And at my state with her proud hornes did push,
   In hope my fame being yet but yong to crush.

56.

The Roman king that bore great *Cæsar's* name,
Twelue aged sires in senate did select,
Men of renowne and all of noble fame,
Who as graue legats his great will t'effect,
Through Neptune's wauie empire did direct
   Their course to our sea-bounded Britanie,
   To menace vs with their proud ambasie.

57.

Where when they came, seeing our court abound,
With honor's sonnes emploi'd in deeds of fame,
Not in still waues of court-deepe pleasures drown'd:
For vse in deeds of armes and martiall game
Exiling sloth the pride of lust doth tame:
   They thought their antique Romane emperie,
   Had been transferr'd from Rome to Britȧnie.

58.

Yet getting audience one amongst the rest,
With graue demeanor and great maiestie,
Thinking with words our greatnesse t'haue represt,
Began t'infold with high authoritie,
The thundring threatnings of his ambasie:
   For he vnbidden boldly tooke his place,
   And thus did threaten me vnto my face.

59.

" *Arthur*," said he, " from ample-streeted Rome
Where mightie *Cæsar* thy liege lord doth reigne
T'effect his will, to thee, loe, we are come,
And in his name to claime our right againe,
Which wrongfullie from vs thou dost detaine :
    For long time since ye Britaines well do know
    That Britanie to Rome did tribute owe.

60.

He doth dislike thy farre commanding minde,
Nor thy proud bold attempts will he allowe
In any thing, by him not being design'd,
By vs he bids thy haughtie stomack bowe
Vnto the bending of his kinglie browe,
    And wils thy kingdom stoop, though so renown'd,
    To Rome, the mistris of the world's wide round.

61.

But if thy hart do harbor haughtie pride,
And that thy people still stiffnecked bee,
If that our words in scorne thou set aside,
Then to thy face I here do threaten thee,
That ere thine eyes one summer more shall see,
    More troopes of men gainst thee we will imploie
    Then erst did Greekes against the sonnes of Troy."

62.

This threatning speech did set my thoughts on fire,
And made me to returne this sharpe replie :
" Doting old wretch," said I, " thou dost aspire
In vaine by vanting words to terrifie
The hart of him that scornes thy ambasie,
    Nor can our person patiently permit
    Those barbarous taunts, signes of thy doting wit.

63.

Do Romaines harbor such a base conceit
That Britain's *Arthur* is of lesse renowne
Then is their king, in empire, though so great?
Or that vsurping *Cæsar* with a frowne
Can make vs yeeld the title of our crowne?
    O sillie sots to thinke vs such a sort
    As your base speeches whilom did import.

64.

Is not our noble nation by descent
Sprung from the warlike Troian's roiall race?
And shall our thoughts be then so baselie bent,
As with subiection seruilie t'embrace
The yoke of loftie Rome the world's disgrace?
    Her fame shall fall, our Britaine state shall rise,
    She ore the world no more shall tyrannize.

65.

With swiftest speed returne thou this replie,
That we a people free will still maintaine
'Gainst all the world our ancient libertie,
And that thou well maist know how wee disdaine
The seruile yoke of Rome's insulting reigne,
    Ile bring reuenge, which Rome shall neuer shun
    For that great scath which *Cæsar* here hath done."

66.

This said, they all amaz'd at my replie
Dismist, made no abode in this our land:
But with winde-winged sailes did swiftly flie
Ouer the depths of Neptune's high command,
Of whom their *Cæsar* soone did vnderstand
    How his command with scorne we did deride,
    In tempting our disdaine with such vaine pride,

67.

A which inrag'd, he in a fatall houre
The tribune *Lucius* for the warre design'd,
Who into France came downe with all his power,
Where many legionaries he did finde
Vnto that quarter of the world assign'd,.
　To keepe it peacefull by warr's threatfull stroke,
　Which then began to shake off Roman yoke.

68.

And as he did prepare to greedie fight,
So did we arme vnto the bloodie field
And from each quarter of our land did cite
All such as able were with strength to wield
Or launce, or bowe, or dart, or sword and shield,
　Whom we did muster vp in armes well dight
　To make them apt and skilfull for the fight.

69.

And in our absence in those forren warres,
To guard our state against all aduerse feare,
We left at home to manage all affaires,
Mordred the brother of my *Gawin* deare,
Our faithlesse nephew, that false hearted peere,
　Th'ignoble sonne of *Loth* the Pictish king:
　From whose blacke treason my sad fall did spring.

70.

Whose loyaltie I little did suspect,
Though on my death his hopes did then depend:
But who so wise hath been that can detect
The meanes and houre, by which the fates intend
To mortall life to adde the finall end?
　Though both the meanes and houre most certaine bee,
　Yet most vncertaine is the time's decree.

71.

But being most secure of future chance,
My thoughts to meete the foes being set on wing,
Who did ordaine, that Augustence in France
Should be the place for each assistant king,
Vnto the Romane aid their powers to bring:
　　With warre's loud trumpe from all parts of the land,
　　I call'd my Britaines downe vnto the strand.

72.

Where our blacke barkes all readie furnish't lay,
In which departing from the barren shore,
Wing'd with full gale, the ships did force their way,
So swiftly with their bending bulkes before,
That 'bout their brests the giuing waues did rore,
　　Through which we kept our course without mischance,
　　And did at Harflew safe arriue in France.

73.

Where thousands troop't in armes the shoares did show
Sent from those princes by alleageance bound,
T'assist vs in our warres against the foe,
Who when our feet did presse the sandie ground,
Did welcome our approch with shouts loud sound:
　　In euery place *Bellona* loud did sing,
　　Of horse and foot the countrie round did ring.

74.

Our powers being ioyn'd and euerie seuerall band
Digested for the fight, without delay
We marched from the salt sea's slimie strand,
And sent our scouts before vs in the way,
To know where *Lucius* host encamped lay:
　　But hearing nought we forward did aduance,
　　Vntill we came to Augustence in France.

75.

And there vpon a chosen plot of gronnd
The Roman host with their especiall aides
Arm'd in strong steele for fight prepar'd we found,
The blaze of whose bright shields and glittering blades,
Did cast a sunshine in the darkest shades:
  With whom we thought t'haue then begun the fight,
  Had setting sun not shew'd approching night.

76.

But when from vnderneath the siluer vaile
Of Thetis lap Apollo did arise,
And to the batlements of beau'n exhale
Night's dewie drops, which fell before from skies,
Our bands t'applie for fight we did deuise,
  And euerie one did buckle to the field,
  Thirsting to bloodie fight their strength to yeild.

77.

Then did the trumpet shrill sound out alowd
To bring them bold to the insatiate field,
And on the plaine both parts in thickest crowd
Opposing sword to sword and shield to shield,
Not fear'd with death, but with stout conrage fild,
  Began the fight, and none their backs did turne,
  In euerie place the skirmish hot did burne.

78.

But where the kinglie eagle Ioue's faire bird
Great *Cæsar's* standard did maintaine the fight,
There both on horse and foote the slaughtering sword
Made greatest hauock, where with most affright
To my bold Britons, *Lucius*, that stout knight,
  Did beate the field or turning troops of men,
  As if the battaile onlie there had ben.

79.

Which when I heard, with my victorious lance
Thirsting to do where deeds of worth were done,
I towards that part my standard did aduance,
The virgin mother of great Ioue's owne sonne,
Vnder whose badge I many a field had wonne,
　　Where 'mongst the foes I rusht with my bold bands,
　　T'auenge my slaughtered friends at *Lucius'* hands.

80.

Then prudent Ioue vpon the foes did frowne,
And in his ballance holding either fate
Of both our fortunes, made their lot sinke downe,
Vpon our steps in fight did conquest wait,
Death's terror did the foe-men's strength abate,
　　Whose hands fell strengthlesse downe, being all inclin'd
　　To flie with shame, and leaue vs fame behind.

81.

They fled, and we did eager pursuit make:
But sad report on fame's vnluckie wing,
With fatall tidings did vs ouertake,
How all our Britaine ocean round did ring
With *Mordred's* deeds aspiring to be king,
　　Which strooke more terror to my grieued mind,
　　Then if the world 'gainst me in armes had shin'd.

82.

Yet with late conquest won in mind made bold,
Returning to our fleet we launcht from land,
And being out at sea we might behold
Our owne rebellious kingdome's rockie strand,
Strengthen'd about the coast with many a band:
　　Which did my vexed soule with sorrow sting,
　　To see false subiects bent to braue their king.

83.

As lions rob'd of yong with hideous rore
All raging wood, makes th'echoing forrest shake
And beasts to dread : so sailing towards the shore,
My souldiers charging, with loud shouts did make
The stoutest hearts on th'aduerse part to quake :
  A wrongfull cause makes fortitude giue backe,
  And guilt of treason courage doth aslacke.

84.

Yet on the land at Sandwich port, before
We could set foot, we lost much life and blood :
For with stones, darts, and shafts thicke sent from shore,
Our men as on the deckes they stoutly stood
Were ouerturn'd into the wauie flood,
  'Mongst whom without all helpe before our eies,
  Did many sinke, and neuer more did rise.

85.

For many 'mongst the rest being wounded sore,
Rising againe, to shun their timelesse graue,
Their fainting browes aboue the billowes bore,
And when their lips did ouerlooke the waue,
For helpe cri'd out their loued liues to saue :
  But they, alas, made weake, with losse of blood,
  Sinking, poore soules, were strangled in the flood.

86.

To wreake such harmes with sharpned arrowes store,
Steele-headed iauelins, stones and singing darts,
We charg'd the bold defendants on the shore,
Which did impresse deepe wounds in their best harts,
And made the rest retire t'escape such smarts,
  From whom our men the firme land hauing won,
  'Twixt them and vs a dreadfull fight begun,

87.

Where noble *Anguisell* the Scotish king,
Amidd'st the foes in fight incircled round,
Did in our cause endure death's fatall sting:
And valiant *Cador* after many a wound,
Did sinke downe dead vpon the flowrie ground:
   Whom my deare *Gawin* did consort in death,
   And in our right, with them expir'd his breath.

88.

For making slaughter with his mightie lance
Vpon the aduerse troopes, though many a band
Inclos'd him from all helpe, where he by chance
Was wounded by a fatall souldier's hand,
Yet 'gainst them all alone he made his stand,
   And with his life halfe spent in their despight,
   Did make retreate vnto his tent from fight.

89.

Where through his wound, before his life did fleet,
These words hee spake vnto the standers by,
" With sad farewell my soueraigne I doe greet,
In whose defence against his foes, though I
In death triumphant ouer death do die,
   Yet brother's treason wounds my heart with woe,
   For which with griefe vnto my graue I goe.

90.

Yee powers of heauen, on whose dispose diuine
The gift of conquest doth depend alone,
Let our dread king in battaile victor shine
Against his foes, let traytors falling grone
Beneath his sword, that do aspire his throne:
   But cease my words, death doth my breath exhale,
   Adue my liege, I die, my life doth faile."

91.

This said, he slept in death, yet neuer sleepes.
The fame of his admired loyaltie,
Seal'd with his blood, record for euer keepes,
His name a mirror of true constancie
To his liege lord for all posteritie:
  For vnto vs he in true loyall loue
  Gainst nature's selfe to death did constant proue.

92.

Nature's affect leuel'd by rule of reason,
The due respect of common good doth binde
Gainst nature's selfe, and when the hand of treason
Inuades the state of kings, the noble minde
To shun the taint of blood 'gainst their owne kinde,
  Aduerse in nature seeme, that loue to showe,
  Which first to care of common good they owe.

93.

Which this illustrate knight in hart did keepe,
And with his blood in death did seale the same:
Which when I heard sad sorrowe seated deepe
In my grieu'd hart my thoughts did so inflame,
That on the foes I rusht with loud exclame,
  And with heroicke wreake my harte's true loue
  To my deare *Gawin* dead, I did approue.

94.

In our reuenge such slaughter we did make
With furious onset on the aduerse part,
That vnto flight themseleus they did betake,
Nor durst the brest that bore the boldest hart
Stand forth 'gainst vs to shake his threatning dart:
  False traytor's hearts the coward's feare doth feele,
  Nor can an edge be set vpon their steele.

95.

The Saxon *Cerdicus* and *Mordred* both
Confederates in this treason 'gainst our state,
Did flie t'escape the meed of their vntroth,
Whom we did fast pursue with deadly hate
From place to place, vntill vntimely fate
 Did by one battell shut vp all our strife
 In *Mordred's* death, and losse of my deare life.

96.

A second field at Winchester we won,
Where many foes in fight were stricken dead,
'Mongst whom false *Mordred* his blacke death did shun,
Who with his friends although from field he fled:
Yet t'hazard fortune once more he made hed,
 And on a plaine by Glastenburie towne,
 Fatall to all this land his tents pight downe.

97.

Whom I as one, that of his owne accord
Had sought to hasten death in armes bedight,
In person follow'd with reuengefull sword,
To shew my selfe as well the first in fight,
As first in name, though with respectiue right
 To common good, whose state depended then
 Vpon my life: I might haue absent ben;

98.

Yet could not this disswade me from the field,
But in the morne when as the daie's bright king
The mountaine tops with golden shine did gild,
No sooner did the warlike trumpet sing
Warre's fearfull song, the sound of which did ring
 About my eares, but rous'd from rest I rose,
 And arm'd me for the field to meet my foes.

99.

With trumpet's blast Bellona summon'd out
My Britons to the field, and then began
Each seuerall band t'enranke themselues about
My royall standard, while each captaine ran
From troope to troope enabling euerie man
  To charge the rebels with their vtmost might,
  Who in the field stood brauing vs for fight.

100.

With trumpets, drums and dreadfull shouts of men
The battailes ioyn'd, earth's batter'd pauements vnder
Did seeme to shake, heauen sounded lowd, as when
Bold Boreas clad in darknesse, stormes and thunder,
Doth cuffe the cloudes and rends their ribs in sunder:
  Both parts being eager bent the day to winne,
  The fight at first with furie did begin.

101.

And as the hunter his shrill horne doth winde,
Breaths forth lowd shoutes and vseth all his art
To make his dogs to pinch the game behinde:
So euerie where I chear'd vp euerie hart,
And vrg'd my men against the aduerse part,
  Exciting them by mine owne valiancie
  To charge through death for fame and victorie.

102.

So long as faire Aurorae's light did shine,
All valiantlie themselues in fight did beare:
But when the king of flames began decline
From steepe Olympus top, th'whole host with feare
Affrighted was, all troopes disordered were,
  Who giuing back from field had fled awaie,
  If I through death had not regain'd the day.

103.

For loe, a Pictish souldier 'mongst the foes
Spake in the British tongue: " Yeeld (O friends) yield,
No more your selues to death in vaine oppose,
Arthur is dead, and with him dead in field
His knights are laid, on whom our hopes did build:"
  This spake he with lowd voice in th'heate of fight,
  Thereby to turne our battaile into flight:

104.

But I that heard and knew his close intent,
In front of all the field my selfe did shoe
Whereby my Britons, that before were bent
To turne their backes, turn'd head vpon the foe,
'Twixt whom the fight againe did feruent grow,
  With whom I brake into the dangerous fight
  In hope to meet with *Mordred*, that false knight.

105.

My launce and sword did many a bosome sacke
Of life's rich spoiles, which were all men of name,
The common sort my hand in troopes did wrack,
For through deepe wounds and death in martiall game
I did enforce my way to win me fame,
  Till wounded in the head with fatall speele
  My death's approch in fight I gan to feele.

106.

Yet when warme blood through my crackt veines flow,
And subtle aire gan pierce the liuely braine,
The eager anguish did my valor show:
For manie foemen in my furie slaine
Did pay my wreake with death and deadlie baine:
  Still did I fight, although with fainting breath,
  Vntill in fight I heard of *Mordred*'s death.

107.

Whose tragick fall when true report did tell,
His souldiers fled away, and in their flight
Vp flew their heeles, in slaughter fast they fell,
Darts thick as haile their backs behinde did smite,
Farre more in chase did fall, then in the fight:
  Yea none had scap't the furie of that day
  Had not my bleeding wounds stood in my way.

108.

In manie a fight before in death's despight
Vpon my head ten wounds I did sustaine,
With life vntoucht: but in this fatall fight
Remorslesse fate to end my life and reigne
With one deepe wound did wound my vitall braine:
  For in the chace with torment of that wound
  Deathe's touch I felt and fell vpon the ground.

109.

From whence conuei'd to Glastenburie by
By my deare friends, who did in vaine pretend
To saue my life, loe, as I there did lie
In th'armes of death, perceiuing how each friend
Did shew his ruth, in teares for my sad end,
  These words I spake, before my vading breath
  Did flie away vpon the wings of death.

110.

" Grieue not," said I, " to see your wounded king
Wrapt in the ruine of his life now done:
For Phœnix-like from death new life shall spring,
Which in this life I by my death haue wonne,
I dead, that left to liue, when I am gone,
  Yea, this in death shall liue my future grace,
  I di'd a conquerour iu cold death's embrace.

111.

The kingly ruth which our sad soule attends
Is our deare countrie's sight, which setled deepe
In depth of my deare loue (O noble friends)
To you I tender 'gainst all spoile to keepe,
When I in peace haue laid me down to sleepe,
   Death now triumphs, my mortall daies are done,
   My houre is spent, my glasse is quite outrun."

112.

This said, when I twice thirteene yeares had been
The stout defendant of my countrie's right,
My soule did leaue th'abodes of mortall men,
My liuelesse limbes in secret hid from sight,
Interred were at Glastenburie hight:
   Thus hast thou heard the truth of all my storie,
   My life, my death, and my nere dying glorie.

113.

In which as in a glasse, seeing men may see
That action only dignifies the name,
That vertue betters euery bare degree,
That vading pleasures vpshot is but shame,
And silent sloth the opposite to fame,
   Commit to mind, what I commend to thee,
   That vnto men a Mirrour it may bee.

THE LIFE AND DEATH
of King Edmvnd, svrnamed
Ironside.

THE ARGUMENT.

" THIS was a worthie prince," quoth Memorie,
" Peerelesse amongst the kings of Britanie,
After whose death the British rule did cease,
And th'English power did more and more increase:
For not long after on the Britaine throne
The Saxon kings did rule and raigne alone,
Who did at first agree in one consent
To make seuen kingdomes of this regiment,
Which did in that confused sort remaine
Till the beginning of king *Egbert's* raigne:
About which time from Denmarke with strong hand
Inguar and *Hubba* came t'inuade this land,
With whom the Saxons manfully did fight,
And turn'd them oftentimes to coward flight:
Yet did they heere long time beare great command,
Though many a valiant king did them withstand,
'Mongst whom I find this one, whose tragedie
Is not recited in our historie,
Which *Edmund* call'd, surnamed *Ironside*,
A famous prince, in battell often tride,
Whom fortune still did grace with victorie
In fight against *Canute* his enemie:

Yet by the cruell fates vniust command
He lost his life by wicked traytor's hand,
Whom vp from graue let fame with summons call,
To take his turne and tell his tragicke fall."

ANOTHER ARGUMENT.

Fame calles vp *Edmund* from his graue below,
His life and lamentable death to show.

1.

WE are not borne vnto our selues alone,
Deeds done, though good : yet from a greedy mind
Intending priuate weale, when life is gone,
Vading away, leaue no record behind
In fame's faire booke, for future age to find :
  Self-loue to priuate good, no good can craue,
  When life is gone such loue lies dead in graue.

2.

The fruits of loue, which after life do liue,
To grow from loue of common good are seene,
To reape such fruit, whoso his life shall giue,
Though dead, yet liues: his fruit aye waxeth greene,
Of which my life a Mirrour might haue been:
  But whose sad muse my tragedie doth sing,
  Or who to light king *Edmund's* deeds doth bring?

3.

Now from my graue, the bed of my long rest
Rous'd vp by fame, through shades of silent night,
Behold I come obeying her behest,
As Mirrours vnto men, to bring to light
My deeds, oft done in my deare countrie's right:
  Heare then (thou sleeping wight) whose mournefull muse
  To sing my storie Memorie doth chuse.

4.

I am the sonne of that vnhappie king
Hight *Egelred*, whose daies were wrapt in woe,
And on whose head false fortune downe did fling,
Such miserable scath and ouerthrow,
That he was forc'd his kingdome to forgo:
  For subiect's treacherie did him constraine
  To leaue his kingdome vnto bloodie *Swaine*.

5.

To bloodie *Swaine*, who from our Albion shore,
Vnto the Norman duke to saue his life,
Forc'd him to flie, whose sister he, before
My mother dead, had made his second wife,
In hope thereby t'appease domesticke strife,
  And by the aid of Norman valiancie,
  To quell the force of forren enemie.

6.

But hence did rise the ruine of the state,
And fourth decay of Albion's emperie,
This was the gap, which by decree of fate
Was open laid for time's posteritie,
Vnto the Norman conquerer's victorie:
  For by these fatall nuptials in the end,
  The Norman duke his title did pretend.

7.

My sire being thus constrain'd by forren force,
And subiects treason, in such miserie,
Amongst his Norman friends to seeke remorce
Of his mishaps, the land meane time did lie
Groaning beneath the victor's tyrannie,
  For nere did captiu'd men sustaine such woes,
  As did the english of the conquering foes.

8.

O noble England, nurse of my renowne,
Queene of all ilands canoped of heauen,
How was thy towring state then troden downe?
How were thy sonnes from their sad mother driuen?
Thy daughter's beautie vnto rapine giuen?
  My words, alas, will thy sad heart compell
  To bleed with woe, these woes to heare me tell.

9.

The simple hinde, who with day-labour stroue
In fruitlesse field to furrow vp his bread,
Nor for himselfe the earth with paine did proue,
But for another, whom his labour fed,
Although in heart he often wisht him dead,
  In euery house lord Dane did then rule all,
  Whence laysie lozels lurdanes now we call.

10.

The nuptiall bed, the lodge of chaste delight,
Was common vs'd in wedlocke's foule disdaine,
Sweet virgins daily forc'd to deeds of night,
Faire ladies beautie set to sale for gaine,
Children made bondslaues, wretched husbands slain,
   Who to such rufull spoile were iustly giuen
   For their offence against the king of heauen.

11.

Let such, whose peacefull eares from sad affright
Of warre's dread voice the hand of heauen doth close,
Who lull'd in that dame's lap of sweet delight,
The queene of peace do sleepe sccure of foes,
Thinke it humane, to thinke on other's woes:
   And in such thoughts fear such like woes to come,
   For their offence ordain'd by Ioue's iust doome.

12.

The life of state lay stifeled in the smoke
Of blacke despaire, till death tooke life from *Swaine*,
Then th'english peeres shooke off the heauie yoke
Of forren pride, which they did erst sustaine,
And did recall my father home againe,
   Who did enforce by power of his strong hand
   Canute the sonne of *Swaine* to leaue this land.

13.

Then did he seeke to reerect againe
The ruines of his crowne's collapsed state:
But he, t'whom at his birth heauen did ordaine
In all his deeds ineuitable fate
Of bad euent, euen to his daie's last date
   His wishfull hopes in vaine did seeke t'aduance,
   Vpon th'vnsteadie wheele of fickle-chance.

14.

For ere those sprightfull horse of heauenly breed,
That draw the chariot of the golden sunne,
Who day by day do vse their swiftest speed
From east to west their yeare's full race had runne,
Our fatall foe *Canute* king *Swanus* sonne,
   To wretched England made returne againe
   From Denmarke shores with many a thousand Dane.

15.

Who taking land at *Sandwich* in their ire,
Deuoid of pitie in the spoile of good,
Senselesse of humane woes with spoilefull fire
All things did burne, that in their passage stood,
Nor yet suffic'd : but thirsting after blood,
   All doom'd to death, none kept for captiue bands,
   Were slaine in troopes by their remorcelesse hands.

16.

T'oppose their powers in field I soone did cite
My father's subiects from all quarters by :
But when prepar'd we were in field to fight,
Th'unhappie tidings through our host did flie
Of false duke *Edrick* and his treacherie,
   Who with his troope in depth of darkest night,
   Vnto *Canutus* campe did take his flight.

17.

Whereby made weake vnable to withstand
Th'augmented powers of our insulting foe,
We backe return'd with our disabled band,
And to our kingly father we did show
Duke *Edrick's* treason, which, alas, with woe
   So wounds his heart, that he expires his breath,
   Poore aged king, and ends his woes in death.

18.

He being dead, to me his eldest borne,
Was left the reliques of a ruiu'd state,
By rage of Mars a kingdome rent and torne,
A diademe by sterne decree of fate
Ordain'd for prize of bloodie warre's debate,
  Which was the end, for which *Canute* and I
  In martial field did many a battell trie.

19.

O wretched end of glorie thirsting pride!
O vaine pursuit of empire and renowne!
What lot the land of discord doth betide
But wastfull spoile and all turn'd topsie downe?
What doe we purchase but a carefull crowne?
  A crowne of care, the cause of froward strife,
  The cause for which I lost my loued life.

20.

For after that against th'inuading foe
Six bloodie battailes I had fought in field,
I that in warre away did victor goe,
On whom (O England) thou thy hopes didst build,
Vanquish't in peace to death was forc'd to yeeld:
  The chance of warre my chance could not apall,
  But trust in traytors wrought my wretched fall.

21.

When as the crowne my head did first adorne,
These thoughts vnto my selfe, I thus did frame:
Vnto my selfe I am not onlie borne,
My countrie deare the cheefest part doth claime,
Who to my care now kneeles and craues the same,
  To saue the remnant of her ruin'd soile
  From cruell focs that threat her vtter spoile.

22.

The thought of this did spirit bold inspire,
And smart of wounds receiu'd from foes of late
Did with swift furie feather my desire,
Which of itself by nature's gifts did hate
To linger time, deferring vtmost fate
   In doubtfull chance of battaile to be tride,
   For which I was surnam'd, hight *Ironside.*

23.

This fire of expedition in affaires
And height of resolution t'vndergoe,
Compar'd to strength of limbes and restlesse cares,
Redoubled in my thoughts t'oppugne the foe,
And yeeld releefe to England in her woe,
   Did touch *Canutus* hart with feare, though bent
   To trie his fortunes in the warre's euent.

24.

Distracted thus with doubt, in any place
By doubtfull fight t'ingage his hopefull fate,
False *Edrick* hoping for to purchase grace,
Who for his treason to my sire of late,
Had run in danger of my deadlie hate,
   Did plot the downfall of mine emperie,
   And in the end did act my tragedie.

25.

From prince *Canutus* campe in dead of night,
Like the Greekes subtile *Synon*, to effect
His wicked plot, to vs he tooke his flight,
And at our feete himselfe he did proiect,
And spake, as if his thoughts had no respect
   To his owne life: for he with craftie wile
   Of seeming sorrow thus did me beguile.

26.

" O noble prince," quoth he, " loe, I am come
As guiltie to my selfe, and do require
To suffer shamefull death by righteous doome
From thine owne mouth, against whose royall sire
And gainst thy selfe I did of late conspire:
  Pronounce then death, a doome more sweet to mee,
  Then aged dayes in loathed life can bee.

27.

Ay me the dayes, on you I may exclaime,
In which to foule defame my life I lent :
Alas, the nights, that testifie my shame,
Your secret treasons I too late repent:
O wrongfull world, that made my thoughts consent:
  Nor dayes, nor nights, nor world in future time,
  But will for aye record my gracelesse crime.

28.

In vaine mine eyes, that shame yee do lament,
Which follows me where euer I doe wone,
In vaine my sighs, in vaine yee now are sent
From wofull hart to waile my trespasse done:
For should I liue, foule shame how shall I shun?
  Then welcome death, 'tis death must end my woe,
  Vnto my graue my greefe with me will goe."

29.

This said, he wept and I began relent
And take remorse on his calamitie,
His hoarie head did moue me to lament
His wretched state, whom I from miserie
Restor'd againe to former dignitie:
  For I, whose thoughts nere double dealing knew,
  Did also thinke his thoughts vnfan'd and true.

30.

He being restor'd againe to liue in grace,
Did cloake beneath the vaile of loyaltie,
Th'intent of treason and did maske the face
Of foule deceit with fawning flatterie,
Till time-borne truth did shew his treacherie,
   For many a field and many a dreadfull fight
   His treason shew'd, which time did bring to light.

31.

The scourge of peacefull pride, the god of warre,
The prodigue spender of sweet plentie's store
Did ride about our coast in iron carre,
Whose thundring wheeles like Neptune's dreaded rore,
Were heard to rattle on our Albion shore,
   So long, vntill the pale-fac'd queene of night
   Had twelue times borrow'd of her brother's light.

32.

In six fierce battels fought in martiall field,
Fortune my sword with conquest did renowne,
Six times *Canute* ore-match'd in fight did yeeld
And fled away, by froward fate cast downe,
Leaning to me the hope of England's crowne:
   Whose hopes my sword had smothered in the dust,
   If I to traytor's words had giuen no trust.

33.

For, after that I had with foule affright
Dispers'd the bold *Canutus* mightie host,
That had begirt my loyall London bight,
Lest any breathing space might haue been lost,
I follow'd him vnto that rockie coast,
   Ouer whose mountaine tops the daie's great guide,
   The golden sunne appeares each morning tide.

34.

And there where Medway with his siluer streames
Runs gliding downe the lowlie dales of Kent,
Vntill he meetes his elder brother Thames,
Vpon a hill I pight my warlike tent,
Expecting how the foes, that night stood bent,
  If till the morne they did determine stay,
  Or daunted with late foile would flie away.

35.

The night we past in quiet sleepe's repose,
And when the bright-cheekt ladie of the light
Tir'd with night's toyle from Tython's bed arose,
And in her saffron-coloured robe bedight
With her approch brought vse to mortall fight,
  We troopt our men in Mars' his best array,
  Vpon the foes in field to giue th'assay.

36.

The foes stood firme vpon the sandie ground,
Shaking their deadlie darts with countnance proud:
Then did the trump the song of battaile sound,
And Danish kettle drums did beate alowd,
While euerie one in midst of martiall crowd
  Insatiate in reuenge vndaunted stood,
  Imbruing their bold hands in humane blood.

37.

While thus oppos'd both parts in fight did stand,
Hopefull of conquest, on the right side wing
Of all the host, nere to the slimie strand,
Where the sweet herbes by Medwaie's streames do spring,
The cries of wounded souldiers high did ring,
  For there *Canute* did charge with violent sway
  Of his horse troopes, in hope to win the day.

38.

But to represse the fire and quench the flame
Of his hot courage, with a troope of horse
I rusht amongst his men with loud exclame,
Whom with fierce furie in our winged course
We did so charge, that we did soone inforce
　　Their faint retire, which we did swift pursue,
　　Vntill with open flight from field they flew.

39.

Then were the Kentish vales imbru'd in blood,
Then death was set on foote and thousands fell,
The brackish waues of Medganara's flood
With slaughtered bodies 'boue the bankes did swell,
Whose blushing streames the fight far of did tell
　　Painting the bankes with crimson in the way,
　　As they did glide into the Orean sea.

40.

Here heauen did smile on me with gracious looke,
And fortune put faire conquest in my hand,
On bald occasion hold I might haue tooke
And thence-forth freed the subiects of my land
From seruile yoke of forraine king's command:
　　But what we purpose heauen doth still decree,
　　In vaine we wish what heauen wils not to bee.

41.

The treacherous duke, the faithlesse man at armes,
Ignoble *Edrick* thus did counsell mee:
" My liege," quoth he, " we hazard now more harmes
In pursuit of the flying enemie,
Then earst we did before the victorie,
　　'Tis best we sound retreate and fall to spoile,
　　Of these dead foes vpon the sandie soile.

42.

Your men, though bold, yet wearied with the fight,
Be faint, and fortune may the foes so grace,
That they, constrain'd with desperate feare from flight
To backward death againe to turne their face,
May charge our troopes disordered in the chace:
  Distraction heartens feare in desperate deeds,
  Constraint in coward thoughts rash valor breeds."

43.

This did he speake despairing hope to come
For prince *Canute*, if we pursu'd the chace:
Some did approue his counsell sound, and some
Did vrge against the same, yet found it grace
With those both rightlie wise and best in place:
  By whose aduice retreate I did command,
  Losing the chance then put into my hand.

44.

Thus did Troye's helme-deckt, *Hector* when in chace
He had the Greekes vpon Scamander's plaine,
And made them house their heads with deepe disgrace
In their owne fleet: whom then hee could haue slaine
And burnt their ships, which did their hopes containe:
  But then being crost by lucklesse destinie
  He did omit the profferd victorie.

45.

Thus did Rome's scourge, the famous *Hanniball*,
For when he might with his victorious powers
Haue made that towne beneath his sword to fall,
And leueld with the ground her high topt towers,
Then did he let passe those auspicious ho ers,
  In which with ease he might haue queld the foe,
  Who after wrought his and his coun rie's woe.

46.

Securefull thoughts do foster fond delay,
Bewitching hopes breed carelesnesse of minde,
Occasion set on wing flies fast away,
Whose backe once turn'd no hold fast can we finde,
Her feet are swift, bald is her head behinde,
   Who so hath hold and after lets her goe,
   Doth lose the lot which fortune did bestowe.

47.

Euen as a fire supprest, if yet remaine
A sparke not quite extinct, whence growes a flame,
Wil soone resume his former strength againe:
Euen so *Canutus* power, which I did tame,
And with one blow might then haue queld the same,
   Resum'd proud strength, which little time did yeeld,
   And oft times after brau'd me in the field.

48.

The bainfull'st battaile we did euer fight,
At Scorstan was, in fruitfull Worstershire,
Where vnto both the hosts in open sight
Duke *Edrick*'s treason plainly did appeare,
Which in his hart 'gainst me he still did beare :
   The heart once tainted with foule treason's staine,
   Possest with guile, seldome proues true againe.

49.

Two dayes in field we stood in doubtfull fight,
And after mutuall wounds with equall fate,
Both parts were parted by approching night:
But in the next daye's fight this traytor's hate
Did shew it selfe, for seeing the foes in state
   Of strength declin'd, he sought by treacherie
   To iue the day vnto the enemie.

50.

In midst of martiall throng my folk t'excite,
As I did stand in skirmish 'gainst the foe,
A man of armes there was, which *Osmeare* hight,
So like to mee, that scarse you could him know,
By whom this traytor sought to worke vs woe:
  For as in fight he stood without all dread,
  False *Edrick* vndiscern'd did strike him dead.

51.

Whose liuelesse lims in endlesse sleepe fast bound,
After he had despoil'd and headlesse made,
He tooke himselfe vnto an higher ground,
And piching *Osmear's* head vpon his blade,
He held the same on high and thus he said:
  " Flie, wretched countrimen, your king is dead,
  The day is lost, see here king *Edmund's* head."

52.

The suddaine horror of this vncouth sight
With suddaine fright my folke did so dismay,
That they which were not in that part of fight
Where with my launce and sword I did display
Th'extreamest of my strength to win the day,
  Away had fled and lost the victorie,
  Had I not heard of *Edrick's* treacherie.

53.

With speed on top of an adioyning hill,
My selfe I did conuey, where I in sight
Of all my host thus spake with voice most shrill:
" Fellowes in armes," quoth I, " let not this slight
Of traytor's practise your bold thoughts affright:
  Behold yet free from death's captiuitie,
  I liue to be reueng'd on th'enimie."

54.

This said, each one which had begun to flie
Turn'd head againe, and stoutly kept his place,
Then rushing with exclaimes on th'enemie,
Eager with furie of their late disgrace,
They gaue the charge so fiercely on the face
    Of th'aduerse force, that by their violent might,
    They brake the rankes, and turn'd their foes to flight.

55.

With whom the Mercian duke fled fast away,
The traytor *Edrick* hopelesse now of grace,
Who wing'd with feare of his decreed decay,
Outstript our pursuit, yet with greedie chace
We did pursue, vntill the day gaue place
    T'approching night, whose wished presence gaue
    Time to the foes themselues from death to saue.

56.

Canute being fled, did slacke no breathing space,
Once more to trie the chance of doubtfull fight:
But gathered his dispersed powers apace,
With whom I by a place, which Dearehurst hight,
In sea-side bordering Glostershire should fight,
    Where I with resolution did intend
    In single fight this spoilefull warre to end.

57.

When on the fishie Seuerne's bordering costs
Oppos'd for fight, the battels ranged were,
A noble knight confronting both the hosts,
Did boldly in the midst aduance his speare,
At which both armies did from fight forbeare,
    For straight my men I staid, because I knew
    His purpose then, which thus he did pursue.

58.

" Yee glory-thirsting sonnes of Mars," said he,
" To what I speake, with good aduice giue eare,
Let not my words by you contemned be,
If any loue to humane good ye beare,
Yee will esteeme my exhortations deare,
   If either part my counsell shall refuse,
   No good can happen in these warres we vse.

59.

Not th'haplesse fate, which followes hostile warre:
Nor terrible euents of bloodie fight,
Nor spoiles, that spring from contumelious iarre,
Nor woes produc'd from strife for lordly right,
To you, my countrimen, need I recite,
   For woe, alas, this land can testifie
   The rauenous rage of Mars his tyrannie.

60.

Pitie the teares of this our mother Ile,
Whose fame which 'bout the world once shone as bright
As Phœbus shine, now dim'd, alas, the while,
With clouds of carefull strife hath lost her light,
That to behold her in this wretched plight,
   Like sorowe's image drown'd in waues of woe,
   Would make the hardest flint with teares to flow.

61.

Her fertile wombe, which goodly fruit did beare,
Now barren made, war's stormie breath hath blasted,
Her buds of gaysome youth, which whilome were
The flowers of chiualrie, haue headlong hasted
Their timelesse end, while she in woe hath wasted,
   And we the cause, we wretches, that delight
   By wicked warre to worke her more despight.

62.

O noble princes, let not warre's blacke hand
Put out for aye the shine of England's light,
About whose right, both in contention stand,
But combate for it in a single fight,
And he that conquers, his be it by right:
   Faire conquest's gift is in the hand of heau'n,
    Which vnto truth, for truth's owne sake is giuen."

63.

He hauing said, forthwith 1 forth did step,
And cast my brazen gauntlet on the plaine,
To which *Canute* with courage bold did lep
And tooke it vp, casting in deepe disdaine
His rich grau'd gauntlet on the ground againe,
   Which 1 accepted and propos'd the day,
    When we in fight each other should assay.

64.

For battell was design'd a plot of ground
Within a little ile, which Olney hight,
Whom Seuerne with his armes incircleth round,
Where we as combatants in single fight
Should d'araine bettell in both armie's sight,
   While they assigned were by our command,
    Ou th'other side of Seuern's streame to stand.

65.

The day of fight being come and order giuen,
Through either host to euery seuerall band
To keepe their stand, my souldiers vp to heau'n
Did cast their eyes, beseeching loue to stand
By me in fight, and grace my powerfull hand
   With conquest 'gainst *Canute,* by whom cast downe
    They did expect the rise of my renowne.

66.

As they thus prai'd, I arm'd me for the fight,
And being mounted on a sprightfull steed,
When 'twixt both armies I appear'd in sight,
My terrible aspect did terror breed
Vnto the aduerse part, but hope did feed
  My souldier's sight to see my goodly grace,
  My stout demeanor, and my stately pace.

67.

As Priam's Hector on the barren plaine,
Manag'd his horse before the walles of Troy,
When he in single battell did maintaine
Troye's right 'gainst Telamon, who did imploy
All his best strength bold Hector to destroy,
  So on my steed I trotted to and fro,
  Waiting th'approch of my expected foe.

68.

Who came at length all arm'd in seemely wise
Into the lists, and when the trumpe did sound,
Our steeds as swift as birds of wings in skies,
Their course did run, and we with speares sharpe ground
Did fiercely meete each other to confound,
  In which swift course our shattered speares did flie,
  Like feathers borne by winde into the skie.

69.

As two fierce buls fights twixt an heard of kine,
Whose violence doth increase, when in their sight
The crimson blood doth from their wounds decline,
So wounds giuen equally in doubtfull fight,
Our eager thoughts did to reuenge excite,
  The anguish arm'd our armes with strength to strike,
  And made vs both incounter lion-like.

70.

On horsback first the fight we did maintaine,
And when our horse did faile, dismounting straight
On foote the fight we did begin againe,
In which my foes haut courage gan to abate,
I with my sword laid on such wounds of weight,
  That his faint knees did stoope at euerie blow,
  And in the fight did stagger to and fro.

71.

Who tir'd with toile and fearing least my sword
Should beare away the palme of victorie,
Thus spake to me : " Forbeare," quoth he, " braue lord,
This doubtfull fight, and let vs both agree
To ioyne our harts and hands in amitie,
  Least that our swords each other do destroy,
  Leauing this land for others to inioy.

72.

Right well thou knowst the chance of victorie
Vncertaine is, and though the crowne thou claime
As due to thee and thy posteritie,
So, noble prince, I, in my father's name,
As my inheritance do craue the same :
  In one consent then let vs both agree
  That England's bounds twixt vs may parted bee.

73.

Let not the inward hands of dogged hate
Teare thy great minde, but supple it with grace
Of heauenlie loue, let loue end our debate,
Which if in thought thou trulie canst imbrace,
Then in my hart thou hast a brother's place,
  To which all-seeing Ioue I witnesse call,
  Who is the supreame souereigne of vs all."

74.

To this I pausde a while, but at the length
Conceauing well the combat's doubtfull chance,
" *Canute*," said I, " since God hath giuen thee strength
In fight to trie the manage of my lance
And slaughtering sword without thy life's mischance,
   I thinke right well his will likewise it bee,
   That in my kingdome thou haue part with me."

75.

This said, our swords we sheath'd in th'armie's sight,
And with kinde armes each other did embrace,
Happie it seem'd to those, that did delight
In happie peace, to see such loue take place
Twixt two such mortall foes in so short space:
   But haplesse I that did accord thereto,
   Th'euent whereof did breed my after woe.

76.

The traytor *Edrick*, preordainde by fate
To act my fall, whom for his treacherie
I daylie did pursue with deadlie hate,
Did instigate his sonne by villanie
With impious hands to act my tragedie,
   Who to impietie by nature free,
   After this tragick sort did murther mee.

77.

Vpon a time, when in the Muse's bower,
England's Parnassus, famous Oxford hight
Was my abode, there in that fatall houre,
When as expedient vse did me excite
To do the deed of nature requisite,
   Vnto the draught as was my wont I went
   Vnto my nature's vse to yeeld content.

78.

Where loe, the sonne of this false duke did lie
Hid in the vault, to further his intent
With weapon arm'd : for on the draught while I
Secure did sit, with fatall instrument
This villane gor'd my bodie's fundament,
   And there to death his due I timelesse gaue,
   At Glastenburie I was laid in graue.

79.

Thus after twice sixe months, and as much space,
As from the time the swallow leaues her nest,
Till Phœbus baue the lion in full chace,
With th'angrie dog, that from his burning brest
Breaths mortall plagues, hot feauers and vnret,
   When I had raign'd, I lost my life and crowne:
   With which our English name lost her renowne.

80.

Thus hast thou heard the sad catastrophe,
And fatall period of my life and raigne,
In which thou seest, that where false treacherie
Hath toucht the heart with her foule finger's staine,
There seldome constant truth returnes againe,
   Which that it may to future times be knowne,
   Forget not what was said, when I am gone.

THE LAMENTABLE LIFE

and death of Prince Alfred, brother

to King Edmund Ironside.

THE ARGUMENT.

" By death of this braue prince," quoth Memorie,
" The English lost both fame and libertie,
Too cruell were inexorable fates,
On him so swiftly t'execute their hates:
Yet with his brother *Alfred's* wofull end
For tragicke act, his death may not contend,
Who liues an exile all his infancie
With his deare vncle, duke of Normandie,
Whence he in riper yeares recall'd againe,
Returning is betray'd, and on the plaine
By Guilford towne his friends betray'd by night,
Are tith'd to death by *Godwin,* that false knight,
The prince is sent to Elie, where his eyne
Being both put out, with hunger he doth pine,
Till th'instruments of *Harrold's* tyrannie
Do butcher him with barbarous crueltie,
Who is the next in course, that must commend
To thee, the maner of his wofull end:
Let fame then call his mournefull ghost to tell
The woes and vncouth death, which him befell."

ANOTHER ARGUMENT.

Prince *Alfred* summon'd, tells to Memorie
His life, his death, and *Godwin's* treacherie.

1.

Of all the sonnes of men, vnhappie fate
With spight pursues the borne of high degree,
Where tyrant wrong vsurpes the chaire of state
The baser subiect sits from danger free,
Wofull it is of royall birth to bee,
   Of which my woes a witnesse may remaine,
   Such tragicke woes no prince did ere sustaine.

2.

Vp then (thou saddest of the sacred nine)
Cause of sad sorow, neuer hadst thou more,
Vp (rufull ghosts and shew some dolefull signe
Of heauie griefe) powre out your teares in store,
Cause of sad sorow neuer had yee more:
   And (thou) the pen-man of my historie
   Prepare sad verse for my sad tragedie.

3.

I am that *Alfred,* famous *Edmund's* brother,
Who in the time of my minoritie
Was by queene *Emma* our beloued mother,
Sent to mine vncle duke of Normandie,
There to remaine safe from the enemie,
 While heere at home against the sonne of *Swaine,*
 My brother *Edmund* battell did maintaine.

4.

Who being slaine, as thou before didst heare,
By treacherous *Edricke* and his bloodie sonne,
They for their fact a guerdon due did beare:
For whereas praise by it they thought t'haue wonne
Of king *Canute,* they both to death were done,
 Whose hands with blood, whose hearts with treason floe,
 Seldome in peace vnto the graue do goe.

5.

Canute being seated on the English throne
By ioynt consent of the nobilitie,
To sit sole monarch in the same alone,
Did daily seeke by wisdome's policie,
T'establish it to his posteritie,
 While I, and *Edward* hight my elder brother,
 Did liue in exile with our wofull mother.

6.

Meane time *Canute,* th'vsurper of our right,
Hug'd in the armes of peace, and finding none
That could oppose themselues against his might,
After all stormes of warre were ouerblowne,
By blood gan tyrant-like t'vsurpe the throne :
 For without cause the royall blood he spilt
 Of *Edmund's* brother *Edwin,* void of guilt.

7.

King *Edmund's* sonnes, those faultlesse infants twaine,
Edmund and *Edward* by his sterne decree,
Were sent vnto the Norway king hight *Swaine,*
He being design'd to act their death: but hee
Lamenting their mishaps, did set them free,
    And sent them both vnto th'Hungarian king,
    Who kept them safe beneath his soueraigne wing.

8.

Canute being freed from doubtfull feare of those,
That to the diademe might make iust claime,
To peacefull pleasure did his thoughts dispose,
And gan to thinke how with some royall dame,
He in chast bed might amplifie his name,
    No sonne he had t'enioy this wretched soile,
    But *Harrold* basely borne of beautie's spoile.

9.

Vpon our mother he did cast his loue,
On whose dislike of loue we both did build
Our future hopes, but she, alas, to proue
The weakenesse of her sexe, as prompt to yeeld,
Leauing vs both, whom she from harme should sheeld,
    Did cast her wauering thoughts vpon *Canute,*
    And in the end did grant his vniust suit.

10.

(O) who doth know the wandring eye, that feeds
Th'vnstedfast fancie of weake women's heart,
Constant in nought, but in inconstant deeds,
In weaknesse strong, as if the soule's best part
Composed were by fond loue's artlesse art:
    Alas, that faithlesse faults shouldso excell,
    Where faultlesse faith with reason ought todwell.

11.

She bath'd in blisse, while we lay drown'd in woe,
She grew in pride, while we did pine away,
She soft embrac'd in th'armes of our false foe,
Did smile at our mishaps, while day by day
We did expect our loued liues decay :
   For fatall 'tis to princes royall borne
   Where tyrant's browes the garland doth adorne.

12.

So long with her *Canute* she liu'd in loue,
Till with loue's fruit her wombe to wex begun, . .
Which being brought to light, a sonne did proue :
But when that twice nine times the golden sun
In heauen's bright zodiack through the signes had run,
   The clouds of care began the dolefull night,
   Which did eclipse the shine of her delight.

13.

Then the deare daies of her dread lord were done,
The stroke of death no mortall may withstand,
The kingdome *Harrold* his ignoble sonne,
The bastard did aspire, by whose command
Our wretched mother was exil'd the land,
   And in despight despoil'd of all that store,
   Which her *Canute* had giuen to her before.

14.

But death's cold touch so soone did close mine eies,
That I beheld not my sad mother's woes,
The base vsurper did my death deuise
Before her fall, in court soone finding those,
Whom he to act my tragicke murther chose :
   The courts of kings with sycophants do swarme,
   Tyrants do want no instruments of harme.

15.

An English earle there was, which *Godwin* hight,
Whose name about the world report did blaze,
A man of wicked wit, in fortune's sight
So highly grac'd, that he himselfe did raise
To be the greatest peere in those our daies,
 The king was only then a king by name,
 While he perform'd the office of the same.

16.

And in the ruffe of his felicitie,
Prickt with ambition, he began disdaine
His bastard lord's vsurp'd authoritie,
Plotting by priuate counsels, how to gaine
Th'emperiall garland after him to raigne:
 Greatnesse in sway of state giues wings t'aspire,
 Aduancement feeds ambition with desire.

17.

In broken sleepes he did consume the night,
While his liege lord lay lull'd in th'armes of shame,
Hope of a kingdome was his sole delight,
While *Harrold* senselesse of all kingly fame,
To idle ease himselfe did only frame,
 Which set th' insulting *Godwin's* hopes on wing,
 Whence woe is me, my woes did after spring.

18.

My brother and my selfe, alas, the while,
Vnto his hopes to make the passage free,
Were markt for death, nor could our sad exile
Suffice hard fate, my wofull tragedie
Must be the subiect of his treacherie,
 We were the obiects of proud *Godwin's* frowne,
 We only stood betwixt him and the crowne.

19.

T'effect his purpose, he did soone excite
The tyrant king, whose actions he did sway,
To thinke, that while mine eyes beheld beau'n's light,
He liu'd in reach of danger day by day,
His safetie liu'd vpon my liue's decay :
 For I, he said, being of an haughtie spirit,
 Would seeke by might my father's right t'inherit.

20.

The bastard king to bloodie deeds inclin'd,
To rob me of my life stood fully bent :
Letters forthwith by messengers design'd,
Forged by wicked wits for their intent,
In our queene mother's name to me were sent,
 Which I accepted as vnfain'd and true,
 The tenor of the which doth heere ensue.

21.

" *Emma*, but only England's queene in name,
Edward and *Alfred*, her two sonnes doth greet
From England's chiefest peeres, who do reclaime
You both from exile, and do thinke it meet,
That you in Normandie should rigge some fleet,
 And crosse the seas your father's right to claime,
 They all will be assistant in the same.

22.

Strike the hard steele, while yet the fire is in,
Slip not occasion put into your hand,
The tyrant *Harrold* daily seekes to win
The peeres vnto his aid, who yet will stand
In your defence, and hazard life and land :
 Then come with speed, for warre we will prepare,
 The way is plaine, the time doth proffer faire."

23.

This in effect their letters testifie,
Which did my forward thoughts so much excite,
That though my brother then in Hungarie
Were absent farre, yet to obtaine our right,
I tooke the seas with many a Norman knight:
   But cursed be that voyage euermoe
   Whose end did end my life with bitter woe.

24.

Woe worth the ground, where grew the towring mast,
Whose sailes did beare vs through the water's rore,
Woe worth the winde, that blew the banefull blast,
Woe worth the waue, whose surge so swiftlie bore
My tragick barke to England's fatall shore,
   Woe worth the mast, the sailes, winde, waues and all,
   That causelesse did conspire poore *Alfrede's* fall.

25.

Why were not they by cruell fates assign'd
To giue that due to death? which death did craue,
On ragged rockes, O why did I not finde
A milder death? why was the darksome waue
Vpon my way not made my bodie's graue?
   Ah why, why did they let my forward feete
   Once touch the shore, such cruell death to meete?

26.

After our ships had brought vs to the shore
And giuen vs vp as captiues to the land,
At Guilford downe, a place so call'd of yore,
A fatall place to me, did *Godwin* stand
To entertaine me and my Norman band,
   Who with the shew of true fidelitie
   Did maske the face of his false treacherie.

27.

He did imbrace me round with treason's armes,
And fawnd vpon me with a villaine's smile,
His lookes were blith to hide his purposde harmes,
His words, which graced were with sugred stile,
Made musike in mine eares, and to beguile
 Suspition's self a solemne vow he made
 Against all aduerse power my part to aide.

28.

At Guilford he gaue counsell as a friend
To make abode with all my companie,
For there hee said my fauorites did intend
To meete me with their powers, who would applie
Their best indeuours 'gainst mine enemie:
 In which being confident, with ioynt consent
 Of all my friends, I vnto Guilford went.

29.

There did the chorus to proud *Godwin's* play
First tell the sequele of my miserie,
There first appear'd the plot of my decay,
There the sad scene of my black tragedie
Was first begun by *Godwin's* treacherie,
 And there my friends took hands in death and led
 The tragick daunce, which I did after tred.

30.

When vnto Guilford with my troope I came,
Godwin of purpose did augment our traine,
And for one place could not containe the same,
Lodging in diuers Ins he did ordaine,
Which might twice tenne or thirtie men containe,
 Which he before with *Harrold* did deuise,
 The better to effect his enterprise.

31.

Plentie, the childe of peace, in euerie house
Did furnish out the tables with her store,
Lyæus fruitfull cup with full carowse
Went round about, mirth stood at euerie doore,
The oliue branch deceitfull treason bore,
   Vsing the voice of peace which sweet did sound,
   To vs at feast that were, in solace drown'd.

32.

The greedie gorge repleat with plentious feast,
Besots the sense and duls the spritfull minde,
Th'infeebled braine with strength of wine opprest,
Losing all quick conceit, soone waxed blinde,
The depth of *Godwin's* plots we could not finde:
   Deceit workes surest, where the wit before
   Hath weakned been by plentie's feastfull store.

33.

This fatall banquet, that did then forerun
The day that death put many soules to flight,
To soone did end, too soone the golden sunne
Fell to the ocean, and the dismall night
Came vp from seas to work my foule despight,
   The woe which chearefull day before did hide
   To end our cheare, the night too soone descride.

34.

When in my naked bed my limbes were laid
And I enchain'd in deepest sleepe did lie,
The rufull clamors of my friends betray'd
Did ring about mine eares: with whose sad crie
I rose from sleepe, and from my bed did flie:
   But by the armed men and doores fast made,
   My weapons gone, I knew I was betraid.

35.

Then did I looke, when death would at the doore
Come in, to sease my life with violent hand :
My chamber shooke, my hart gan tremble sore,
And as in horror I did silent stand,
Vp flew the doores, in rusht an armed band,
   Who laid rude hands on me in spightfull hate,
   Without respect vnto my princelic state.

36.

But when Aurora left her Tython's bed,
And through each part of heau'n disperst her light,
My Norman friends fast bound in bands were led
To Guilford downe, to whom in dolefull plight
None gaue releefe, false *Godwin* tooke delight
   With sight of their sad death his eyes to feed :
   Such sight would cause the hardest hart to bleed.

37.

By casting lots they were ordain'd for death :
Of ten, still nine did beare the bitter fate,
And in strange torture did expire their breath :
The tenth reseru'd did liue in wretched state
Of bondage, till the day of finall date :
   And thus six hundred vnto death being done,
   All faithfull friends did my sad fall forerun.

38.

My friends thus slain, through couert shades of night,
That none to my abode might priuie be,
Conuey'd I was to th'ile of Elie hight,
There to abide, till *Harrold* did decree,
What kinde of death from thrall should set me free :
   Where I with care consum'd for death did call
   Vntill a fate far worse then death did fall.

39.

Then cause thy muse with me to mourne her fill,
And all yee nightlie birds, that do appeare,
As gastly signes, shrieke out your deadlie ill,
Let all that wofull is and voide of cheere,
That may augment my dole, to me draw neere,
    And helpe me with their vncouth companie
    To tune the song of my sad tragedie.

40.

Despoil'd by foes of all my princelie state,
And lockt in dungeon deepe from sight of heauen,
Sweete dame delight, with whom I liu'd of late,
Farre from my sad abode away was driuen,
And carefull sorrow for companion giuen:
    The youthfull spring of my delight was done,
    And winter's state now in my youth begun.

41.

And with the winter of my woes begun
The frostie seasons winter bore apart,
Whose vnkinde cold did through my bodie run,
While gnawing hunger to increase my smart,
For want of foode did feed vpon my hart:
    Thus I with cold and hunger long foreworne,
    Did nought but mourning pine and pining mourne.

42.

My greene of youth with griefe's sad sighes was blasted,
The sap of my life blood began decay,
My flesh through fast and euill fare was wasted,
My hart did faint, my strength did fleete awaie:
Ah God that death oft wisht so long did stay,
    Why did not fates preuent my bloodie foes,
    And with keene knife in death cut of my woes?

43.

My woes, alas, as yet were to begin:
For though my foes were priuie to my cries,
Yet could my rufull plaints no pitie winne,
To take from me at length they did deuise,
The last of all my comforts, both mine eyes:
　Ah cruell foes, too cruell were ye bent,
　Why could my death to you not yeeld content?

44.

When first the instruments of *Harrold's* ire
Did come prepar'd to rob me of my sight,
Hoping that death, which I did long desire,
Had then been sent to me, the last despight
That can be done to man in wretched plight:
　These words I spake to moue remorse of mind,
　While teares in plentie downe my cheeks declin'd.

45.

" Thrice happie men, if ye the tidings bring '
Of happie death my dolefull daies to end,
From whose long houres my lasting death doth spring,
This last request to you I do commend,
That pitying my sad plaints, you may befriend
　My wretched soule with quicke dispatch in death,
　And not with torture, when I yeeld my breath.

46.

Behold this bodie pin'd away with woe,
This starued carkas in such rufull plight,
That who, alas, can poore prince *Alfred* know,
These cheekes, whilome so full of fresh delight,
Now wexed pale and wan, are dri'd vp quite
　For want of dew : yet dew'd with sad supplies
　Of mournefull teares still flowing from mine eies.

47.

Yeeld then, O yeeld some comfort in this case,
And do not yee augment my deadly smart,
Ile hug sweet death, and with kind armes embrace
His grizly shape, and wooe him with his dart
To end my woes, by wounding my poore heart:
 Only make ye dispatch when ye begin,
 And heau'ns impute it not to you for sin."

48.

This did 1 speake, supposing they were come,
With violent hands to make my life the prize
Of wished death: but by more grieuous doome,
I first adiudged was to lose mine eies:
For while that vnto heau'n with pitious cries
 Vpon their crueltie I did complaine,
 They reft me of my sight with bitter paine.

49.

Thenceforth, as caytife cast in dungeon deepe,
Where with fresh griefe my hart did hourely bleed,
As Philomel that spends her time of sleepe
In mournefull tunes recording his misdeed,
Whose lust in wastefull woods her shame did breede,
 Night's endlesse houres till death did end the same,
 Against my foes I wasted in exclame.

50.

Famine, the childe of want did feast my soule,
And in my brest her hungrie arrow steepe,
The black night's shreeking bird, the ghastlie oule
With balefull notes in waking woe did keepe
My greeued soule, when nature craued sleepe,
 With whose shrill shreekes my plaints did beare a part,
 And kept true time with sighes from sorrowing hart.

51.

Sorrow and griefe with waste of teares drawne drie,
Suppli'd the place where eyes did once remaine,
Whose want of teares my hart did still supplie
With drops of blood, fresh bleeding with the paine
Of wounding griefe which it did long sustaine,
 Of which impatient to despaire being driuen,
 Cursing my birth, I thus did crie to heauen.

52.

Woe worth the wombe, which nature did inforce
To bring me forth and leaue me in neglect:
Woe worth the starre, that did direct my course,
If anie starre the course of life direct:
Woe worth the houre, which did my birth detect:
 Woe to you all, that did conspire with foes
 To drowne my better dayes in bitter woes.

53.

Why do I liue? ah, why liue I the space,
Of half a day in this my mournefull mew?
Why doth grim death so often shew his face?
The woefull waste in me why doth he view
Of nature's worke: and yet not craue his due?
 Why do I liue, yet daylie die with paine?
 Why do I die, yet daylie liue againe?

54.

To you therefore ye heau'ns, whose cheerefull face
With mortall eyes I neuer more shall see,
To you and all your powers I crie for grace:
Let me, ah let me now no longer be,
But by swift death from foes do set me free:
 My dayes be ouer long, for death I crie,
 End then my dayes (O God) and let me die.

55.

Wanting the salue of patience, wherewithall
To cure the sore of sorrow growne so rife
In my grieu'd hart, thus forc'd I was to call
For death to launch the wound with his sharpe knife,
Which griefe had festerd in my loathed life:
  Who in his horrid shape himselfe did show
    To me poore wretch, with too much paine and woe.

56.

For death at last with such vnkinde constraint
Did force my soule from th'house of her vnrest,
That neuer prince had cause of more complaint:
Nature's vnkindest children will detest
My death's vnkindnesse, and the flintest brest
  Wil learne t'expire sad sighes with sorrow's breath,
    To heare me tell the manner of my death.

57.

From thence, where in grim darknesse I did dwell,
I forth was fetch't, and by my foes that been
First stript I was, and then (O woe to tell)
My wombe was opened with a rasor keene,
With paine of which downe sinking, I did weene
  That then my gasping ghost would haue expir'd
    The breath of life, which I so oft desir'd.

58.

But after grieuous groane, when as my sprite
With feeling sense reuiued was againe,
My sterne tormentors, seeming to delite
In this their bloodie game, while I in vaine
Did beg dispatch of my tormenting paine,
  With vnremorsefull hands againe began
    T'inflict more woes on me most woefull man.

59.

At that smart wound, which in my wombe they made,
One of my intrailes ends they forth did take,
Which, out alas, (that ere it should be said
Of any prince) they fasten to a stake,
And with sharpe needles (yet my ghost doth quake
  To thinke on it) my tender sides they wound
  About the stake to make me go around.

60.

With painfull wounds they wound me in each part,
When still I stood to ease me of such woe,
Yet worse then painfull wounds increast my smart
As oft as I about the stake did go,
Then in this pitious plight, what should I do?
  Death's touch I felt: yet by my foes made blind
  The readie way to death I could not find.

61.

At length my soule vnable to withstand
Th'afflictions of my foes, in heart made stout
With torment of my wounds, I hand in hand
Went on with death that deadly stake about,
Vntill my bowels being winded out,
  With death I fell, and in that fall did find
  An end of woe, an end of griefe of mind.

62.

Men light of credence warned be by me,
To deeme no profer'd friendship firme and sure,
Till truth haue triall made, for flatterie
Makes fained loue the fittest cloake t'obscure
Falsehood from truth, which practise puts in vre,
  Of which that henceforth I a Mirrour bee,
  My storie told, I leaue it vnto thee.

THE TREACHEROVS

Life and infamovs Death of Godwin,

Earle of Kent.

THE ARGUMENT.

" THE banefull plot of *Godwin's* treacherie,
And *Alfred's* rufull end," quoth Memorie,
" With doubt may shake a weake belieuing mind,
Which to resolue, no better proofe I find
Then *Godwin's* selfe, who in his turne shall tell
After prince *Alfred's* death, what him befell,
How he in seruice of *Canute* his king,
In forren warres himselfe in grace did bring,
How he in state did rise, with what increase
Of noble issue, heau'n his house did blesse,
His life produc'd to length of many yeares,
Foure kings he serues, in *Edward's* daies appeares
His treason t'*Alfred*, till that time conceal'd,
Which by the hand of heau'n is then reueal'd,
His oath, his periurie, bread stops his breath,
Heau'n plagues his issue for prince *Alfred's* death,
The truth of which, that we at large may heare,
Let fame's trumpe cause his guiltie ghost t'appeare."

Godwin. *(a guilty ghost)* 623 *(primitive)*

ANOTHER ARGUMENT.

Godwin as guiltie tels th'ambitious ayme
Of his desire, first cause of all his shame.

1.

FAIRE fall the steps, that happily do end
Their course begun in vertue's painfull race,
Many begin that steepie hill t'ascend,
Where vertue dwels; but few do find such grace
As not to faint, ere they attaine that place,
  To tread the path of praise I first begunne,
  But lost true praise, which I did weene t'haue wonne.

2.

Ambition tooke me by the haplesse hand,
And with delight led me another way,
Both blood and treason in my way did stand,
Which heau'n with vengeance failes not to repay,
Although reuenge of men escape they may:
  Of which that I a Mirrour be, giue eare,
  And in thy mind my fatall storie beare.

3.

I am that *Godwin*, sometimes earle of Kent,
Who with king *Harrold* did conspire to shed
Prince *Alfred's* blood, which I too late repent :
For whereas I vpon the glorious bed
Of spotlesse honor, might haue laid my hed,
 This one blacke deed of my false treacherie,
 Doth brand my name with spot of infamie.

4.

If from that way, my steps had neuer strai'd,
Which in my youthfull daies I first did tread,
My famous acts, which now are all decai'd,
Had liu'd in lines of gold, and in the stead,
Of foule defame, with praise had crown'd my head :
 But partiall fame lets passe our deeds of praise,
 Our worser deed she keepes for future daies.

5.

When bold *Canutus*, that victorious king,
O'er Danes and English did in triumph raigne,
Desire did set my youthfull thoughts on wing
In pursuit of renowne, which to attaine,
From pleasure's idle bed I did refraine :
 Ease duls the sprite, each drop of fond delight
 Allaies the thirst, which glorie doth excite.

6.

About this time we being secure of warre,
Fame by report did giue to vnderstand,
That the bold Vandale threatned to inferre,
Such strong inuasion both by seas and land
Vpon the Danes, that all the force of hand,
 That they for warre could make, would scarce suffice
 To giue repulse vnto their enemies.

7.

Which when *Canute* did heare, his Danish force
He mustred vp, and I inspir'd by fame,
Troopt vp my Kentish friends, both foot and horse,
With whom deckt in braue armes and skill'd in frame
Of varied fight, vnto *Canute* I came,
   With whom to Denmarke I design'd did goe,
   Conductor of the English 'gainst the foe.

8.

The seas we launcht, but long we had not wau'd,
Vpon the deepe, when all our ships did scatter,
Proud Nereus fom'd, the sea lookt blacke and rau'd,
The billowes rude rouz'd into hils of water,
Cuffe after cuffe the earth's greene bankes did batter,
   Which with their force our scattered nauie bore
   In great distresse about the Norway shore.

9.

Tost to and fro, the storme at length ore-blowen,
We did arriue vpon the Danish coast,
Where, in the field the Vandale dreadlesse growen,
Their valours to auouch, did vaunt and boast
Of spoiles and captiues in their conquering host,
   'Twixt whom and vs the fight had then begun,
   Had night, to part the fray, not twixt vs run.

10.

The night, that giues each deathlesse creature rest,
In chaines of darknesse all the earth did bind,
And in our tents, each one as seem'd him best,
Did passe the time: but in my labouring mind
Nor rest, nor sleepe could entertainment find,
   Care kept me waking, how I best might bring
   My selfe in credit with *Canute* the king.

11.

The time, I thought, did fit occasion yeeld,
The foes with fond neglect of vs at shore
Did sleepe secure, dispread about the field,
Their guard slight kept, their men were wearied sore
With hunting after spoile the day before,
    Whom to *Canute* vnknowne could we confound,
    Our names I thought, would euer be renown'd.

12.

These thoughts, but newly borne in my great mind,
By secret messengers I did conuent,
The English chiefetaines all, whom I did find
In heart so well inclin'd, that all were bent
With readie hands to strengthen my intent,
    And in each point their minds to mine did frame
    For this affaire, all thirsting after fame.

13.

Our English quarter, which did vtmost lie,
We vndescri'd, drew forth, and on our way
With silence we did passe, the windes blew high,
And night her darksome wings did wide display,
Lest th'aduerse scout our purpose might bewray :
    So forth we went, and gain'd with good euent,
    The drowsie Vandale's vtmost regiment.

14.

The outward watch, and courts of guard being slaine,
Through all their rankes by slaughter making way,
We did at length their fatall tents attaine,
In which, as in neglect they sleeping lay,
Without respect all went the common way,
    That leads to death, as well the noble kind
    As the ignoble, were in death confin'd.

15.

Then was th'alarum giuen, and euery where
The foes with fearefull shouts did pierce the skie,
Heere one affrighted silent stands, and there
Another dreading death doth mercie crie,
Heere one cries stand, another there bids flie:
   In euery place death's terrour did abound,
   And all on heapes our foes we did confound.

16.

At length, troopt vp in haste the foes made head,
Twixt whom and vs ensu'd a deadly fight,
Grim death in darknesse hid, did bring more dread
With his approch, the foes, through sable night,
Their friends from foes could not discerne aright,
   In which distresse vnable long to shield
   Their campe from spoile, they fled and left the field.

17.

Darknesse suborn'd their flight, and did preuent
Our purpos'd pursuit for th'intended chase,
Their campe laid waste, we found in euery tent
Rich spoile and captiues, men of no meane place,
With more renowne our deed of worth to grace,
   Of which *Canute* our king did nothing know,
   Vntill the morning's light our deeds did show.

18.

For when in east Aurora did appeare,
Canute intending to begin the fight,
When he of our supposed flight did heare,
In rage he vow'd reuenge for such despight,
And forth in furie marcht: but when in sight
   The Vandale's campe appear'd despoil'd with fire,
   And all their host dispers'd, he gan admire.

19.

The Danes, in troopes all gathered, stood amaz'd
To see through what great dangers we had run,
Vpon the slaughtered Vandales wounds they gaz'd,
Vpon the captiues and the rich spoiles wonne,
Applauding all with praise, what we had done,
    The king himselfe, in heaping praise on praise,
    The worth of this our deed on high did raise.

20.

The good successe of this high conquest won,
My name in credit with the Dane did bring :
And to encrease this honor new begun
In th'horrid warre betwixt the Norway king
And prince *Canute*, of which the world did ring,
    I by my deeds vpon the Norway coast,
    Did saue *Canutus* and his fainting host.

21.

When *Olauus* and *Vlfe* those brothers stout,
With their Norwegians in a dangerous fight,
Against *Canute* successefully had fought,
I with my English souldiers in his sight
Regain'd againe, what he had lost by flight,
    And forc'd proud *Olauus* to flie the field,
    Who to our king his crowne did after yeeld.

22.

Grac'd in all warre affaires without mischance,
With king *Canute* in such great grace I came,
That he, my name and fortunes to aduance,
His sister gaue to me for wife, whose name
Hight *Thira* faire, a ladie of great fame,
    Whom I with earnest suite did often proue,
    And in the end obtain'd her for my loue.

23.

Thus with auspitious lookes the heau'ns beheld,
The new borne infant of my towring state,
Which growing vp, with proud ambition swell'd,
Flattering it selfe with hope of happier fate,
Which to obtaine I long did lie in wait,
 And left at length true honor's path to tred,
 To trace the footing which ambition led.

24.

When death did end *Canutus'* life and raigne,
I standing in contention, t'whom the right
Of England's vnswai'd empire should remaine,
Canute's base sonne, ambitious *Harrold* hight,
Did step into the throne in my despight,
 Being backt by diuers peeres, that sought to clime
 By his support in this new change of time.

25.

'Gainst whom I stood with fained loyaltie
To those two princes, sonnes of *Egelred,*
The true borne heires to England's emperie :
In which affaire, had fortune false not fled
And turn'd her backe, the crowne had grac'd my hed:
 For had I gain'd the garland in their name,
 Neither of them should haue enioy'd the same.

26.

But al-seeing heau'n, that did my drift perceiue,
To take effect would not permit the same,
Those strong built holds I was constrain'd to leaue,
In which defiance I did first proclame,
Against the bastard in prince *Alfred's* name:
 Wherefore my oath I vnto *Harrold* past,
 To be true liegeman, while my life did last.

27.

Yet did not this my mounting thoughts beat downe,
Nor quell the pride of my aspiring mind,
My heart still aim'd at England's royall crowne,
Aspiring hope did th'eies of reason blind,
To all impietie I was inclin'd,
   Of which prince *Alfred*, whom would I had neuer
   Betray'd to death, a Mirrour liues for euer.

28.

The maner of whose death I shame to tell,
Such was the cruell torment of the same,
And such the noble vertues, that did dwell
In th'heart of that sweet prince, whose liuing name
To all posteritie records my shame,
   The more his vertues were, whose blood I spilt,
   Remorselesse wretch, the greater was my guilt.

29.

Curst be the gracelesse heart's vnswayed pride,
Which tempted me to act so foule a deed,
Why as at first did not faire vertue guide
My steps in path of praise? why in her steed,
All grace abolisht, did foule vice succeed?
   With state and greatnesse, vertue seldome dwels,
   State fosters pride, pride all good grace expels.

30.

After the murder of this guiltlesse man,
Long time I flourisht with prosperitie,
In slothfull *Harrold's* daies my house began
With many valiant sonnes to multiplie,
Who after came to great authoritie,
   Of whom hereafter I intend to tell,
   Hearken meane while what vnto me befell.

31.

Hearken ye glory-thirsting men, and heare
Iudgement of wreakful wrath powr'd downe by Ioue
On me, and on my house, that all may feare,
Aspiring honor's height those plots to proue,
To which vaine pride the heart doth often moue,
   Of which, both I, and all my progenie,
   May Mirrours be to all posteritie.

32.

When *Harrold* had, the tearme of three yeares space,
Vpon the English throne borne supreame sway,
He dying left a name of foule disgrace,
T'obtaine true fame, he neuer gaue th'assay,
His idle life in sloth did fleet away:
   In houres of ease, who euer spends his daies
   To future time, leaues seldome any praise.

33.

Vpon the throne, his brother did succeed
Prince *Hardiknute*, *Canutus'* lawfull sonne,
Whom I did feare, lest for my bloodie deed
By his edict, I should to death be done,
Which I in lawfull triall could not shun,
   To murdred *Alfred* he was borne halfe brother,
   Got by *Canute* on *Emma* his queene mother.

34.

Yet I being right expert in euery thing,
Which did pertaine to subtile policie,
˙Both tooke a solemne oth before the king,
That I from guilt of *Alfred's* blood was free,
With which his friends had often charged mee:
   And also, that mine oth might fauour finde,
   With golden gifts I did corrupt his minde.

35.

If that the powre of gold doe conquer kings,
Corrupts the noble, and deceaues the wise,
Subdues the valiant: yea, the brother brings
To sell his brother's blood for golden prise,
Wherewith to glut his greedie auarice:
  No maruell then, if that my gold did bring
  This fained oth in credit with the king.

36.

Of *Hardiknute* this fauour I did finde,
I liu'd in grace and great felicitie,
To me the rule of all things hee resign'd,
He onely kept his kinglie dignitie,
All things were swaid by my authoritie:
  But after two yeares space, by suddaine death
  In midst of mirth, he lost his vitall breath.

37.

Being at a feast vpon a solemne day,
At Lambeth house, within the bishop's place,
With cup in hand his life did fleet away,
To ground he fell and did cold death imbrace,
Leauing few friends to waile his woefull case:
  In loue of drinke he liu'd, in drinke he dide:
  Such drunken death oft drunkards doe betide.

38.

Prince *Edward, Alfred's* brother, he being dead,
Was left the lawfull heire vnto the crowne,
Which I did claime as due from *Edgelred,*
And on his seeming foes I seem'd to frowne,
That sought with violent hands to pluck him downe:
  For well I did perceaue, he being king,
  To good effect my purpose I should bring

39.

Zealous he was, and did so much delight
In sacred precepts of .pure sanctitie,
That farre more fit he seem'd in all men's sight,
To liue religious in a friarie,
Then sway the sceptor of a monarchie :
 Yet seing the right did vnto him pertaine,
 He was permitted ouer vs to reigne.

40.

Vpon whose minde more pliable to yeeld
To rule of others, then to rule alone,
The hope of future fortune I did build,
And after him, vnknowne to anie one,
I laid my plot to step into the throne :
 For vnto him my daughter I did wed,
 Twixt whom I knew would be a barren bed.

41.

Although the choycest eye could not select
A virgin with more sweets of beautie fild :
Yet for in hart he iustlie did suspect
His brother *Alfred's* blood by me was spild,
Her beautie with delight he nere beheld,
 My dreaded power, which might haue dangerous beene
 To his estate, was cause he made her queene.

42.

Whereby in future time my valiant sonne,
My *Harrold* stout a title did pretend
Vnto the crowne, who by his valor wonne
High credit with the king, who in the end
So far to him his fauour did extend,
 That after his decease, he did ordaine
 The crowne and kingdome should to him remaine.

43.

Thus did I sit in top of fortune's wheele,
Knit to the royall blood of England's crowne,
Till death did strike, mischance I nere did feele,
Fortune at my successe did neuer frowne,
Who in the hight of pride pluckes manie downe:
    Dreadlesse I liu'd, being dreaded still of all,
    Fearing no lucklesse chance, that might befall.

44.

Beneath the sway of my securefull power
I from the king my guilt did long conceale
Of *Alfred's* death, vntill that fatall houre,
When fate appointed did my soule appeale,
And in my death my bloodie deed reueale:
    Blood for due vengeance neuer calls in vaine,
    Heau'n will reuenge, when we remisse remaine.

45.

Once sitting at the table with the king,
My son, whose office was the cup to beare,
By chance did stumble, as he did it bring,
And lightlie did himself againe vpreare,
At which by me these speeches spoken were:
    " Ha, ha, my liege," said I, " see how one brother
    In time of need can well sustaine the other."

46.

To which the king return'd this sterne replie
With browes contract, signes of his angrie minde,
" Most true it is," said he, " and so should I
My louing brother *Alfred* liuing finde
To helpe me now, but for thy self vnkinde."
    With which neere toucht: yet all distrust to shun,
    Bread streight I took, and thus my oth begun.

47.

" This bread," quoth I, " I neuer wish to take
Downe through this throat into my hollow chest,
But choaking me, God grant, that it may make
My death a scandall, to my soule vnblest,
Which heav'n henceforth for euer may detest,
  If I your brother *Alfred* did betray,
  Or gaue consent to take his life away."

48.

No sooner had I spoke, and taken bread,
But of the heauens, my wish I did obtaine,
Vnto the ground I instantlie fell dead,
While yet the bread did in my throate remaine,
Through which to passe, the breath did striue in vaine:
  In death did heau'n detect my villanie,
  In death did vengeance iustlie seise on mee.

49.

Which in my suddaine downefall tooke not end,
This dreadfull iudgement could not satisfie
The wrath of righteous loue, who did intend
The extirpation of my progenie,
In the reuenge of *Alfred's* tragedie,
  With seu'n sonnes done to death, all valiant men,
  My name did vade, as it had neuer ben.

50.

My eldest sonne, hight *Swaine*, in his rash moode
With rage incen'st, with his vnhappie hand,
Did beast-like spill his vncle *Byorn's* blood,
For which a pilgrim to the holie land
He was inioyn'd by churche's strict command:
  Where rouing Saracens vpon the way,
  With murther did his vncle's death repay.

51.

The next was *Harrold,* who in *Edward's* reigne,
After my death grew famous in this land,
Manie great victories he did obtaine
Against the Welsh, who with rebellious hand
Against the king themselues did proudlie band:
  For which in name and fame he was renown'd,
  And by the king with manie merits crown'd.

52.

But the third brother did thereat enuie,
Tostie by name, a man of mickle pride,
Which when his brother *Harrold* did espie,
His angrie hart did swell, and rage did guide
That reason, which doth man and beast diuide:
  For on a time inrag'd with anger's sting,
  They fell at ods in presence of the king.

53.

Where *Harrold* caught young *Tostie* by the haire,
And with his fist did smite him on the face:
But by well-wishing friends they parted were:
Yet *Tostie* in his minde for such disgrace,
Did vowe reuenge in more conuenient place,
  And forthwith from the court with angrie looke,
  To *Harrold's* house his readie way he tooke.

54.

Where when hee came, the seruants hee did finde
Preparing all things for the king's repaire,
On whom he wreak'd the vengeance of his minde:
For not a man his wrathfull sword did spare,
In his reuenge they all alike did share:
  Yet could not this his furie's heat asswage,
  Their limmes he hew'd in peeces in his rage.

55.

Which he amongst the hogsheads of pure wine,
Vessels of ale and cydar did bestow,
And in the lomes of meath, and tubs of brine,
And other sorts of liquor he did throw
Heads, legs, and armes, whence yet warme blood did flow:
   Then sent he word, that at his brother's honse
   The king should find good store of poudered sowce.

56.

For which offence, he was exilde the land,
And *Harrold* after *Edward* as his right
The crowne did claime, 'gainst whom no peere did stand :
Yet *Tostie* did the Norway king excite,
In battaile gainst his brother for to fight,
   In which by *Harrold* vpon Stamford plaine,
   Both *Tostie* and the Norway king were slaine.

57.

Stout *Harrold* in the field his death's wound tooke,
With his two bretheren *Girth* and *Leowin*,
At Battaile abbey 'gainst the Norman duke:
For in ist iudgement then did heau'n begin
To plague this land for my detested sinne,
   Which from that time twice thirtie yeares and foure,
   With Norman bondage was oppressed sore.

58.

Thus by decree of fate without remorse
By the keene sword fiue sonnes to death's doome past,
The sixt in riding on a head-strong horse
Into the siluer Thames dark deepe was cast,
In which his soule the pangs of death did taste :
   The seuenth and last was in close prison kept,
   Vntill in death the conquering Norman slept.

59.

Yet beere heau'ns heauie iudgement did not end,
My wretched mother, though forworne and old,
Vntimely fell, who, while she liu'd, did send
Yong dames to Denmarke, where for gaine of gold,
Their virgin beauties vnto lust were sold,
 For which offence, to all the world a wonder,
 She stricken was from heau'n by horrid thunder.

60.

And that on earth, my shame might neuer die,
The sea's proud waues haue ouerrun my lands,
Which did of yore by Sandwich hauen lie,
Where now bound vp in Neptune's watrie bands,
They at this day are called *Godwin* sands,
 And since are made of pasture-springing-ground,
 A dangerous gulfe the sea-man to confound.

61.

Thus for prince *Alfred's* blood, which I did shed,
loue in the tempest of his wrathfull mood,
Powr'd downe his wracke vpon my wretched hed :
Of all foule ils most aduerse vnto good,
Vengeance pursues the blushing sinne of blood,
 Blood out of earth with cries importunes heau'n
 To grant reuenge, vntill reuenge be giuen.

62.

Vnto a sinfull wight, though time do seeme
With wings of waste his shame away to wipe,
Although the king of heau'n secure he deeme:
Yet when his sore of sinne is waxen ripe,
Of his smart scourge he feeles the bitter stripe,
 The truth whereof, that I may testifie,
 Amongst thy Mirrours place my tragedie.

THE LIFE AND DEATH

of Robert svrnamed Cvrthose,
Duke of Normandie.

THE ARGUMENT.

" When Ioue," said Memorie, " for Normans slaine
Through *Godwin's* treason vpon Guilford plaine,
From English birth his wreake would not reuoke,
But made it stoope to conquering *William's* yoke:
In that sad time, that noble prince I find
Most worthie of record, that Norman blind,
The stout duke *Robert,* who in th'hopefull spring
Of his greene youth, rebels against the king,
His hopes deluded sets his heart on fire,
He fights succesfully against his sire,
Is absent, when his father leaues to liue,
Who to his second sonne the crowne doth giue,
The duke returnes, finds *Rufus* on the throne,
Both rise in armes, but gold doth make th'attone,
Robert to Palestine with *Godfrey* goes,
Wins fame in field against the Pagan foes,
Hearing of *Rufus'* death, he thence returnes,
Finds *Henrie* king, with indignation burnes,
Meets him in field to wreake it with his sword,
But peeres on either part make them accord,
After in peace they liue like brethren,
The duke's kind nature wronged by the queene,

Againe he armes him to reuenge his wrong,
Fights with the king, whose part he finds too strong:
In fight is taken and to Cardiffe sent,
Where long captiu'd, in seeking to preuent
The fate of loathed thrall by secret flight,
He taken is, and is depriu'd of sight,
And after with long life in thrall opprest,
He pines away with hunger and vnrest,
Whose princely ghost let fame from graue vpraise
To make those deeds a Mirrour for our daies."

ANOTHER ARGUMENT.

The Norman prince tels fame, how he was borne
To be a king, yet dies a duke forlorne.

1.

In that great booke of loue's decrees in heau'n,
Compiled ere time had any wings to moue,
The wofull wight, to whom blacke fate is giuen,
To cancell it in vaine doth after proue,
No change of time can change the will of Ioue,
   What power so potent is, that can controle
   The first decree that he did there inrole.

2.

Let fortune hold a crowne aboue thy head,
And at it with wit's best direction aime,
Rise to it royally from honor's bed,
Iustly deserue it for thy deeds of fame :
Yet shall thy carefull brow nere beare the same,
 If thou in that star-text of euery thing
 Foredoom'd for fate, be not inrol'd a king.

3.

Of which that thou a lasting Mirror haue,
Behold me heere a wretched prince of yore,
To whom true birth a crowne and kingdome gaue,
Whom vertue did inrich with all her store
Of goodly gifts, to make me fit therefore,
 Of which depriu'd by destinie's decree,
 Woe and alas was only left to mee.

4.

Behold this feeble bodie pin'd away
With hunger's waste, which once so stoutly bore
Our Sauiour's badge in many a bold assay :
Behold the place where eyes haue stood before,
Now filled vp with blacke congealed gore:
 Behold blind *Beauchampe* duke of Normandie,
 New crept from graue to tell his tragedie.

5.

A prince I was borne of the Norman blood,
To that victorious king the eldest sonne,
Who with his Normans, like a furious flood
From southerne seas did England ouerrun,
And to his heires the golden garland wonne,
 Though heau'ns and fortune neuer would agree,
 That of the same I should possessor bee.

6.

When fortune's gentle hand had set the crowne
Vpon his happie head, when all assaies
Of his bold foes in field were beaten downe,
To me his eldest borne my state to raise,
The Norman dukedome with such long delaies
 Assigned was, that I being set on fire
 For such protract, turn'd rebell 'gainst my sire.

7.

Like lustie Phaeton, that gaue th'assay,
To guide the head-strong horses of the sunne,
Puft vp with pride to seeke his owne decay,
Gainst conquering *William* his rebellious sonne,
T'aspire the dukedome violently begun,
 And fier'd with heat of gaysome youth did venter,
 With warlike troopes the Norman coast to enter.

8.

The false French *Philip* dreading euery houre,
The towring state of my vnconquer'd sire,
Gaue life to my attempt, and sent a powre
Of tall strong men, as fuell for the fire
Of my ambition, lest I should retire,
 And faint in pursuit of the warre begun,
 Betwixt my sire and me his gracelesse sonne.

9.

As th'hungrie flame growen powerfull by degrees,
And flying on wings of winde throughout a wood,
With thirstie tongue lickes vp the leauie trees,
Or as the rising of some stormie flood:
So blinded with neglect of humane good,
 My natiue Normandie I did inuade,
 Making her soile the spoile of Mars his blade.

10.

To whose distresse the wrathfull conqueror came
Through sea's rough waues, wilde furie was his guide,
Cursing my birth, 'gainst me he did exclame,
And in reuenge affection set aside,
He vow'd to scourge my most vnnaturall pride,
  Setting his second birth yong *Rufus* hight,
  Before me in his loue, and in my right.

11.

At Archenbraie, both battels first did braue
Each other with proud proffer for the fight,
There th'ensignes with the wanton winde did waue,
The plume-deckt helmes with gold all horrid bright,
With pale reflection glitter'd in the light,
  And 'bout both hosts in troopes the horsemen stood
  Like loftie cedars in a thicke-set wood.

12.

When as the trumpe the banefull blast begunne,
In clamorous noise we clos'd on either side,
Brother 'gainst brother, father 'gainst the sonne
Themselues oppos'd, nature in fight defi'd
Euen nature's selfe, the sun in heau'n did hide
  His glorious head, denying vs his light,
  As lothing to behold so strange a sight.

13.

The soules of mortall men were put to flight,
Blacke deeds of death each one did vndergo,
Need boldned cowards, hope gaue wings to might,
And made each one his best strength to bestow,
To purchase fame by downefall of his foe,
  Death set on foot ran round about the field,
  Whole troopes of men t'her conquering stroke did yeeld.

14.

In th'heate of fight, I caus'd a troope of horse
To breake vpon the rereward of the foe,
Who brauely gaue the charge, and with such force
Their fainting troopes in heapes did ouerthrow,
That they their rankes were forced to forgo,
   Whom I well mounted on a tall strong steed,
   To the maine battell did pursue with speed.

15.

Where vnder th'ensigne of his royall armes,
T'encounter with the king it was my chance,
Who bent with his owne hands, to wreake his harmes,
Did fiercely charge me with his well-aim'd lance,
'Gainst whom vnknowne my selfe I did aduance,
   And in my winged course with staffe in rest,
   I gaue the charge vpon his royall brest.

16.

But heau'n did calme false fortune's threatfull brow,
And did auert the point of my sharpe speare:
Yet by his ribs the flesh it vp did plow,
And running through his arme made blood appeare,
The stubborne staffe the king to ground did beare,
   Who falling from his horse in mind dismai'd,
   Vnto his men aloud did call for aid.

17.

The voice descri'd my error, and with speed
I downe dismounting to my royall sire,
Did take him vp, and for my gracelesse deed
His pardon vpon my knee, I did require,
Pleading mistake t'appease his kingly ire,
   Whom I remounted, and from field conuey'd,
   Lest danger should his noble life inuade.

18.

Meane time the horse troopes, who by me design'd
Gaue charge vpon the flankers of the foe,
So beat the field about, that conquest shin'd
Vpon our helmes, slaughter and ouerthrow
On the aduerse part inforc't such workes of woe,
    That all by flight sought saftie, none durst stay,
    Rufus disgrac'd, and wounded went his way.

19.

Conquest in triumph on my brow did stand,
Fame did renowne my sword in euerie place,
Fortune with fame did ioyne her helping hand
With my displeased sire to winne me grace,
T'whom nature pleaded my vnhappie case,
    And forc't him yeeld (that both in loue might liue)
    What reason would, and rage denide to giue.

20.

Restor'd to grace like Saturn's god-like sonne,
To England I returned with the king,
Where *Malcome* in his absence had orerun
The north from Tuuidale, where Tweed doth spring,
Vnto the Tine, whose streames such profit bring
    Vnto that towne, which on her bankes doth stand,
    Now call'd Newcastle built by my command.

21.

T'oppose the furie of th'inuading foe,
The king my late tri'de valor did imploy,
The Tine with wafting waues did seeme to woe
My swift accesse, to saue her from th'annoy
Of her proud foes, who daylie did destroy
    The towres and townes, which did themselues enranke
    About her streames, vpon the pleasant banke.

21.

Where with my troopes, when I appeard in sight
Beneath the kinglie lyon marching on
Towards Tuuidale, to seeke the foes for fight,
Malcolme retirde beyond the Tweede, and none
In England's bounds durst stay to looke vpon
   Our angrie host, for peace the foemen su'd,
   Which for the common good I did conclude.

23.

But leaue I now, to speake of blessed daies,
In which I liu'd true subiect to my king,
Leaue we a while to memorize the praise
Of my best deeds, thy muse againe must sing
My rebell pride, whence worse effects did spring,
   Mischiefe now tracts each step, that I do tread,
   Vnlookt for plagues falles downe vpon my head.

24.

Suppose thou seest me on the German coast,
Clad in rebellious armes against my sire,
Trooping vp men, to make a compleat host,
Waging th'vnwilling mind with golden hire,
And hope of spoile, to furnish my desire:
   Bent once againe, vnto my sire vnknowne,
   To claime the Norman dukedome, as mine owne.

25.

But ere my wicked sword I could vnsheath,
Vpon the bed of fraile mortalitie
Lies conquering *William*, in the armes of death,
T'whom enuious fame in his extremitie,
Brings tidings of his sonne's impietie,
   Debatefull enuie, finding once the thing
   That breeds our shame, sets euill newes on wing.

26.

Could enuie find a darker cloud of shame,
Wherewith t'obscure the shine of my renowne?
Could fate for future woes more fitly frame
The houres of time, to cause the conqueror frowne,
Then when in death, he should dispose the crowne?
　Enuie, fate, time and all things else agree,
　To crosse that man, t'whom fortune crosse wil bee.

27.

The sickly king my sire, whose daies were done,
Thinking my course did threaten sure decay
To the rich trophie of his conquest wonne,
What nature gaue to me, did giue away,
To set the state vpon a surer stay:
　For leauing life, he left by his decree
　His crowne to *Rufus*, and his curse to mee.

28.

Tell me ambition, whence hadst thou that might,
To stirre vp nature in bold *Beauchamp's* brest
Gainst God, 'gainst king, 'gainst nature's selfe to fight,
Enacting by my hand such deeds vnblest,
From the first motion of my mind's vnrest?
　From hope of rule, and empire's blind desire,
　Thou hadst that power to make me first aspire.

29.

Reason strooke blind euen from my youth's first spring
With fond-bewitching hope in state to clime,
That hope made frustrate by the powerfull king,
Did but prefigure out for future time,
Th'vnfortunate effects of my foule crime,
　The losse of crowne, the losse of all my right,
　The losse of freedome and my bod'ies sight.

30.

Scarce had the hand of vnimpeached death,
Clos'd vp the eyes of England's conquering king:
But fame, whose listning eares feeles euery breath
Of whispering rumour, set him selfe on wig,
And ouer seas to vs did tidings bring,
 That our dread sire was to his graue gone downe,
 And vnto *Rufus* had bequeath'd his crowne.

31.

Heart-swolne with furie to reuenge such wrongs,
And claime the priuiledge then almost lost,
Which vnto birth by nature's gift belongs,
Lest *Rufus* pride in my disgrace might boast,
My quarrell strengthned with a mightie hoast,
 I did arriue on England's southerne shore,
 Gainst whose white rocks the British billowes rore.

32.

The English peeres abhorring *Rufus* pride,
In me expecting a more milde command,
Both by affection and by dutie tide
T'aduance my cause, each with his armed band,
Gainst *Rufus'* powers in field did stoutly stand,
 Whose wilder nature knowne in former daies,
 Now many friends to my attempt did raise.

33.

Th'vnconquered Kentish in the English east
With that stout bishop *Odo*, first made head,
The actiue people, coasting on the west,
Marcht beneath *Mowbraie's* ensigne proudly spread,
The northerne rout the valiant *Bygod* lead,
 And the bold Britaines fauouring my right,
 Were troopt by braue *Mountgomerie* valiant knight.

34.

Th'vsurping king seeing such sterne stormes to frowne,
On the first spring of his ambitious raigne,
Fearing the fall of his new-borne renowne,
Sought by insinuating words to gaine,
What by the sword he could not now maintaine,
  His golden gifts with many faire sweet words,
  Did turne the edge of our reuengefull swords.

35.

He did not seeke t'vsurpe the crowne by might,
Such pride his loyall heart did nere inuade,
He knew my senior birth did claime that right,
He, we being absent, tooke in hand, he said,
In our behalfe the scepter then vnswai'd,
  The which, since now, he did the same enioy,
  He crau'd to hold of vs, as our vice-roy.

36.

His gifts still flowing from him in excesse,
Did giue full power to euery mouing word,
And that in me he might all doubts suppresse
Of fraudulent deceit, he did accord
That he of me, as of his supreame lord,
  Should hold the crowne, and yearely I should claime
  Three thousand markes, as tribute for the same.

37.

Fraternall loue so well her powers appli'd,
To end these iarres begun betwixt vs twaine,
That he constrain'd t'appease his wonted pride,
And I respecting glorie more then gaine,
Did reunite our selues in loue againe:
  The frowne of Mars did bring his stomacke downe,
  And golden gifts did calme our martiall frowne.

38.

Farre from the fruitfull Albion's peacefull shoare,
For th'easterne world thy muse thou now must wing,
Who in her flight a loftie pitch must soare,
Of those stout pilgrims in high straine to sing,
Which th'holy hermit did to Salem bring,
   Imploring aid of princes in the west,
   Against the Pagan's bloodie acts in th'east.

39.

I as a partner in that great affaire,
With my support that iourney to vphold,
My wants with store to furnish, did not spare
My Norman dukedome, which for summes of gold
Till my returne the king did morgag'd hold :
   Gold doth men's thoughts to high attempts prepare,
   And ouergilds the danger of the warre.

40.

Hearken how fame vpon the Norman coast
With her shrill trumpe from kingdomes far away,
Summons vnto an head my warlike host,
Behold the sackfull troopes in braue array,
Beneath my ensignes for this bold assay,
   Who martiall'd by my hand, with ample traine,
   Do crowne the vtmost bankes of Belgike Seine.

41.

Behold the English famous for his bow,
Sharpning his angrie arrowes for the field,
The Scot with his long pike his cunning show,
The Britaine big-bon'd-bold, not borne to yeeld,
Addressing brauely both his sword and sheeld,
   See how the Norman manageth his horse,
   The Irish shakes his dart with manly force.

42.

As wak'd from sleepe, with christians wofull cries,
Bound by the Saracen in captiue bands,
And often blushing at the late surprise
Of those milke-hony-flowing holy lands,
Now made the spoile of Pagan's conquering hands,
  Hence did we march with heau'ns great king for guide
  Into the east, to beate downe Pagan's pride.

43.

Inglorious age, made drunke with dregs of peace,
Heere iustly may I taxe thy peacefull time,
Heere must our muse's warlike song surcease,
A carping straine, a more inuectiue rime,
Doth best befit the nature of thy crime:
  Looke backe at vs, mourne thine owne want of praise
  And glorious deeds, to glorifie thy daies.

44.

Say glorie, say, hath peacefull follie furl'd
Thy flag of honor? li'st thou dead in graue,
With great *Heroes* of the elder world,
Who led vs ouer Hellespontus waue
Beneath his badge, whose blood the world did saue?
  Arise, arise, call forth the christian man,
  Against the house of tyrant Ottoman.

45.

Hearke, how Thessalian woods records the cries
Of captiu'd Greekes vpon Penæus shore:
Behold how sacred Salem wasted lies:
See, see, how Sion mournes, where saints of yore
Did in sweet hymnes the king of heauen adore:
  Behold that blessed land, the cursed seat
  Where raignes th'Arabian Turkish Mahomet.

46.

O warlike nation, where is now that name,
Which th'English sword did graue on Acon's wall,
Why do your valours sleepe, vp, vp for shame,
Let not your countrie's ancient glorie fall:
Go, free poore christians from proud Pagan's thrall,
    Redeeme his sepulchre, who did redeeme
    The world from death, with blood of such esteeme.

47.

Transport thou now thy muse to Bosphorus' brim,
Ouer whose waues from Iuno iealous dame,
To Asian meades of yore did Io swim,
From whom transform'd the streame then tooke his name,
And since that time hath still retain'd the same,
    Ouer whose waues as we did waft our host,
    Much christian blood we 'gainst the Bulgar lost.

48.

Hence did we march to Hellespontus flood,
Where Helle, with yong Phrixus, put to flight
By stepdam's rage, of which in feare they stood,
Flying, alas, and falling with affright,
Into the waue sunke downe in Phrixus' sight:
    Yet still to liue, in leauing her deare breath,
    She left her name to Pontus at her death.

49.

The coast we tooke, where once Abydos stood,
Whence nak'd Leander, wafted by the light
Of Hero's loue, so often swom the flood,
Till Helle rauisht with so sweet a sight,
Enuying Hero's hap, in her despight
    Into the deepe her deare Leander drew,
    Where to his loue he sigh'd his last adew.

50.

There on the plaines, where Troye's sad ruines stand,
Whence Agamemnon's troopes haue often run,
To shun the furie of great Hector's hand,
Against the Pagan many deeds were done
Beneath our standard of Ioue's powerfull sonne,
   There all the host, as towards Nice we past,
   With spoilefull hands laid all the countrie wast.

51.

The noble citie Nice, so strongly wall'd,
·We with our conquering host begirted round,
Her gates we wonne, her turret's tops we scall'd,
Her towring walles we eqnall'd with the ground,
And all her pride did in the fire confound:
   Amongst whose spoiles great Solyman's faire make,
   With her deare children we did captiue take.

52.

Then did stout Heraclêa stoope her pride
And seeing the Niceans yeeld, did yeeld with them,
From thence to Tarsus we our host did guide,
Fast by the bankes of Cydnus, whose sweet streame
Did seeme t'inuite vs to that stratageme,
   Wafting vs, with slow wateis sliding downe
   From mountaine Taurus, vnto Tarsus towne.

53.

Where when we came with sp'rite infus'd from heauen,
We through the walles did force our dreadfull way,
The mightie towne into our hands was giuen,
The captiue foes in pitifull dismay,
With teares bemoan'd the imminent decay
   Of their strong walles, which Perseus so renown'd
   Had long before erected from the ground.

54.

Thence our triumphant standards we aduance
To Syria-ward with *Godfrey* for our guide,
Where on the way, with seruice of my lance
In many a fight against the aduerse side,
I with fresh strength our fainting host suppli'd,
 And forc'd the Pagan *Pyrrus* from the field,
 Who fled, and made faire Antioch wals his shield.

55.

Whom we pursu'd, and by the siluer streames
Of swift Orontes, where the king of light
Vpon our armes did cast his golden beames,
Our troopes did tracke the foe-men, turn'd to flight,
'Till Antioch towers shot vp themselues in sight,
 Whose pride we menac'd with victorious armes,
 And shooke it in long siege with loud alarmes.

56.

Nine times the pale-fac'd queene of peacefull night,
Did lose that siluer lustre in her wane,
Which she receiu'd from Phœbus cheerefull sight,
And nine times did her brothers light againe
Renue that losse, which she did erst sustaine,
 While Antioch walles our armie did enclose,
 And stood in daily skirmish with the foes.

57.

In the ninth month, vpon the topfull brow
Of the towne-gate, the flag of truce did waue,
The captaine *Pyrrus* haughtie heart did bow,
The citie stoopt her pride, and for to saue
Her selfe from spoile, her gates wide open gaue,
 Whose wealth, as due reward of our long toile
 To th'vniuersall host, was giuen for spoile.

58.

Should I assay to tell each conquest wonne,
Which at that time the christian host did crowne,
Or bring to light each high atchieuement done,
Before we could attaine that sacred towne,
Which God's sonne's sepulchre doth so renowne,
  Our muse, though willing all at large to show,
  Yet were too weake such taske to vndergo.

59.

See how the Persian fronts vs in the field,
Vnder the sway of whose huge horse-arm'd host,
The earth with bowing backe doth seeme to yeeld,
Whose troopes in number infinite doth boast
Our swift decay, ere we do crosse their coast,
  Hemming vs round, in hope t'enrich their hands,
  With noble conquest on our conquering bands,

60.

With shouts, and war-like instruments loud sound,
Hid all in clouds of smoake they toward vs came,
In fearefull fight vpon the groaning ground
Both hosts incounter'd, glorie did enflame
Both bent to fight, both greedie after fame,
  Standerd 'gainst standerd stood, and band 'gainst band,
  Troope clos'd with troope, men singl'd hand to hand.

61.

Corbona hight, a Persian farre renown'd,
Chargeth our host with all his troopes of horse,
Stiffe stands each regiment, no ranke giues ground,
Power beats backe power, and force repelleth force,
The foes repell'd doth often shift their course,
  Oft charging and recharging euery ward,
  Where they do find the rankes most vnprepar'd:

62.

Then thicke as haile from aire's darke regiment,
When in blacke clouds a tempest raues in skie,
Steele-headed shafts from th'English bowes are sent,
Threatning the armed men as they do flie,
With singing slaughter, thicke prepar'd on high,
   Who in their flight, though some fall short of wounds,
   Yet some againe both men and horse confounds.

63.

Here th'angrie courser chaf't with deadlie sting
Of wounding shaft, for verie paine and woe
Doth stampe, doth plunge, and vp from ground doth fling,
Doth snuffe, doth puffe, doth boggle, snore and blow,
Till from his back his rider he doth throw:
   Then ranging through their host with sinewie shankes
   He wounds his friends, disturbing all their rankes.

64.

There one with shaft infixed in his brest,
As the stalke stoopes his top orecharg'd with seed,
Hangs downe his head: another here opprest
With feare of death, forsakes his wounded steed,
Each place throughout the field our eyes did feed
   With ruine of the foes dispred on ground,
   Gasping for breath with many a bleeding wound.

65.

Greate Ioue the god of conquest, who from harme
Did garde our host in euerie such assay,
Did through the cloudes stretch out his mightie arme,
And on the foes did powre downe swift decay,
Slaughtering their men on heapes, few fled away:
   Twice fiftie thousand dead in field did fall,
   With stout *Corbona* their cheife generall.

66.

Here could I tell the sack, which did decline
The pride of Salem, whose high walles withstood
Our fierce assaults twice fifteene dayes and nine,
How euerie street polluted with the blood
Of Pagans slaine, did seeme a crimson flood:
  How Egypt's Soldan did before vs fall,
   Whom to these warrs, this towne distrest did call.

67.

But back to England we must turne our eye,
From whence, since first to Palestine I came,
Fiue times bright Pisces in the azure skie
Had in their yerelie course outrun the Ram,
Whose iust returne againe begins the same,
  Where in our absence let vs view in state,
   What changes haue ben wrought by time and fate.

68.

Our brother *Rufus* with vnrighteous hand,
Swaying the scepter in the English throne,
Did so oppresse the people of his land,
That, when he left to liue, he then left none,
That would as friends his suddaine death bemone:
  He in that forrest did death's cup carowse,
   Which fatall was vnto the conqueror's house.

69.

A goodlie place, that forrest once had ben,
Where manie a towne and manie a temple stood,
Made sacred with the prayers of holie men,
All which without respect to common good,
My father did conuert into a wood,
  Intitling it New Forrest, and for game,
   Did after keepe wild beasts within the same.

70.

Which stir'd the stormefull wrath of heauen's great king,
Who seeing his temples equald with the ground,
And where his priests sweet pæans once did sing,
And oft with thankfull prayers his altars crownd,
Hearing the crie of th'hunter and his hound,
   Did in that place punish th'impietie
   Vpon my sire, in his posteritie.

71.

His second sonne, my brother *Richard* hight,
A hopefull youth, whom nature's hand had sto 'd
With sweetes of youth, as he, for his delight,
Did range this wood, was through the bodie gor'd
By saunge beasts, whose death my sire deplor'd
   With bitter teares: yet could not quench the fire
   Of loue's fierce wrath, so moued was his ire.

72.

Rufus, his third borne sonne, in that same wood,
When he had strook an hart that fled his sight,
Was by another crost, where as he stood,
At whom one *Tirrill* call'd, a Norman knight,
A shaft let flie, which in the lucklesse flight
   Missing the deere, and glancing on the ground,
   Vpon the brest the king to death did wound.

73.

He dead, yong *Henrie* for his learning skill
Surnamed *Beauclerk*, did aspire the crowne,
And wonne the English peeres vnto his will:
Fortune once more vpon my state did frowne,
Aud from ambitious throne did keepe mee downe,
   Mocking my hopes, denying mee command,
   When she had put a scepter in my hand.

74.

After the conquest of Ierusalem,
The princes did amongst themselues accord,
To crowne my temples with the diademe,
That my abode might in distresse afford
Comfort t'all christians gainst the heathen sword:
   But tidings of my brother *Rufus* fall,
    From Palestine to England me did call.

75.

That sword renownd with fall of Pagan foes
 I ow did brandish gainst my brother's brest,
That sheeld, which did the Persian oft oppose
In skirmish in the field, was now addrest
Against my friends, to worke mine owne vnrest:
   And all mine ensignes fam'd in forraine fight
    At Winchester did waue in *Henrie's* sight.

76.

Where, close to swords in fight we would haue stood
Had not our friends foreseene the future harmes
Of our debate, who tending either's good,
To calme the tempest of warre's threatfull stormes,
First caus'd vs lay aside our angrie armes, '
   Then counsell'd *Henrie* to such couenants yeeld
    As *Rufus* did, when he the state did weeld.

77.

As he, while he did liue, for England's crowne,
Inioyned was by general states decree
Three thousand markes each yeare to pay me downe,
So *Henrie*, younger borne by birth, then he,
To like conditions thenceforth should agree,
   To which we both consenting did depart,
    One from the other seeming pleasde in hart.

78.

But hooded with the shew of outward loue,
Beguiling my simplicitie of mind,
He in the end a deadly foe did proue,
In my franke brest by nature too too kind,
A cunning way to catch me he did find:
  Into the best minds pliable to good,
  Deceit soone enters maskt in truth's plaine hood.

79.

His queene, a woman sweetly tongu'd and faire,
By whom the king at his desire did aime,
With speech so affable did so insnare
My princely pliant thoughts, that in the same,
She could impresse, what forme she pleas'd to frame:
  So free was I, that what her heart could craue,
  As was my wont, with prodigue hand I gaue.

80.

The tribute due for England's emperie,
At her request I freely gaue away,
Whereby my title and my dignitie
I lost, in that I could not then gain-say
A queene's request, proud *Henrie* had his prey:
  A woman's power to proue my power but vaine,
  What I had done did soone vndoe againe.

81.

Wanting in after times necessitie,
Those golden sinewes of my dukedome's state,
To strengthen my much weakned royaltie,
I gaue the king words of despitefull hate,
And for reuenge tooke armes: but froward fate
  With clouds of shame did now eclipse the shine
  Of all my conquests, won in Palestine.

82.

Ore the sea's narrow brest from England's coast
To Normandie my furious brother came,
Gainst whom, my cause being good with my small host,
Before the fort of Tenerchbray by name:
Though fewer farre, in battel's bloodie frame
   We did aduance, where though *Mortaigne* and I
   So stoutly fought, our folke the field did flie.

83.

Vpon that day, when fortie yeares before,
My sire to conquer England gaue th'assay,
In which he first set foot on England's shore,
The king and I did meet in battell ray,
In which, alas, we Normans lost the day:
   For on that day the Normans England won,
   Was Normandie by English men orerun.

84.

Where, though false fortune turn'd her treacherous face,
And then began to worke our future woe,
Though dreadfull Pallas did denie vs grace,
And 'gainst our side her selfe in field did show,
Yet did we scorne, as scar'd, to flie the foe,
   Mortaigne and I 'gainst them alone did fight,
   Till multitudes did ouermatch our might.

85.

Let Pallas cease to sing of armes oppos'd,
Sorrow must be the subiect of her song,
In stead of greaues with golden buttons clos'd,
In which she marcht amidst our martiall throng,
Now in sad straine, while we relate our wrong,
   She in the sock the tragicke dance must lead,
   Whose dolefull measures, we captiu'd do tread.

86.

Thy muse, that in warre's bloodie hew was sent
To Palestine, must now in blacke be found,
Each word with heauie fall she must accent,
Each symphonie must yeeld a dolefull sound,
Each measure with a captiue band be bound,
    And euery couple's sad catastrophe,
    Double the woes of our captiuitie.

87.

Now Normandie's great duke in *Henrie's* hand
Vpon the rouling billowes running high,
Is carried captiue from his natiue land,
To which oft turning backe his heauie eie,
It seemes a farre to follow him and crie,
    " Adew, deare lord, adew, who neuer more
    With one step's touch shall grace my sandie shore."

88.

With griefe arriu'd on Cardiffe's rockie coast,
Where Seuerne first meets Nereus wanie brood,
Through whose blacke waues faire Sabrine's guiltlesse ghost,
T'Elizium bankes did passe the fatall flood,
In whose defence king Locrine lost his blood,
    The tyrant king, in dread what might befall,
    Did confine me within the castle wall.

89.

As bird in cage debarr'd the vse of wings,
Her captiu'd life as nature's chiefest wrong,
In dolefull dittie sadly sits and sings,
And mournes her thralled libertie so long,
Till breath be spent in many a sithfull song:
    So heere captiu'd, I many daies did spend
    In sorowe's plaint, till death my daies did end.

90.

Where as a prisoner, though I did remaine:
Yet did my brother grant this libertie,
To quell the common speech, which did complaine
On my distresse, and on his tyrannie,
That in his parkes and forrests ioyning by,
 When I did please, I to and fro might goe,
 Which in the end was cause of all my woe.

91.

For on a time, when as Aurora bright
Began to scale heau'n's steepie battlement,
And to the world disclose her cheerefull light,
As was my wont, I with my keeper went
To put away my sorrowe's discontent :
 Thereby to ease me of my captiue care,
 And solace my sad thoughts in th'open aire.

92.

Wandring through forrest wide, at length we gaine
A steepe cloud-kissing rocke, whose horned crowne
With proud imperiall looke beholds the maine,
Where Seuern's dangerous waues run roling downe
From th'Holmes into the seas, by Cardiffe towne,
 Whose quicke deuouring sands so dangerous been
 To those, that wander Amphytrite's greene.

93.

As there we stood, the countrie round we ey'd
To view the workmanship of nature's hand,
There stood a mountaine, from whose weeping side
A brooke breakes forth into the low-lying land,
Here lies a plaine, and there a wood doth stand,
 Here pastures, meades, corne-fields, a vale do crowne,
 A castle here shootes vp, and there a towne.

94.

Here one with angle ore a siluer streame
With banefull baite the nibling fish doth feed:
There in a plow'd-land with his painefull teame,
The plowman sweates, in hope for labor's meed
To get the earth with childe of Ceres' seed:
 Heere sits a goatheard on a craggie rock,
 And there in shade a shepheard with his flock.

95.

The sweet delight of such a rare prospect
Might yeeld content vnto a carefull eye:
Yet downe the rock descending in neglect
Of such delight, the sunne now mounting high
I sought the shade in vale, which low did lie,
 Where we reposde vs on a greene wood side,
 Afront the which a siluer streame did glide.

96.

There dwelt sweet Philomel, who neuer more
May bide th'abode of man's societie,
Lest that some sterner Tereus then before,
Who cropt the flower of her virginitie,
Gainst her should plot some second villanie:
 Whose dolefull tunes to minde did cause me call
 The woefull storie of her former fall.

97.

The redbreast, who in bush fast by did stand
As partner of her woes, his part did plie,
For that the gifts, with which Autumnus hand
Had grac'd the earth, by winter's wrath should die,
From whose cold cheekes bleake blasts began to flie
 Which made me think vpon my summer past
 And winter's woes, which all my life should last.

98.

My keeper with compassion mou'd to see,
How griefe's impulsions in my brest did beate,
Thus silence broke: " Would God, my lord," quoth he,
" This pleasant land, which nature's hand hath set
Before your eyes, might cause you to forget
   Your discontent, the obiect of the eye
   Oft times giues ease to woes, which inward lie.

99.

Behold vpon that mountaine's top so steepe,
Which seemes to pierce the cloudes and kisse the skie,
How the gray shepheard driues his flock of sheepe
Downe to the vale, and how on rockes fast by
The goates frisk to and fro for iollitie:
   Giue eare likewise vnto these birds sweet songs,
   And let them cause you to forget your wrongs."

100.

To this I made replie: " Fond man," said I,
" What vnder heau'n can slack th'increasing woe,
Which in my grieued hart doth hidden lie?
Of choice delight what obiect canst thou show,
But from the sight of it fresh griefe doth grow?
   What thou didst whilome point at to behold,
   The same the summe of sorrow doth infold.

101.

That gray coat shepheard, whom from farre we see,
I liken vnto thee, and those his sheepe
Vnto my wreatched self compar'd may bee:
And though that carefull pastor will not sleepe,
When he from rauenous wolues his flock should keepe:
   Yet here, alas, in thrall thou keepest me,
   Vntill that woolfe my brother hungrie bee.

102.

Those shaghair'd goates vpon the craggie hill,
Which thou didst shew, see how they friske and play,
And euerie where doe run about at will:
Yea when the lion markes them for his prey,
They ouer hils and rockes can flie away:
　But when that lion fell shall follow me
　To shed my blood, O whither shall I flee?

103.

Those sweet-voic'd birds, whose aires thou dost commend,
To which the echoing wood returnes replie,
Though thee they please, yet me they do offend:
For when I see, how they do mount on hie,
Wauing their out-stretcht wings at libertie:
　Then do I thinke, how bird-like in a cage
　My life I leade, and griefe can neuer swage."

104.

Heere sighes broke off my speech, and that in mind
I vndisturb'd might in that place bemone
The lot adiudg'd to me by fates vnkind,
I did command my keeper to be gone,
And there to leaue me to my selfe alone,
　Who doubting nothing what I would assay,
　Left me, as was his wont, and went his way.

105.

He being gone, I wandring to and fro,
Began t'imagine how I might preuent
My wretched thrall, doom'd endlesse by my foe,
T'attempt all danger I stood fully bent,
Finding the meanes to perfect my intent,
　Which at the last I found, alas, the while,
　Since fawning fortune did my hopes beguile.

106.

Alone long wandring through the desert wood
Farre from the castle, I did chance t'espie,
Whereas a lustie gelding grasing stood,
Whom straight I backt, and did for freedome flie
Through vnknowne waies, that none might me descrie:
  But what is hid from heau'n, or who can shun
  God's firme edict, by which all things are done?

. 107.

In swift careire, as I did heedlesse passe,
And through a meadow greene did make my way,
In midst of which a muddie quauemire was,
Into the same my horse did fall, and lay
Vp to the bellie, which my flight did stay,
  Where striuing, as I was from thence t'haue past,
  They that pursu'd me, found me sticking fast.

108.

To Cardiffe thence they bore me backe againe,
As one whom frowning fortune did despise,
And to the king of me they did complaine,
Who with himselfe did tyrant-like deuise,
That I for this offence should lose mine eies:
  Which when he tooke, what did he leaue behind,
  But woe in captiue bands to leade the blind?

109.

My bodie thus the darkesome caue was made,
In which my soule abode, as it had been
Confin'd to dwell in house of endlesse shade,
The windowes shut, no light could enter in,
The light put out no comfort could be seene:
  And left thus blind, I seeke to flie my foes,
  Both soule and bodie Cardiffe doth inclose.

110.

Bidding farewell vnto the world for euer,
There in my chamber, as a forlorne guest,
My wretched selfe I wilfully did seuer
From all resort, where with long night opprest
(For day did shun the place of mine vnrest)
  To yeeld griefe passage, after sad sighes giuen,
  Thus oft I call'd, with hands vp-lift to heau'n.

111.

" Thou powerfull God, whose champion I haue been
Fiue cold bleake winters, both by day and night,
In field against the cursed Saracen,
Although I seeme forgotten in thy sight,
Yet now behold me heere a wofull wight:
  And seeing I liue in such calamitie,
  Send death to end my dolefull miserie.

112.

Can I distinguish day from darkesome night?
Or do I know the seasons of the yeare?
Know I when spring deokes earth with sweet delight,
When summer's sun glads earth with his bright cleare,
Or when in woods Autumnus' fruits appeare?
  O no, of nought but winter can I tell,
  Whom by his boystrous blasts, I know right well.

113.

Where is become that azure concauite,
That doth so many wonders rare infold?
Where all the host of starres, so infinite?
Where daie's great monarch drawne in carre of gold?
Where night's bright queene, so beautious to behold?
  O still, they do remaine in heau'n's faire frame,
  Although I neuer more shall see the same.

114.

Where now the valley greene, and mountaine bare,
The riuer, forrest, wood, and crystall springs,
The hauke, the hound, the hinde, the swift-foot hare,
The lute's sweet straine, the voice that sweetly sings,
And princely sports in courts of mightie kings?
   Where now are these? O let not memorie
   With thought of these augment my miserie.

115.

Heere do I sit in shades of darkenesse grim,
While others walke in light at libertie:
Heere I in waues of wofull teares do swim,
Condoling my vnhappie miserie,
While others laugh, and sing for iollitie:
   Send then, O God, send death for my reliefe,
   Too heauie is the burthen of my griefe."

116.

Thus many times, with bitter plaint and mone,
To vtter woes in words I did assay,
Witnesse ye wastefull walles, whose flintie stone
Haue euen dropt teares, to heare me night and day,
With pitious voice lament mine owne decay,
   Oft wishing death, which sorow in the end,
   And *Henrie's* vnkind scoffe did timelesse send.

117.

For as he should vpon a solemne day
Make triall of a scarlet vestiment,
The cape being straite, the which he did assay
To put vpon his head, by chance did rent,
Which with this scornefull scoffe to me he sent,
   " Vnto our brother beare the same," said he,
   " We know he hath a sharper head then we."

118.

The garment being brought, the rent I found,
At which my troubled thoughts so grieued were,
That many doubts did in the same abound,
Which made me aske of him, that did it beare,
If any one before the same did weare:
  Who told me of the king's disdainfull scorne,
  And how by chance the same by him was torne.

119.

Affliction bleeding fresh at this wide wound,
My heart griefe's burthen could no longer beare,
But downe I cast my selfe vpon the ground,
Where I with wretched hands, the hoarie heare
From off my aged head, alas, did teare,
  And when my tongue was free, against my foe
  I forc'd it vtter forth these words of woe.

120.

" Woe, woe is me, that I was euer borne
Of halfe so many yeares to liue the space,
And in the end to liue my brother's scorne,
Yea trebble woe to me, since such disgrace
Doth in despight my former deeds deface:
  Then perish all my deeds, be neuer seene,
  Die fame with shame, as it had neuer beene.

121.

Could not disdainfull *Henrie* be content,
Into his hands my kingdome to surprise,
Could not my thraldome cause him to relent,
Nor th'vnsustained losse of both mine eyes
His rage 'gainst me his brother yet suffice?
  But must he thus my princely state abuse,
  And as an almesman his owne brother vse?

122.

Why haue yee then, ah why, haue yee thus long,
Ye vnremorsefull fates produc'd that thread
Of loathed life, by life to lengthen wrong?
Why clip ye not my clew? why am I fed
With breath of life, and yet in life am dead?
  Curst be such fate, and curst that fatall hower,
  When first begot, I came within your power."

123.

Hardned with griefe, in spight of death to die,
Thenceforth as loathing life I stopt mine eares,
When hungrie food for appetite did crie:
And while with hunger nature slowly weares,
My food was sighes, my drinke griefe's mournfull teares,
  Famine at length did blow the banefull breath,
  Whose bitter blast did strike my soule with death.

124.

Euen as the naked woods, whose greene is lost,
Clad in hoare, their ruth do seeme to show,
In teares turn'd t'ysicles by wintrie frost:
So I my head made white with age and woe,
While from th'eyes organs teares downe drizeling flow,
  When as I did perceiue approching death,
  Thus tooke my last farewell with fainting breath.

125.

" Adiew the daies, that did my dole prolong,
Adiew the nights, that vexed me so soare,
Adiew false fortune, cause of all my wrong,
Who laughes to scorne the fame I won of yore,
Adiew O wrongfull world for euermore:
  Ye that conspir'd my sorowes to renew
  Both daies, nights, fortune, world and all adew.

126.

These hands to thee (O God) that for a gift
Thine owne deare Sonne for sin to death did yeeld,
These hands, I say, to thee I now do lift,
Which once did beare thy badge in brazen shield,
Against the Pagan foes in many a field,
 Beseeching thee, from whom all mercies flowes,
 To grant such grace, as death may end my woes.

127.

Twice fortie yeares and more, my daies haue ben,
And twice fifteene the Ram his race hath runne,
Since first, O Cardiffe, as in darkesome den,
Within thy walles mew'd vp from sight of sunne,
Forlorne, to mourne my fortunes I begunne:
 Then pitie take, O God, on th'aged blind,
 Death now begins my captiue bands t'vnbind.

128.

Leade on, leade on, vnto that heau'nly place,
Where in eternall blisse my soule must dwell,
Flie faith before, sue penitence for grace,
Backe, backe, my griefe, and vnto *Henrie* tell,
Beauchamp is dead, Cardiffe adew, farewell:"
 This said, I downe did sinke into my bed,
 In which my soule did leaue the bodie dead.

129.

Thus hast thou heard the Norman's blind duke tell
His fame in forren parts, the wretched wracke
Of his renowne, and cause for which he fell:
The iudge of heau'n to punish is not slacke,
Where men do cast heau'n's gifts behind their backe:
 Of which let my sad life in Cardiffe lead,
 A lasting Mirrour be, though I be dead.

THE MEMORABLE LIFE

and death of King Richard the
first, surnamed Cœur de Lion.

THE ARGUMENT.

" This prince," quoth Memorie, " did liue too long,
At his sterne brother's hands to beare such wrong,
Which yet reuenged was by God's owne hand,
Vpon himselfe, his children, and his land:
Two sonnes he had, of daughters also twaine,
Of which three drown'd, were swallow'd in the maine,
The fourth a daughter was, which *Maud* by name,
Of whom *Plantagenet's* two houses came:
Duke *Gefferie* of Aniou, noble knight,
Vpon this *Maud* begate that worthie wight,
Duke *Henrie*, second king that bore that name,
Though second to no king in deeds of fame,
Who   ong, yet forc'd th'vsurper *Stephen* in fight
To leaue to him the crowne, his due by right:
Le in chast bed begot three sonnes and one,
ight *Henrie*, *Richard*, *Gefferie*, and *Iohn:*
ongst whom that *Richard* when both *Henries* dide,
n *England's* throne did sit as supreme guide,
nce *William's* conquest, only he of kings
is host in person gainst the Pagan brings,
e sackes Messina, beats the Cypriotes bold,
aptiues their barbarous king in gyues of gold,

Takes Acon's towers, is of the French enuide,
And left forlorne, yet after quels the pride
Of *Saladine* in field, after whose flight
He makes all Syria subiect to his might:
Prince *Iohn* rebels, the valiant king is sold.
To captiue bands, and bought againe for gold:
At his returne he crownes himselfe againe,
And is by traytor's hand vntimely slaine:
The truth of which that we exactly heare,
Fame sound thy trumpe, and cause his ghost t'appeare."

ANOTHER ARGUMENT.

Fame's siluer trumpe's farre-flying sound, doth make
King *Richard Cœur de Lion's* ghost t'awake.

1.

THE wrath of heau'n doth most pursue those men
With secret iudgement of disaster fate,
That gainst their parents haue rebellious ben,
Nature displeas'd at such vnkindly hate
Against it selfe, it selfe doth aggrauate,
    Causing the starres at such abortiue birth,
    With bad aspects to frowne vpon the earth.

2.

Seldome such cursed insects in our kind
Escape the scourge of hatefull destinie,
Vnhappie chance in iudgement is assign'd
Till death, to follow such impietie,
Which to the world my life might testifie,
   If any in this age with painefull pen,
   Had made the same a Mirrour vnto men.

3.

Why should the glorie of so great a king
Be darkned by obliuion's cloudie frowne?
Why should this age, as loathing euery thing
Of th'elder world, my trophies all cast downe,
And let my deeds in waues of silence drowne?
   As if twixt best and worst no ods there were,
   When both alike are laid vpon the bere.

4.

Long hauing slept, and now rouz'd vp by fame
That keepes the due reward of doing well,
In hope thy pen will helpe to raise my name
Out of obliuion's den where it did dwell,
In course I come my storie's truth to tell:
   That by the praise, or dispraise of my name,
   Others may make a Mirrour of the same.

5.

Of noble *Henrie*, second of that name,
The second sonne I am of sonnes twice two,
Yet second vnto none in worthie fame,
If yeelded were to me my praises due,
As may appeare by that which shall ensue:
   First *Richard* call'd, first true borne English king,
   That wore the crowne since Normans conquering.

6.

In large discourse to light I will not bring,
The obloquie of that now loathed crime,
In stubborne youth against my lord and king,
Blushing, I wish all such records of time
In darknesse dead, and wrapped vp in slime:
  Yet seeing that truth bids hide no part of blame,
  I will in briefe blaze out mine owne defame.

7.

My father's browes with prints of age repleate,
Fortune that erst did smile, began to frowne,
Abus'd by flatterie and his owne conceat,
As bent with wilfull hands to hasten downe
The statefull dignitie of his renowne:
  His eldest borne he made his fellow king,
  From whose ambition his distresse did spring.

8.

Yong *Henrie* sharing equall dignitie,
And hauing set one foot within the throne,
Puft vp with pride to make a monarchie
Of his new state, he would be king alone,
A partner in the crowne he would haue none:
  Which pride of mind with bad aduice borne higher,
  Caus'd him rebell against his royall sire.

9.

To strengthen his ambition yet but yong,
The false French king in person did support
His part in field: and to be yet more strong,
The Scot and Flemming he did both exhort
With them gainst aged *Henrie* to consort,
  To whom both I and *Gefferie* my brother
  Did giue consent, excited by our mother.

10.

Not one of vs whom nature's band did bind
With due alleageance to our sire and king,
Did vnto nature's selfe not proue vnkind,
Yet could not power preuaile, nor enuie's sting
Against our sire, whom heau'n did helpe to bring
  Our stubborne neckes againe beneath his yoke,
  Our knees did stoope to his victorious stroke.

11.

Oft did we threaten ruine to his state,
His Norman dukedome with warre's wastefull spoile
We did deface, and sought to set debate
Twixt him and his: yet after all our toile,
At his weake hands we did receine the foile:
  So iust is heau'n to patron right gainst wrong,
  And guard the weake with strength against the strong.

12.

To future time the king to leaue report
Of our rebellion and his long vnrest,
Did cause to be depainted in his court
A pellican, who breeds beneath his brest
Foure yong with tender care in his warme nest,
  Of which three waxing strong, vnkindly rise
  And pecke his brest, the fourth peckes out his eies.

13.

By the three first, he did decipher forth,
Geffrie, my selfe, and *Henrie* his first sonne:
The fourth was stubborne *Iohn* his yongest birth,
Of whom when he was likewise left alone,
He beat his manly brest with age foredone,
  And ending griefe in death, to vs vnkind,
  My selfe and *Iohn*, he left his curse behind.

14.

The sinne that drew these plagues vpon his head,
Was wanton lust and loose lasciuious life,
Burnt with desire, he left his lawfull bed,
For which the iealous queene his angrie wife,
Twixt him and vs stirr'd vp debatefull strife:
   Mischiefe pursues the steps that false do proue,
   In the firme couenant of sinlesse loue.

15.

Vnhappie we, his gracelesse sonnes that were
The rods of heau'n's reuenge for his misdeed,
Did the reward of our rebellion beare,
In vs our father's curse, the plaguefull meed
Of disobedience after did succeed,
   The rods, with which Ioue executes his ire,
   He oft in iudgement casts into the fire.

16.

When *Henrie* crown'd a king in royall throne
And made in state coequall with our sire,
Attempting oft the soueraignetie alone
In sway of scepter, which he did aspire,
And yet could neuer compasse his desire:
   With indignation at his fortunes crost,
   Being stricken to the heart his health he lost.

17.

And seeing in sicknesse with repentant eies,
The vglie shape of sinne, heart-freez'd with cold,
Of death's pale terror, he for mercie cries,
And begs but this, that he may but behold
Our father's face, ere he be wrapt in mould:
   Which last request our father him deni'd,
   Doubting deceit in death, when *Henrie* di'd.

18.

My yonger brother Britaine's *Gefferie*,
A partner with vs in rebellious pride,
To pay iust paines for his disloyaltie
Vnto our father, bruzed on the side
With fall from off his horse, vntimely dide:
   In youth cut off, as most vnworthie life,
   That with his father liu'd in rebell strife.

19.

This vengeance for such disobedient sin,
Vnto my brethren as in mercie sent,
Might to my future deeds haue caueats bin:
But I in heart too stubborne to relent,
And proud prince *Iohn* did once againe consent,
   /To lift rebellious hands against our sire,
   \In his last daies when age did rest require.

20.

The French king's power we did support in field,
And did in armes the aged king constraine
To such dishonor'd tearmes of truce to yeeld,
That he in heart vnable to sustaine
The griefe of such disgrace, with sorow slaine,
   In those last words which dying he did breath,
   To vs his curse most iustly did bequeath.

21.

After his death, to shew that griefe and shame
Of my misdeeds, did put his soule to flight,
His cold dead corps, as I beheld the same,
Streaming out blood did shew the great despight
That it conceiu'd at my detested sight:
   Which forc'd griefe's drops to dew my manly face,
   Toucht at the heart with shame of such disgrace.

22.

Thus hauing blaz'd out those vnnaturall crimes,
The wicked brood of my degenerate pride,
I will no longer vilifie thy rimes:
Thou now to tell what after did betide
Vnto the house of fame, thy muse must guide,
   And mount her thoughts to th' highest pitch of glorie,
   In loftie straine to sing my golden storie.

23.

No sooner was the kingdome's scepter seene
In my right royall hand, but that in mind
Transform'd I was from what I once had beene,
And turn'd my back to fore-past shame: heau'n shin'd
Vpon my head, thoughts only now enclin'd
   To actions of true praise did heau'n aspire,
   Forren affaires gaue wings to my desire.

24.

For absolution for my trespasse done
Against my sire, when I did vnderstand
How *Saladine*, the Pagan prince, had wonne
The sacred Salem and the holy land,
Which christian princes did of late command:
   The christian badge I bore vpon my brest,
   And did direct my iorney towards the east.

25.

The ablest men through my large emperie,
That I could chuse for this so great affaire,
From England, Guien, Poyctou and Normandie,
From Britaine and from Aniou did prepare,
Themselues in best habilliments of warre,
   T'insue their father's steps, and gaine againe
   What they had wonne, and we could not retaine.

26.

Report from Rome did tidings daily bring,
Who stood in feare of th'heathen's bold assay,
How mightie *Saladine* the Pagan king,
Had proudly purpos'd Palestine's decay,
To glut the gulfe of his vnsaciate pray,
   Wishing vs hasten to the christian aid,
    Who ouer-matcht with power, were much dismai'd.

27.

The warre-god rouz'd with ratling drumme's alarme,
Rose vp and left his louely lemman's bed,
Himselfe he for the field did brauely arme,
Tooke vp his mightie launce, and boldly led
Our battels forth, with crosse-fam'd ensignes spred,
   On which as marching we infixt our eies,
    We hastned on to meet our enemies.

28.

Leauing my kingdome's state beneath the sway
Of foure estates, in peace to keepe the same,
I crost the seas and tooke my readie way
To Lyons that French towne: where when I came
The king 1 met, then *Philip* call'd by name,
   Who for this great affaire had vow'd to goe
    With his support against the common foe.

29.

Our armies being ioyn'd, we marched on,
Where that strong bridge that ouerlookes the waue
Of Rhodanus, beneath our feet did grone,
And brake, where many, whom no helpe could saue,
In that blacke strugling streame did find their graue:
   At which dismai'd, to part we did agree,
    And after both to meet in Scicilie.

30.

From hence ore aged Tython's purple bed,
For Scicilie thy muse must take her flight
To mount Pelorus, on whose loftie head,
Let her insist and view our nauall might
Afloat vpon those seas, so faire a sight
    King *Philip* on the shore with his French powers
    Did then admire from off Messanae's towers:

31.

There do behold my men in thickest throng,
Scaling Messanae's walles, and beating downe
The citie gates in wreake of that foule wrong
Done gainst vs all by that iniurious towne,
Who with first conquest did our sword renowne:
    Vpon whose walles our banners we did pight,
    Which did the false French *Philip* much despight.

32.

In spight of hate the cause we did protect
Of our queene sister, *Ioan* of Scicilie,
Whose husband dead, prince *Tancred* late elect
To sway the scepter of that emperie,
Did with vnfit repulse her due denie,
    Till now at length he by our power compell'd,
    Did yeeld her dowrie, which he long withheld.

33.

Keeping the feast of his natiuitie,
Whose birth true peace t'all humane soules did bring,
In *Tancred's* court, there first the treacherie
Of faithlesse *Philip*, that ignoble king,
Did shew it selfe: who did intend to bring
    All my designements for the christian aid,
    To ill effect by plots which he had laid.

34.

The stout Scicilian king he did excite
T'inuade my campe, and that he might not faile,
He wisht him take th'aduantage of the night:
And lest my dreaded might his mind might quaile,
He with his power would helpe him to assaile:
 So much did he maligne my name's renowne,
 Which all true noble hearts with praise did crowne.

35.

But I that did preferre a royall minde
Before base thoughts of griping auarice,
And prince-like did with bountie's hands strike blinde
The eyes of enuie in mine enemies,
Did finde such grace, that none could preiudice
 My name or state, but euen amongst my foes
 I found such friends as would the same disclose.

36.

Tancred that did admire the royalties,
That in my kingly brest did make repose,
Could not conceale the French-man's treacherie:
But with a kingly sp'rit, disdaining those
That traytors were, this treason did disclose:
 Seldome base treacherie it selfe can seat
 On the high pitch of kingly bred conceat.

37.

Philip disgrac'd, did launch into the deepe,
Being bound for Acon that besieged towne,
Where leauing him, thy muse her course must keepe
Vnto that land, whose name did first renowne
The queene of loue, and her first altars crowne:
 Whence she may safely see how Neptune raues,
 And wrackes my ships in the Pamphilian waues.

38.

When launcht vpon the seas my ships were seene,
From the Scicilian shore with that sweet maid,
Nauare's faire *Berengaria*, my new queene:
Neptune as if he did intend t'haue pray'd
On my late chosen loue, began t'inuade
 My blacke fleete's wooden walles, which he did batter
 With bounding billowes of his rough rouz'd water.

39.

Tempestuous winds, whose swelling cheekes did draw
The louring clouds full burthened with blacke showers,
Flew on the waues, which breaking with the flaw,
Foaming white froth, did rise like loftie towers,
In roring traine, trooping vp all their powers,
 Darknesse did hide the chearefull face of heau'n,
 Our ships disperst, were each from other driuen.

40.

T'encrease our feare, and make the night more grimme,
Through heau'n's thicke clouds pale lightning still did flie,
Whose dazeling flash our mazed sight did dimme,
While the world's soueraigne in the thickned skie,
Aboue our heads did thunder horriblie,
 From whence his darts with sulphurie flash he threw,
 Which brimstone-like did sauour as it flew.

41.

The seas did swell, and proudly braue the heau'n,
The windes did bellow and the billowes rore,
Many tall ships with gust of tempest driuen,
To saue themselues from spoile, all desperate bore
Vnto the hauens of the Cyprian shore,
 Vpon whose strand the barbarous Cypriotes stood
 T'encrease their woes that did escape the flood.

42.

Of those whose barkes did perish in the deepe,
Some hauing gain'd the shore with life halfe drown'd,
They tooke, whom as their captiues they did keepe,
And some by swimming hauing foooting found,
Comming on shore with death they did confound:
  Which when I heard, the storme once blowen away,
  Such wrong with iust reuenge I did repay.

43.

The depth of danger we did vndergo
To gaine the shore, such ods there was in fight:
Yet at the last our foes their backes did show,
And left the shore to vs, but after flight
Isakius their stout king resuming sp'rit,
  Troopt vp his people, summon'd far and neare,
  And threatned fight when day light should appear.

44.

But to preuent his threats, before the day
His treasure, standard, horse and royall armes
In field we tooke, from whence he fled away
Despoil'd and naked, fearing th'horrid harmes,
Which through his tents did ring with our alarmes:
  That night, whose next daie's light did promise faire
  Vnto his hopes, did end them in despaire.

45.

Heere could I tell the conquest and rich spoile,
Which for those wrongs, that we did erst sustaine,
My souldiers made on Cyprus fruitfull soile:
How false *Isakius* yeelding did remaine
With me in hold, and fled away againe,
  Whom after taken for his trespasse past,
  In guines of gold I then did shakle fast.

46.

But deeds of more import are to be told,
Thy muse must launch with vs from Cyprus shore,
That on the surging seas she may behold
Prince *Salphadine's* huge barke, whose bosome bore
Such furniture for warre, sent to restore
    The weakned strength of Acon almost lost,
    Then round besieged by the christian host.

*Salpha-
dine* the
brother of
Saladine.

47.

To whom like ▆▆ing *Delos* on the waue
We gaue the chase, till turning backe from flight,
With all her fights set vp she did vs braue,
And fifteene hundred men all arm'd for fight,
Vpon her deckes did shew themselues in sight,
    Whom in our gallies thronging in thicke croud,
    My souldiers did assaile with clamours loud.

.48.

Oft times with valour the repulse they gaue
To vs, that sought to boord their ship and scale
Her wooden walles, so high aboue the waue,
Till from our bowes, shafts thicke as winter's haile,
Their stoutest hearts with deadly wounds did quaile,
    Who shrinking from the fight my men did boord,
    And in their furie did not spare the sword.

49.

Then did appeare the ruine of the foe,
Gasping for breath in vaine, sweet life they craue,
The blood of wounded men did streaming flow
Into the flood, and here and there it gaue
A crimson colour to the siluer waue:
    Whereby through th'English fleet each little boat
    In Pagan blood triumphantly did float.

50.

With that great monster barke two hundred men
Reseru'd from death, in triumph we did scower
The seas: to Acon's siege begirted then
By all the christian host, from whose watch-tower
The foe-men viewing my approching power,
 And hearing of my deed vpon the deepe,
 No longer did intend the towne to keepe.

51.

Yet after my arriue they being fed
With lingring hope, did change their first intent,
Gainst vs the towne did proudly beare her hed :
For hearing of a priuate conuoy sent,
With fresh supplie for their prouision spent,
 Though faint for food, yet they did after sheeld
 Their walles with stout defence and would not yeeld.

52.

To frustrate Acon's hopes of such supplies,
And with some high aduenture to renowne
Our English name, finding by my espies
The passage where the carriages came downe,
From Babylon to that distressed towne:
 I with a band of choice selected men,
 Departed from the christian host vnseene.

53.

From vnder couert of a thicke-set groue,
On the carauan first the charge we gaue,
Three thousand burthened camels in a droue
We from the conuoy tooke, who for to sane
The rest from spoile, at first aloofe did waue,
 But when we towards them made, though more they were
 In number farre, they tooke the wings of feare.

54.

With many a thousand mule, and many a beast
Of other burthen, we return'd with speed
Vnto the christian host, where we did feast
Vpon the prey: the towne of this our deed
Inform'd by fame, and forc'd by hungrie need,
　　Her gates did open of her owne accord,
　　To saue her sonnes from warre's reuengefull sword.

55.

Heere must thy willing muse desist to tell
Our happie hopefull conquests in the east,
Canils breake forth, enuie rouz'd vp from hell,
Creepes into false king *Philip's* cankred brest,
Who with old hate of my good hap possest,
　　Doth by his plots the Austrian duke excite,
　　To ioyne with him to worke vs all despight.

56.

As still th'infection of this foule disease,
Contagious venome in their brests did breed,
So my name's greatnesse daily did encrease,
While they on spleene nere satisfied did feed,
Fortune still grac'd me with some glorious deed:
　　Vertue enui'd shines brighter, like the sun,
　　Which breakes through clouds, with which it was orerun.

57.

With enuious eyes, impatient to behold
The golden beames of my sun-shine like fame,
Philip with th'Austrian duke hight *Leopald,*
Without respect vnto our Sauiour's name,
The cause for which to Palestine we came:
　　Seeming heart-sicke, did thence depart away,
　　Hoping to leaue me to the foes for pray.

58.

He gone, the hand of heau'n that doth dispose
The course of things, did beare before my brest
The shield of safetie gainst our Pagan foes:
With my small troope their powers in field supprest,
The bordring christian held his right in rest:
  No crosse euent while I did there abide,
  In honor'd deeds of armes did me betide.

59.

If thou desire those famous acts to know,
Mount Perseus horse, to Ioppa take thy way,
Which at this time that fatall stone can show,
To which the virgin faire Andromeda
In bands was bound, to be the monster's pray:
  There on that rocke thy muse may sit and see
  Those deeds of fame, that then were done by mee.

60.

Assur can speake my praise, before whose wall
Great *Saladine* with all his heathnish host,
In battell did beneath mine ensignes fall,
Who in my passage seeking to haue crost
My way to Ioppa, on that salt sea cost,
  Fought from noone-tide vntill the setting sun,
  And then did flie, the field we christians won.

61.

In fortie yeares before the Saracen
Such losse did not sustaine in Palestine,
Nor in one battell lost so many men:
The towring state of mightie *Saladine*
In this fight shaken, daily did decline:
  That ancient kingdome of the Syrian land
  Did fall from him, and was at our command.

62.

From wel-wall'd Ascalon, that ancient towne
The Pagans fled with all their golden good,
Darus did stoope her pride, Assur came downe
Vpon her knees, Ioppa the port that stood
Vpon the Syrian shore, before the flood
  With generall deluge did the world orespread,
  Did beare the christian badge vpon her head.

63.

To follow fortune brauely marching on,
Who with auspicious looke did seeme to smile,
We did direct our course to Babylon:
But she false ladie did my hopes beguile,
And forc'd me with mine armie to recoile:
  Fame ouer seas on her vnluckie wing
  Sad tidings from the west to vs did bring.

64.

Backe, backe to England, with a grieued heart,
Leauing these blest affaires of th'holy one
Of Israel, we must with griefe depart:
Philip my foe excites my brother *Iohn*
In my long absence to aspire the throne:
  My England's rockie bounds ring with alarmes
  Of factious traytors, *Iohn* is vp in armes.

65.

Warn'd by report, my course I did direct
For England's bounds: but heere thy muse must know
My father's curse began to take effect:
Heau'n seem'd to frowne, the sea became my foe,
And earth conspir'd to worke my greater woe:
  By sea's darke waues and froward winds from heau'n,
  Vnto my foes at shore I vp was giuen.

66.

By tempest driuen, from danger to be free,
I made hard shipwracke on the Istrian strand,
Depriu'd of all my traine, excepting three,
Enforc'd I was to make my way by land
Through Austria, to Vienna, that doth stand
   Vpon Danubius bankes, that dukedome's seat,
   The bulwarke now gainst Turkish Mahumet.

67.

There being descri'd vnto mine ancient foe
The Austrian duke I was giuen vp for pray:
Who like himselfe, himselfe to me did show,
Bearing in mind the malice of that day,
When I at Acon, for his proud assay
   In taking for his lodging in the towne
   The palace vp, I cast his ensignes downe.

68.

Yet with this duke not long was my abode:
For when report of my captiuitie
Was newly set on wing, and flowen abroad,
Henrie then emperour of Germanie,
Forgetfull of emperiall royaltie,
   Of that false duke that had me fast in hold,
   Greedie of prey, did purchase me for gold.

69.

Vpon that man, whom fortune doth begin
To leaue forlorne, who will not seeme to frowne?
When he is sunken vp vnto the chin
In waues of sad distresse, all thrust him downe,
And suffer him in wretchednesse to drowne:
   They that did enuie my great state before,
   Did wish such state might nere betide me more.

70.

Ambitious *Iohn*, and *Philip* that false king,
Taking the time to perfect their intent,
To *Henrie* did a golden message wing,
In hope if he to set me free was bent,
Such purpose with corruption to preuent:
  Which when with terror stricken I did heare,
  No hope I had, no comfort did appeare.

71.

Ignoble age, branded with this foule crime,
This blemish thou canst neuer wipe away:
When true record shall tell to future time,
How most vniust the christian did repay
His backe returne, that did through death assay,
  Gainst paganisme t'aduance the christian name,
  Euen children shall vpbraid thee with the same.

72.

In tempest of this trouble long being tost,
Sore grieu'd in mind for my captiuitie,
At length compounding with my greedie host
Th'emperour *Henrie*, hight of Germanie,
With ransome to redeeme my libertie:
  An hundred thousand pounds I did agree
  To giue to him before I could be free.

73.

Now is my iourney set on foot againe
For my deare England: now false *Philip* stormes,
Now *Iohn* repents, and feare doth him constraine,
In peace to lay downe his rebellious armes,
And by our mother seeke to shun those harmes
  Approching on: t'whom I in reuerence
  Of her estate, gaue pardon for his offence.

74.

In England safe arriu'd, the people greet
My glad returne with bright bone-fires and bels,
My royall London in each seuerall street,
By her large gifts and golden glorie tels
Within her walles what faithfull subiects dwels:
  And I, in hope that heau'n would blesse my reigne
  With better fortunes, crown'd my selfe againe.

75.

But on the swift wings of reuenge for France,
Hasten thy muse to Vernuile that strong towne,
There see French *Philip* flie before my lance,
And at Vandosme how his armes cast downe,
He flies, and leaues vs treasure and renowne:
  Of which two flights, this age doth since that time
  To his disgrace record a shamefull rime.

76.

Disgrac'd, he cals the Britons to his aide,
With their yong *Arthur* sonne of *Gefferie*
My brother dead, for which with wrathfull blade
I entred his rich dukedome Britanie,
And vengeance tooke for his disloyaltie :
  Whence, when my wreake was past, I did aduance
  With ensignes spread into the bounds of France:

77.

Where heau'n did blesse me with such fate in fight,
That *Philip* in each field I did repell :
Let Gamages and Vernon speake his flight,
And at another time let Gysors tell,
How flying from Curseile's, with his horse he fell
  Into the waues of Geth, the bridge brake downe,
  Whom mongst his men the streame did almost drowne.

78.

Repulst with shame, he casting in his mind,
With rags of honor, how to patch the rent
In his wide wounded name, this shift did find:
Out of the greatnesse of his mind he sent
This challenge bold: if I durst giue consent,
     That fiue for him in field should hazard life,
     Against fiue men of mine to end our strife.

79.

To this bold offer I did gladly yeeld,
Yet interposing this condition,
That he as chiefest champion in the field,
Should mongst the fiue vpon his part make one,
Gainst me on th'aduerse part to fight alone:
     From which, without respect vnto a name,
     Mongst men renown'd he did reuolt with shame.

80.

Yet was a truce concluded twixt vs both,
To which with willing minde I did encline,
For that I then had bound my selfe by oath
Once more to shape my course for Palestine,
T'employ my valour gainst great *Saladine:*
     But what I did decree, death soone preuents,
     Heau'n beares the chiefest stroke in our intents.

81.

Thy muse must now put on a mourning weed,
Death doth begin to shew his ghastly face,
With sad teares mourner-like let her proceed,
To Chalus Cheuerell that fatall place,
Where death with his cold armes did me embrace:
     There let her stand, and on that towne's strong wall
     Behold the manner of my haplesse fall.

82.

My treasure spent by my long warres with France,
And gainst the Pagan for the east parts bound,
I was inform'd that in my land by chance
A British vicount, *Widdomer*, had found
A wealthie treasure hidden vnder ground :
  For whom when I had sent, he guiltie fled
  To Chalus Cheuerell to hide his hed :

83.

Whom I did follow, hastned on by fate,
And did besiege the towne, where in mine ire
For such indignitie against my state,
I made my vowes thence neuer to retire,
Vntill I should obtaine my iust desire :
  Three daies with fierce assault I did assaile,
  But all in vaine, my power could not preuaile.

84.

The towne so strongly situated was,
And the stout foes imboldned by the same,
That of our powers they did little passe :
Whose stubborne pride of strength that I might tame,
I chose a captaine, *Marchades* by name,
  To walke with me, and view that fatall towne,
  Where t'vndermine her walles and cast them downe.

85.

Each step I treade doth hasten on my end,
And leads to death vnthought vpon, vnseene :
For as with eyes infixt I did attend
The towne's foundation, loe, an arrow keene
Sent from the towne wall, wounded me betweene
  The necke and shoulder with his venom'd poynt,
  Iust in the natiue closure of the ioynt.

86.

Deepe was the wound and full of deadly paine,
Yet did it not my mightie minde appall,
Before the towne in siege I did remaine,
Vntill her people did for mercie call,
And prostrate at my feet did humblie fall:
  Whom when the raging souldiers in their ire
  Would haue deuour'd, I spar'd from spoile and fire.

87.

But death doth hasten my vntimely end,
The wound lookes blacke, the poison doth appeare
In his effects, and bids me to commend
My soule to God: my friends who held me deare,
All round about me stand with heauie cheare:
  And when I knew that breath began to vade,
  I call'd for him that had my life betray'd.

88.

Vnto the man before me brought, whose name
Bertram de Gord'an was, these words I spake,
" What iust offence," quoth I, " did cause thee aime
At my deare life? or wherefore didst thou take
Me for thy marke, and in thy aime forsake
  Hight *Marchades*, my friend, that by me stood,
  When thou didst shoot thy shaft to shed my blood?"

89.

The man with courage turn'd this stout replie:
" Because," said he, " thou in thy warres didst kill
My father and my brethren, therefore I
Did vow in my reuenge thy blood to spill:
Which since I haue attain'd and haue my will,
  What do I care though all thy friends do weepe,
  Seeing that mine shall not vnreuenged sleepe?"

90.

I did admire that his sterne words were such,
And yet forgaue his fact, and gaue command
That none amongst my friends with violent touch
On him should after lay offensiue hand :
And that he might not in their danger stand,
  I gaue him twentie crownes to beare him thence,
  From those that seem'd to threaten his offence.

91.

Thus with my chiefest foe my peace I made,
And when I sensiblie felt nature's waste,
To friends about me such like words I said:
Quoth I: " Come neere, and since all hope is past
Of longer life, whose line long cannot last,
  Attend my words, and witnesse after death,
  What in my will I to the world bequeath.

92.

To *Iohn* my brother I resigne my crowne:
Arthur is French and rebell to the state:
Seeke not with wilfull hands to hasten downe
What I haue built by future time's debate:
Factions will grow, and I foresee the fate,
  The wofull fate that England will betide
  When I am gone, that did enrich her pride.

93.

Not long thy king, deare England, can I be,
Death's cold begins into my heart to creepe,
No more thy fame can be aduanc'd by me:
To *Iohn* the prince I tender thee to keepe,
When I with death haue laid me downe to sleepe:"
  Thus death when I ten yeares had been a king,
  T'vntimely end my life and reigne did bring.

94.

My deeds I did atchieue with much vnrest,
Death with blacke period did my deare life close
In prime of age approuing heau'ns behest,
Which seldome doth allot long life to those
That to their parents proue rebellious foes:
   Of which that I may testimony giue,
   Let *Cœur de Lion* in remembrance liue.

THE VNFORTVNATE

Life and Death of King Iohn.

THE ARGUMENT.

" This prince to future time," quoth Memorie,
" Remaines a Mirrour of true charitie,
Who at his death that traytour did forgiue,
Whose bloodie hand did him of life depriue:
But *Marchades* for vengeance did suruiue,
The traytour taken he did fley aliue:
Now to the next, whom vp from graue we bring,
Prince *Iohn* the brother of the late dead king:
He takes the crowne as due to him of gift,
At whose good fortunes many hands do lift:
Philip beyond the seas inuades his lands:
Arthur in Anion with his British bands,
Pursues the aged mother of the king,
Who to the rescue all his powers doth bring:
Takes *Arthur* captiue, and for his disdaine
Sends him to Rouen castle, whence againe
He nere returnes: wonders in heau'n are seene,
Treason amongst the peeres, the wrathfull spleene
Twixt Rome's proud *Innorent* and stout king *Iohn*:
The French afresh inuade, the king finds none
To take his part: the Irish do rebell:
The Welch breake forth, both whom he doth compell
To stoope their pride: the curse of *Innocent*,
Against whose pride the king stands stiffely bent:

Philip's huge nauie doth on England frowne,
The king vnto the legate yeelds his crowne:
The lords rebell, the king is left forlorne,
Abus'd, reuil'd, and made his people's scorne:
Seekes th'aid of strangers, and in his fierce ire,
Flies ore the kingdome like a flaming fire:
The barons flie from him, and seeke to bring
The French prince *Lewis* in, to make him king:
He lands in Kent, London receiues his traine,
From th'haplesse king all fals away againe:
The French men's pride the English sore opprest,
King *Iohn's* reuenge, poore England's woes encreast:
In midst of hope t'expell his enemies,
The wretched king at Swynsted poysoned dies:
All which, since many writers in his daies,
Of very malice writ in his dispraise,
That we may heare, let fame with summons call
His princely ghost, to tell his tragicke fall."

ANOTHER ARGUMENT.

Fame cals king *Iohn:* his grieued ghost doth wake,
Comes vp from graue, and heere his turne doth take.

1.

Discord the daughter of dissension,
Home-bel-hatcht furie with bewitching charmes,
Doth sooner ruine *Cæsar's* royall throne,
Then all the imminent inuading harmes,
That can inferred be by forren armes:
    Where people hate, and where the prince doth frowne,
    What might builds vp, dissension soone puls downe.

2.

Of which I once that sway'd this scepter state,
Vniustly wrong'd by peeres, vnkindly sold
To wretched fortune by my subiects hate,
A Mirror might haue been in lines of gold,
If to this age my storie truth had told:
    But th'vnkind age presents to iudgement's eye
    My shame at large, but lets my praise go by.

3.

To whom shall I my many wrongs complaine?
Since false traditions of those enuious times,
Inuented by my foes, do yet remaine,
Liuing to euery eye in forged rimes,
As matter for the sceane obiecting crimes
    Vnto my charge, which firme in censure stands,
    Though nere enacted by my guiltlesse hands.

4.

The long concealed griefe of discontent,
Which for such vniust scandall I sustaine,
Vp from the graue my grieued ghost hath sent,
On such sterne people iustly to complaine,
That vilifie my praise with lips prophane,
    Speaking what then the superstitious wits
    Vnto this age recorded haue in writs.

5.

Could not the enuie of that age be quell'd
With my last houre's vntimely tragedie?
Could not these burning veines with poison swell'd,
Their deadly hate against me satisfie?
O no, in death their malice will not die:
  For which now summon'd by the trumpe of fame,
  I gladly come to put away such shame.

6.

My royall birth *Plantagenet* can show,
Stout *Cœur de Lion's* life declares the same,
Who was the second sonne as thou dost know,
Vnto king *Henrie* second of that name,
Who grew so great in wealth, in strength and fame,
  His yongest sonne I was, by name hight *Iohn*,
  Next after *Richard* seated on the throne.

7.

Thy lines with spot of that disloyaltie
Against my sire, Ile not defile againe,
Nor will I tell that false conspiracie
Against my brother *Richard*, to obtaine
From him his life, his kingdome, and his raigne:
  For he at large doth in his tragedie,
  Declare the manner of my treacherie.

8.

Ambitious ayme at greatnesse in the state,
Most incident to men of mightie mind,
At first did bring me in my brother's hate:
Yet in the end such fauour I did find,
That he to me, though I so most vnkind
  Did oft times seeke the fall of his renowne,
  Forgaue my fact, and gaue to me his crowne.

9.

With free consent of all this kingdome's peeres,
Aduanc'd I was to all the royalties
Of my late brother dead, and thrice three yeeres
Inthron'd I was, before my haplesse eies
Were made beholders of those miseries,
    Which in deep waues of woe did England drowne,
    And brought confusion to my state and crowne.

10.

In my first rise vnto the kingdome's state,
False France did frowne, and stirred vp the fire
Conceal'd in ashes of our ancient hate,
The yong duke *Arthur*, as he did require,
Gainst vs rebell'd, and did with him conspire:
    Both stretching forth their enuious hands, to crop
    My new growen greene vpon our cedar's top.

11.

On the swift whirlewinde of tempestuous warre,
Into Touraine and Aniou th'vtmost bound
Of this our empire, then inlarg'd so farre,
They furiously did breake, where what they found
In my defence, they laid it waste on ground:
    Of which the duke proclaim'd himselfe the lord,
    And sought t'obtaine it by the threatfull sword.

12.

Warre's fearefull earthquake shaking more and more,
The state of Aniou, I did vnderstand,
How th'aged queene my mother *Elinor*,
Besieged was by *Arthur* with strong hand,
Within a tower, which on that coast did stand:
    Who sore opprest, and in her mind dismai'd,
    In such distresse did call me to her aid.

13.

Incens'd to heare my nephewe's vnkind deed
Gainst her now in her age, that gaue him breath :
As dutie bound me, on the wings of speed
I hastned to the rescue, to vnsheath
My angrie sword, whose edge did threaten death :
   A filiall loue to rescue her from harmes,
   Both day and night did make me march in armes.

14.

Before the foes of my approch did heare,
Such expedition thither I did make,
That at their backes my ensignes did appeare :
At which dismai'd, their siege they did forsake,
And most did vnto flight themselues betake :
   Of whom were many slaine that stood in fight,
   Arthur vnhurt was taken in his flight.

15.

T'whom brought captiu'd before me, thus I spake :
" Cosin," quoth I, " what madnesse was that same,
That moued you these warres to vndertake ?
Why do you thus your royall friends defame,
In bearing armes in false king *Philip's* name ?
   Preferre you him in your esteeme more deare,
   Then me, that am to you in blood so neare ?

16.

For shame that French man's company forsake,
Let not his counsell tempt you any more :
Turne vnto me, so shall I euer take
Your cause as mine, and you againe restore
Vnto my wonted fauour as before :"
   With gentle speech thus did I him entreat :
   But thus he made replie with many a threat.

17.

" Tyrant," said he, " thou dost detaine my right,
I am, thou knowest, true heire to England's crowne:
Though vniust fortune in this lucklesse fight
Looke blithe on thee, and on my state do frowne,
Heau'n may again aduance what now is downe:
   My friends be free, though I in bands be bound,
   That will not rest vntill thou be vncrown'd."

18.

The arrogant deliuerie of this speech,
Vnto th'impeachment of our royall right,
Did in our former loue make such a breach,
That with contracted brow for such despight,
We did in rage command him from our sight,
   And did this cruell paine on him impose,
   That he for such offence his eyes should lose.

19.

But when such readie instruments of ill,
Who for reward act any villanie,
To Rouen castle came t'effect my will :
Hubert de Bourgh a man of valiancie,
That then had *Arthur* in his custodie,
   Withstood their purpose, and his part did take,
   Saying, that I those words in furie spake.

20.

The heate of anger cool'd, conscience began
In th'eare to whisper how I had offended,
And when I heard how *Hubert* valiant man,
Prevented had what I in rage intended,
As reason would, his courage I commended :
   Yet after this by *Arthur's* haplesse woes,
   I did incurre the scandall of my foes.

21.

Close kept in Rouen castle by that knight,
Whose wals his steps from starting thence did bound,
Casting in mind how to escape by flight,
At last vnfortunate a way he found
To climbe the wall, that did begirt him round :
   A forward mind impatient to sustaine,
   The losse of freedome did procure his baine.

22.

Haste prickt him forward to redeeme the time,
Greedie desire his freedome to regaine,
Aboue the castle walles did cause him clime:
From whence as enuious fate did first ordaine,
He downe did fall into the riuer Seyne :
   Whose waues against that castle wals did swell,
   Where to the world hc breath'd his last farewell.

23.

He dead, vnto my charge false *Philip* laid
That in his blood I had imbru'd my hands,
And in reuenge thereof did craue the aid
Of many princes, who with warlike bands
Did in their rage depopulate my lands :
   T'whose distresse with aid I could not come,
   Worse fortunes did befall me heere at home.

24.

Mischiefe on mischiefe fals t'encrease my woes,
At home my faithlesse barons do rebell,
The Irish rise, the Welch turn'd treacherous foes,
And enuie, lest this monster I should quell
Of many heads, her selfe comes vp from hell,
   And stirres vp Rome to ioyne her hands with hate :
   No king did fall beneath so hard a fate.

25.

The heau'ns foretold such things before their time,
Before my haplesse hand that cup did take,
In whose blacke deadly wine my death did swim,
Th'whole aggregate of heau'n did seeme to shake,
Sad signes on earth my tragicke fall forespake :
  Seldome such fatall deeds of death are done,
  But prodigies do their euents forerun.

26.

Before the founder of that famous tower,
Which ouer lookes our Thames' siluer cleare,
Did in the senate meet his liue's late bower,
Horrid ostents and accents full of feare,
To many Roman eyes did oft appeare,
  The graues did open, and the dead did rise,
  Filling the streets with lamentable cries.

27.

Before stout *Brutus* that proud Roman lord,
Whose bloodie hand strooke mightie *Cæsar* dead,
With fatall blade his owne deare bodie gor'd,
Strange apparitions, full of feare and dread
Foretold his heart blood should ere long be shead :
  Dead *Cæsar's* ghost spake to him in his tent,
  The night before his tragicke death's euent.

28.

Before proud *Commodus* that Roman king,
With violent poyson did the combate trie,
Heau'n many wonders vnto light did bring,
And many dreadfull meteors blaz'd in skie,
Flames of bright fire out of the earth did flie,
  Before he tooke that fatall cup of wine
  Of faithlesse *Martia*, his false concubine.

29.

Before those mischiefes then were set abroch,
Which did infect the peace of my estate,
Before that lucklesse houre did then approch,
In which that desperate villan did await
With deadly wassaile to abridge my fate:
  Heau'n did behold the earth with heauie cheare,
  And plaguefull meteors did in both appeare.

30.

Fiue moones were in heau'n's concaue nightly seene,
As if that heau'n vpon our state below,
Foreseeing our harmes compassionate had been,
And had foresent them with their shine to show.
To purblind England her approching woe:
  Who not being warn'd by them of future harmes,
  Was after wakened by tempestuous stormes.

31.

The earthquake-making God, to warne vs all,
With violent hand shooke earth's foundation,
And from his thickned clouds in stormes let fall
Such showers of ycie bals, that vnto none
In former times the like had ere been knowne:
  For euery hailestone of such thicknesse was,
  That it in compasse did foure inches passe.

32.

Fire making rupture through the earth did breake
And burned many a towne and steeple high,
Ghosts in high-waies were often heard to speake,
And spirits in shapes of birds in darksome skie,
With fire in their beakes about did flie:
  Wherewith they did afflict much scath and woe
  Vpon the countrie, flying to and fro.

33.

O stubborne England, that with such foresigne
From future euill couldst not warned bee :
When heau'n and earth destruction did diuine,
For thy rebellious sinne to fall on thee,
Why didst thou close thy eyes and would'st not see?
   When God did thunder iudgement in thine eare,
   Why wert thou deafe, as if thou would'st not heare?

34.

For pitie reade thy ruine, drawing nigh,
Vpon the crystall battlements of heauen,
Where grau'd in golden letters to each eie,
Thou maiest behold thy wretched kingdome giuen
Into a stranger's hand : thy sad king driuen
   To flie from thee forlorne and leaue his state,
   Sold to misfortune by his subiects hate.

35.

Let time's blacke hand blot out the memorie
Of that vile age, and let it not be said
That *Iohn* did euer guide this emperie,
That future time with shame may not vpbraid
This nation's name, by whom I was betraid,
   And say that subiects yet did neuer bring
   Such grieuous wrongs vpon a wretched king.

36.

To guide thy muse, that she the cause may know
Whence first these euils in the state did spring,
To blood-built Rome, our Albion's ancient foe,
Nurse of all factions, let her take swift wing,
That when this wofull storie she shall sing,
   She truly may define the Roman hate,
   Which first did broch these mischiefes in our state.

37.

When as our England's metropolitan
Leauing his life, had left at emptie chaire,
I did elect a right religious man,
Who with the best might in those daies compare,
For habitude to manage that affaire:
  In whose behalf at Rome I did entreate,
  That he might be installed in that seate.

38.

Great Rome then in the ruffe of all her pride,
Deiects my suite with proud contempt, and chose
Langton, a man vnfit that place to guide,
On which such trust in state we did repose,
Since he was nurst in France amongst our foes:
  And might in time, bearing such rule in state,
  Vnto my fortunes worke vnluckie fate.

39.

For this with Rome's proud priest thus I contend,
" Thinke not," said I, " that I that right will yeeld,
On which my royaltie doth sole depend,
The same in spight of hate I trust to shield,
While I shall liue this scepter's state to wield:
  No power on earth in my despight shall place
  A stranger in my realme to my disgrace.

40.

If my decreed election may not stand,
I vow by heau'n, henceforth I will restraine
Those passages to Rome out of this land,
Which you hereafter will repent in vaine,
Since by the same you haue no little gaine:
  For what need we to Rome a gadding go,
  Since many learned men this land can show ?"

41.

Hence grew the hate that after did ensue,
Heaping on wrongs vpon my grieued head:
Rome's *Innocent* when he these lines did view,
Kindled with wrath, on raging furie fed,
Which through his brest a deadly venom spred:
  Whose breath did soone infect our subiects blood,
  And bred a plague vnto the generall good.

42.

Thinking it shame to his pompaticke state,
To winke at my contempt of his command,
With lips prophane, big swolne with eager hate,
He breaths his curse gainst me, and gainst my land,
To last so long as I his will withstand:
  And lockes vp all church gates by his great word,
  Forbidding vs accesse vnto the Lord.

43.

Thou proud vsurper of our *Peter's* key,
Behold thy sinne, and blush at thy foule shame,
Why didst thou locke the gate that leads the way
Vnto the holy place? why didst thou name
Thy selfe the rocke on whom that power that came
  To saue the world, his sacred church should found,
  And yet didst cast it then vnto the ground?

44.

My people frightned with the roaring threat
Of wrathfull bulles to England daily sent,
Their due alleageance to their lord forget:
Th'inglorious peeres, as if the gouernment
Had been transferr'd from *Iohn* to *Innocent,*
  Did shrinke from me, and would not by me stand,
  For th'impeacht priuiledge of our free land.

45.

Yet could all this not stoope my noble hart,
The rebell priests, that did at his command
Pronounce his curse prophane, did feele the smart
Of their offence, and from my furions hand
T'escape my vow'd reuenge, did flie the land,
  Leauing their sweet possessions for a pray,
  Which to my friends I freely gaue away.

46.

After this curse it seem'd my blisse begun:
For when the stubborne Irish did rebell,
Meth witnesse be of my atchieuements done:
And let cold Snowden's barren mountaines tell,
How the rebellious Welch my hand did quell:
  No wofull fate befell me at this season,
  Till my false peeres began to practise treason.

47.

Infected with this curse, and hauing lost
My wonted loue, they did with Rome consent:
For as to Wales I marched with my host,
The Scottish king their malice to preuent,
Did send me letters of their whole intent,
  How they were bent, if I did forward goe,
  To kill me, or betray me to my foe.

48.

Perplext in mind, thenceforth I stood in feare
Of ruine threatned to my life and state:
France did oppresse me, and the Welch did beare
Rebellious armes: but such was my hard fate,
None could oppose them through my barons hate:
  Yet I, on whom mine owne no mercie haue,
  In their distresse to strangers comfort gaue.

49.

To me with care opprest, the Scotish king
Letters did send full fraught with lines of woe,
Which vnto me his sonne the prince did bring,
By which he moued me, though once my foe,
On his oppressed age remorse to show :
    For his base subiects gainst him did arise,
    And for his age his person did despise.

50.

A mightie host with speed I did prepare,
With which enrag'd, I into Scotland went,
Where, in that warre my sword but few did spare,
That gainst their aged king their powers had bent,
To take from his crowne and gouernment :
    Guthred mac William cause of all this strife,
    Did with a traytor's death shut vp his life.

51.

But let vs turne vs backe from Scotland's bounds,
At home to view th'effects of Roman hate :
There see how *Innocent* inflicts fresh wounds
Vpon the mangled bodie of our state,
Who since that no old mischiefe could abate
    The spirit inuincible of my great mind,
    To make me stoope, new mischiefes now did find.

52.

By power of his vsurpt authoritie,
He did absolue all subiects in my land,
That by alleageance were oblig'd to me :
Then would he put into king *Philip's* hand,
The crowne and royall scepter of this land :
    If he from hence could me expell by might,
    Or take my life away by treacherous slight.

53.

Thou that dost ride vpon the backes of kings,
Yet feines to walke the steps of our deare Lord,
Thou that dost make a cloake of holy things
To hide thy shame, and leau'st the sacred word,
T'oppose the Lord's anointed with the sword:
  Is this the path that th'Holy One did passe?
  When he to *Cæsar* gaue, what *Cæsar's* was.

54.

How canst thou wash thy hands of these foule crimes,
When thou didst make this kingdome's crowne my shame:
Let not posteritie in future times,
Impute this fact to England's *Iohn* for blame,
That Rome did force him stoope to such defame:
  Since mine owne friends with all the world did frowne,
  Before proud Rome could cause me yeeld my crowne.

55.

See on the seas where France her way doth take,
To plucke me from my throne by force of hand:
See how my faithlesse barons me forsake,
And rather readie be themselues to band
Against their prince, then in his quarrell stand:
  Yea see my houshold folke do me forgoe,
  And lift vp rebell hands to helpe my foe.

56.

The stiffe-neckt priests the subiect to excite
Against his king, a prophet did procure,
Who by the skill of his propheticke sight,
Of peace to come the people should assure,
And that as king I should not long endure:
  To which th'vnconstant people credit gaue,
  Whose minds in state do alterations craue.

57.

In this distresse, in vaine I striue to stand
Against th'approching shame which I lament,
Besieged round with feare on euery hand,
Not knowing how such mischiefe to preuent,
Pandulph the legate comes from *Innocent*,
  To know if yet th'effects of his proud frowne,
  Had in such dangers brought my stomack downe.

58.

O vnkind England now behold and see
Thy wronged king forlorne, and forc'd by feare
To yeeld his crowne vpon his bended knee:
O deepe disgrace, that any prince can beare,
O that such pride in prelates euer were:
  Pandulph in signe that I my sinnes repent,
  Receiues my crowne giu'n vp to *Innocent*.

59.

Remitting former faults with gratious doome,
And hauing kept my crowne for fiue daies space,
As made contributorie vnto Rome,
The same againe he on my head did place,
And with my former title did me grace:
  To the French king likewise with speed he went,
  Charging him leaue his course for England bent.

60.

But he in hope the diademe to gaine,
Would not desist: but with a nauie came
Of twice foure hundred ships vpon the maine:
Whose powers t'oppose, proud *Pandulph* did proclame
That all men should in *Innocentius* name
  Lift vp their hands t'auert those threatned harmes,
  Whereby the shores were stuft with men of armes.

61.

Fiue hundred saile well mann'd against the foes,
I launcht into the seas with them to fight:
And for the generall of the fight I chose
My bastard brother, *William Longspath* hight,
Of those our troublous times the brauest knight,
 Who at this time his valiancie did show,
 In this sea-fight against th'inuading foe.

62.

Gainst whom they fought with such successefull hands,
That on our side the conquest did remaine:
Philip disgrac'd with his dismembred bands,
Vnto his home returned backe againe,
There to recure the losse he did sustaine:
 While I in vaine do seeke to heale my state,
 All rent and torne by mutinous debate.

63.

Out of the ruines of my countrie's woe,
What I to raise did carefull hands applie,
My rebell barons downe againe did throw :
To take aduantage, while my miserie
Is yet but fresh, they me in field defie,
 For that to their demands I gaue no eare,
 Which to mine honor preiudiciall were.

64.

By friends forlorne, they forced me by might
To yeeld to them, to my disgrace and shame:
The thought of which, and of that great despight
Done by Rome's *Innocent*, did so inflame
My heart with furie, that I did exclame
 Vpon my fates that did my daies prolong,
 In which I was ordain'd t'indure such wrong.

65.

Of mine owne seruants left all desolate,
But seuen in number did with me remaine,
Pursu'd by most disloyall people's hate:
Oft with meane food my life I did sustaine,
Lest they by poyson should procure my bane:
    And for my safetie with those few approued,
    In strange disguise I to and fro remoued.

66.

In this distresse into the Ile of Wight
My selfe in secret wise I did conuey,
Where while I did remaine, in my despight
Each slaue, whose heart my name could once affray,
With barbarous taunts vpon the same did play:
    Some call'd me fisherman, some rouing thiefe,
    That fled the land, at seas to find reliefe.

67.

Such wrongs with patience I did seeme to beare,
Dissembling wrath in my reuengefull mind,
To such reports I seem'd to giue no eare:
But still did lie, as vnto peace inclin'd,
Till I fit opportunitie did find:
    For in the end when I return'd againe,
    For such contempt they paid me double paine.

68.

Receiuing aid from friends beyond the seas,
Like to a tempest stooping downe from heau'n,
With spoilefull hands my kingdome I did sease,
All in my furie were to slaughter giuen,
My barons into flight with terror driuen:
    Fled from my face, and sought their heads to hide
    For their misdeeds, in field none durst abide.

69.

They all vnable to withstand my might,
Not with submission milde did mercie craue:
To do to me and mine the more despight,
To France they sent, desiring for to haue
Prince *Lewis* to their king, to whom they gaue
    Their promise to aduance him to the crowne,
    And as a tyrant king to cast me downe.

70.

King *Philip* fostring malice in his mind,
And gainst me such aduantage hauing found,
Though no pretence of title he could find,
Whereon his purpos'd enterprise to ground:
Yet stretcht he out his arme our state to wound,
    And take from me and my posteritie,
    Our diademe and kingly royaltie.

71.

For his proud sonne prince *Lewis* he did send,
With many a troope and many a warlike band,
Whose wisht accesse my barons did attend,
With all their troopes vpon the Kentish strand,
Where with his host French *Lewis* first tooke land:
    Whence with those traytors he to London went,
    Which in this treason did with them conseat.

72.

Then did begin my former miserie,
For those, in whom chiefe trust I did repose,
Those stranger souldiers all from me did flie,
Except some few, that did lament my woes,
And Douer castle kept against my foes,
    Vnto whose trust I did the same betake,
    All other seeming friends did me forsake.

73.

But see the iudgement of almightie Ioue,
On the disloyall people of this land:
The conquering French, whose nature is to proue,
Insulting ouer whom they beare command,
Now being lords of all, with heauie hand
  The English people did begin t'oppresse,
    Who could not helpe themselues in this distresse.

74.

Thus did the King of heau'n iust vengeance take
On them, for their vniust disloyaltie:
My part he did not vtterly forsake,
But in the end did force my foes to flie,
And leaue the crowne to my posteritie:
  For he did chuse out one amongst the foe,
    To be our enemie's chiefe ouerthrow.

75.

There was a noble minded man of France,
Vicount of Melum, and a Frenchman borne,
Who falling sicke did waile the sad mischance
Of th'English, iustly made false fortune's scorne,
That thus had left their king to liue forlorne:
  Yea with remorse his conscience it did sting,
    To see the subiect so oppresse the king.

76.

When death in him began his due to take,
He for my nobles secretly did send,
To whom with fainting voice these words he spake:
" My friends," quoth he, " vnto my words attend,
Which shall ere long for euermore haue end:
  Attend, I say, conscience bids me impart
    The things that now lie heauie on my hart.

77.

Woe to the wretched people of this land,
Which do their soueraigne lord and king forsake :
Woe to your selues, that for your king should stand,
Of whom a scorne vnto the world ye make :
And woe vnto your children for your sake :
   Yea, woe to England euermore shall be,
   Vnlesse with speed ye seeke some remedie.

78.

Lewis our prince of late hath deepely sworne,
And with him sixteene earles and barons more,
That ye, that now haue left your king forlorne,
Shall die the death, or else exil'd deplore
Your case in forren parts for euermore :
   Then let each peere with speed draw forth his sword,
   To helpe himselfe and his distressed lord.

79.

If conscience cause me to bemone the chance
Of this so braue a king, which ye possesse,
To whom I am a stranger borne in France :
Yea once his foe, though now as ye may gesse,
I as a friend bewaile his sad distresse :
   How then should ye that are his liegemen borne,
   For this his sad mishap with sorow mourne?

80.

Assist him then as dutie doth you bind,
Pitie your selues and your posteritie :
And keepe what I haue spoken in your mind,
Of which no more to you I can descrie :
For now my heart doth faile and I must die :
   Adieu pourtant, Adieu à chasqu'amy.
   Adieu ie dis ma vie ce fini."

81.

My peeres forewarned of such treacherie,
And with remorse viewing their natiue lands
Betrai'd to spoile by their disloyaltie,
Did cast in mind how they with helping hands
Might best restore themselues from captiue bands:
　And hoping now my grace againe to win,
　From *Lewis* to decline they did begin.

82.

Vpon th'insulting French to powre my spleene,
Throughout my kingdome's bounds I did proclaime,
That all my subiects that had wronged been
By forren foes, if vnto me they came
With minds for fight, I would reuenge the same:
　Whereby with speed came many a worthie wight
　Vnder my standard gainst the French to fight.

83.

Like raging storme blowne out of *Boreas* mouth,
With violent furie I did force my way,
From east to west, from north vnto the south
Destroying all things, that before vs lay:
Which did our aduersaries so dismay,
　That none durst stand t'oppose vs in the field,
　But readie way vnto our will did yeeld.

84.

Had proud prince *Lewis* met with me in fight,
Our quarrell by the dint of sword to trie,
Soone should I haue obtain'd my kingdome's right,
And made th'vsurping prince from hence to flie,
Who did support my peere's disloyaltie:
　But treason stretched out her deadly hand,
　Who twixt the French and my reuenge did stand.

85.

In Swinsted abbie witnesse of my wrong,
A monke there was, the worker of my bane,
Who heard me vow that if I liued long,
Through England I would raise the price of graine,
To plague my subiects for their proud disdaine:
   Which was the cause, as fates did first decree,
   For which this villan monke did poyson mee.

86.

To vent the poisned thoughts of his false brest,
Loe all alone in dead time of the night,
When euery one had laid him downe to rest,
When aire was husht, when from the welkin bright
The golden stars did cast a glimmering light,
   He forth did walke into a garden by,
   For to effect his wicked treacherie.

87.

There as this villan wandred to and fro,
To find some weed that had the power t'expell
The vitall spirit, or any aduerse foe
To humane life, some kind of serpent fell,
Or any thing that did with poyson swell:
   At last an vglie toad he haplesse found,
   Big swolne with poyson crawling on the ground:

88.

With which full glad he did returne againe,
And to his chamber secretly did goe,
Where with his pen-knife he did pricke and paine
The lothsome toade, from whom the blood did floe,
By which the wicked monke did worke my woe:
   For poison which the toade did vomit vp,
   With wine he mixed in a fatall cup.

89.

With which to me he came, and thus he spake,
" My liege," said he, " a cup of wine I bring,
Of which if that your grace a taste will take,
It will abate the edge of sorowe's sting,
Which deepely seemes to wound my grieued king :
   With it to England's health I will begin,
   Whose woes for euermore be drown'd herein."

90.

Thus did this villan drinke, and dranke his last,
And after vnto me the cup he gaue,
Of which misdeeming nought, I straight did taste,
Which done, not all the world my life could saue,
So deadly was it tempered by the slaue :
   Th'effects whereof before my death were knowne,
   Which came to passe immediatly thereon.

91.

For when the raging venome had dispread
It selfe throughout my bodie by the veines,
My blood did boile, my heart began to dread,
My bodie swell'd, and when no hope remaines
Of any helpe to remedie such paines :
   I for the monke did call to haue his head,
   But one did answere make, that he was dead.

92.

" Then God," quoth I, " haue mercie on my soule,
For of this wretched world no man am I,
Seeing nothing may this venom's force controule :
For sensiblie I feele how it doth lie
Vpon my woefull heart, and I must die :
   Wherefore my sonne fetch hither vnto mee,
   That I before I die his face may see."

93.

The child being brought, for then he was a child,
To him I thus did speake with weeping eie:
" My sonne," quoth I, " on whom my hopes I build:
Come neere to me, where heere in paine I lie,
Come neere and haue my blessing ere I die,
 Nought else to thee is left for me to leaue,
 Since of my crowne my foes do me bereaue.

94.

Wherefore ye heau'ns who do behold my woes,
Now at my death giue eare vnto my prayer,
Protect this child of mine from all his foes:
And for your mercie's sake this infant spare,
Whose tender age doth want your tender care:
 Else will that roring lion *Lewis* kill
 This litle lambe, though he hath done none ill.

95.

And thou, my litle sonne, take heed by me,
That thou thy peeres and people's loue procure,
Contend not thou with thy nobilitie:
So shall thy state and kingdome long endure,
And thou from forren foes liue safe and sure:
 For my false subiects vndeserued hate
 Did worke my woe, which I repent too late.

96.

Renowned *Pembroke*, thou hast left my foe,
Be thou protector to this pretie boy,
And for the father's sake thy fauour show:
When I am gone do thou thy strength employ
Against all those that seeke this child's annoy:
 And ye, my other peeres, who once haue ben
 My foes, proue now true hearted noble men.

97.

Redeeme your countrey from that captiue woe,
Which from the roote of ciuill discord grew :
Ioyne hearts and hands against the common foe :
Forget old wrongs, vnto the prince proue true :
Farewell, my daies be done, I die, adew."

    Thus after twice nine yeares of rule in state,
    I lost both life and rule by timelesse fate.

98.

Behold the last effects of *Henric's* curse
On his last sonne, for his rebellious pride :
Let princes learne, that where debate, the nurce
Of discord, doth the prince and peeres diuide,
Nought but destruction can that state betide :

    Of which let that sad time of my short reigne,
    A Mirrour vnto future time remaine.

THE WOFVLL LIFE AND
Death of King Edward the second.

THE ARGUMENT.

" Writers," quoth Memorie, " were much to blame
Of *Iohn*, that noble prince, to speake such shame :
But little credit vnto them we giue,
Since they were foes to him, when he did liue :
His first sonne *Henrie*, third of that same name,
Did him succeed, and with his sword did tame
That French prince *Lewis*, whom he forc'd by might
To leaue this kingdome, due to him of right :
Edward his sonne, the first that bore that name
Since *William's* conquest made, whose noble fame
Shall neuer die, did in the throne succeed,
And in his daies wrought many a worthie deed :
Yet neither of these princes both did feele
Th'inconstant course of fortune's froward wheele :
That *Edward* of Carnaruan, third from *Iohn*,
Is next in course, whom we must stay vpon :
He in the first spring of his fatall raigne
Recals the banisht *Gaueston* againe,
Exil'd before by his renowned sire,
At whose proud taunts the peeres being set on fire,
Do quench it with his blood : the angrie king
Vowes his reuenge, the valiant *Breuce* doth bring

His powers into the field, and in the fight
At Banokesborne turnes th'English into flight:
Heau'n, dearth, and death foretels the sad euent,
Which did ensue vpon the riuer Trent:
The queene is sent to France the peace t'haue mou'd,
Proues false, returnes againe with her belou'd:
Arriues in armes, gainst whom the king craues aid,
Who left forlorne, and at the last betrai'd,
Imprison'd, and enforc'd by parlament,
Vnto his sonne resignes the gouernment:
On him depos'd, more mischiefe to inferre,
His queene, the bishop, and her *Mortimer*,
In darke enigma do conclude his death:
And, lest that he should seeme t'expire his breath
By violent hand, a torment they deuise
By which the king in Bercklie castle dies:
Of which that we th'vndoubted truth may haue,
Let fame call vp his wronged ghost from graue."

ANOTHER ARGUMENT.

Fame summons vp the king: in briefe he showes
How queene, peeres, people, all did him depose.

1.

THAT subtill serpent, seruile flatterie,
Seldome infects the meaner man, that feares
No change of state through fortune's treacherie;
She spits her poison at the mightiest peeres,
And with her charmes inchants the prince's eares:
  In sweetest wood the worme doth soonest breed,
  The caterpiller on best buds doth feed.

2.

If slie dissimulation credit winne
With any prince, that sits on highest throne,
With honied poyson of soure sugred sinne,
It causeth him turne tyrant to his owne,
And to his state workes swift confusion,
  Aboue his cedar's top it high doth shoot,
  And canker-like deuoures it to the root.

3.

Of which that thou a perfect Mirrour haue,
The wronged ghost of that deposed king,
Carnaruan's *Edward,* hath forgone his graue,
Who does with him such dolefull tidings bring,
That yet thy muse the like did neuer sing:
  Those sad mishaps which she before did show,
  Compar'd to mine are counterfeits of woe.

4.

To strengthen her complaint before she sing,
And drowne her grieued thoughts in depth of woe:
(Yee murdred ghosts, that vnder night's black wing,
In vncouth paths doe wander to and fro,
And oft in sighfull groanes your griefe do show)
  Haste vnto vs, and hauing heard our wrong,
  Help with your shrieks to make a mourneful song.

5.

The quill of some sad turtle's wing applie
That mourn'd so long, till griefe did strike her dead :
Blood be thy incke, which when it waxeth drie,
Moisten with teares : and when all thine are shed,
From euery eye, that haps these lines to reade,
   Let euery verse compos'd, such sad sound beare,
   That for each word it may enforce a teare.

6.

(Sorrow, distresse, and all that can be found
Which once did helpe me waile my woefull smart,
When fatall *Berckly's* buildings did resound
The echoing complaints of my poore hart)
Grant your accesse, and helpe to beare a part,
   That our sad muse more ruthfully may sing,
   The storie of a dead deposed king.

7.

I tell of honie-soothing parasites,
Of stubborne peeres, who louing sterne debate,
Did boldly braue me in two bloodie fights,
Of a proud prelate's plots, of people's hate,
Of the sad ruine of a royall state :
   And of a queene betrai'd to fond desire   ✓
   Who too too cruell did my death conspire.

8.

To the first *Edward*, since the Norman's name
Grew famous for their crown'd grac'd victorie,
The fourth of six of his faire sonnes I am,
Mongst whom I was ordain'd by destinie,
To sway the scepter of this emperie :
   Before my kingly father left to liue,
   The first three borne to death his due did giue.

9.

I did suruiue, the yongest of the foure,
And did succeed my sire in royall chaire:
But did not treade the path which he before
Had with his vertuous foot-steps beaten faire:
Birth binds not vertue to succeed in th'heire,
   Else why did I of such illustrate race,
   Obscure his vertuous deeds with my disgrace?

10.

Had I but tract the steps of such a sire
To perfect that great worke, which he begun,
Had princely thoughts but mounted my desire
T'assay like glorious deeds, which he had done,
O what a prize of honor had I wonne!
   But discord sent from hell did raine bring,
   Euen at that time, that I was crown'd a king.

11.

As th'holy priest with sanctified hand
'The precious vnguent on my head should powre,
And as before the altar I did stand,
Discord the furie sent from that blacke shore
By damned *Dis* where *Phlegeton* doth rore,
   Shapt like th'appointed priest whose hallowed hand
   Should me annoint, by me vnknowne did stand.

12.

Approching nigh, the venome she did shed
Of sad *Cocytus* poole, which she did bring
In her blacke viall, on my haplesse head,
Whose banefull sauour borne on furie's wing,
Did not alone infect th'anointed king:
   But round diffus'd, as sent from peere to peere,
   Did poyson those high bloods that present were.

13.

The ranke contagion of this foule disease
With rauing looke the mightiest in the state,
Whose desperate rage with remedie t'appease,
Warre rouz'd himselfe at home, who had of late
Slept in the bosome of pernicious hate:
   And did incite them in pretence of good,
    With their owne swords to let their bodies blood.

14.

O most remorselesse of that impious age,
That did not only then deny your aide   :
To your deare countrie, when with barbarous rage
The bordering foes her bosome did inuade,
And in her wombe such ghastly wounds had made,
   But as a nation borne of viper's brood,
    O shame to tell, did daily sucke her blood.

15.

Great queene of sea-siedg'd iles, what canst thou show
Of that good hap, when *Edward* thy late king
Did safely bulwarke thee against thy foe?
Thy *Edward* now doth with his minions sing,
While thou thy hands in wretchednesse dost wring:
   And *Brewse* doth mangle thee with many a scarre,
    While thy proud peeres prepare for ciuill warre.

16.

In our discourse, that we a method haue
Of euery action, let vs briefely tell
In his due place, which time and order gaue:
And that we may first know those causes well,
From whence these sad effects produc'd befell,
   In the respectiue scope of this our storie,
    Let vs looke backe to *Edward's* daies of glorie.

17.

In the fresh blossome of my youthfull spring,
Sucking the sugered poison of delight,
Euen then when with strict hand the carefull king
Kept backe my youth, I on the baites did bite
Of *Gaueston* that soothing parasite:
    A yong esquire of Gascoyne in faire feature,
    Shapt like an angell: but of euill nature.

18.

My royall father, who with iudgement's eie
Could sound the depth of things, perceiuing well
How follie did by him her charmes applie,
T'inchant my youth: such mischiefe to repell,
Did him exile, lest by the powerfull spell
    Of his allurements drawne from all renowne,
    I should be made vnworthie of a crowne.

19.

O prudent prince! the depth of that decree
Which heau'n did purpose by my *Gaueston*,
Too secret was for humane sense to see,
Who did ordaine, that exil'd minion
To ruine *Edward* and thy royall throne:
    For though an exile he did then depart,
    Yet with him went thy wanton *Edward's* heart.

20.

Too late it was that obiect to remoue,
To whom in fancie's cup I long before
Had quaff'd so deepe, that surfetting with loue,
Heart-sicke I was till time did him restore,
And set him once againe on England's shore:
    Forgetfull of my faith to *Edward* dead,
    Not to reuoke, whom he had banished.

21.

His bones were yet scarce cold, his royall throne
Scarce warme beneath me was, when in the same
I did embrace my deare, lou'd *Gaueston*,
Who as infected with contagious shame
Of some corrupted place, from whence he came,
   Throughout the land in little space did spread,
   That foule disease which our destruction bread.

22.

In court the leprous spots of his delights
Vnto the palace wals so fast do cleaue,
That from my presence all the noblest wights
Withdraw themselues, and in their roomes do leaue
Those vp-starts base, who them of grace bereaue:
   No man is held to be the king's true friend,
   But he that doth his *Gaueston* commend.

23.

His lips were made the oracles, from whence
I tooke aduice, he in the counsell sits,
Graue states as enemies are banisht thence,
The shallow-brain'd yong giddie-headed wits,
Our wanton humour with best counsell fits,
   The sage instructions of the wise man's mouth,
   Do sound harsh musike in the eares of youth.

24.

This was the spring, from whence at first did floe
Those streames of strife, which rising like a flood
Do ouerwhelme my state in waues of woe,
Which threat confusion to the common good,
Which first in death do coole my barons blood:
   And which yet swelling higher, lastly bring
   A violent downefall to a royall king.

25.

My *Gaueston*, in maiestie's great armes
Being safely hug'd, no change of fortune feares:
He wantons with the king, soothes his owne harmes,
He playes the buffon's part, he flouts and ieers
The courtly actions of the honor'd peeres:
    The great in counsell and the noble borne,
    Are made the subiect of his hatefull scorne.

26.

Sterne wrath to let loose rage, steps vp from hell,
Conducts my peeres from court vnto the campe,
She claps her hands and with a countnance fell,
Gnashing her teeth doth fiercely raue and rampe,
And with her feet vpon the ground doth stampe:
    Then whets them to reuenge in their rash mood,
    Whose furious thirst must be allaid with blood.

27.

Twice was my minion as an exile sent
To forren shores, their furie to restraine,
And twice againe reuokte with their assent,
Who now no longer able to refraine,
Prouokte with daily wrongs of his disdaine,
    He being betrai'd, for vengeance all do call,
    On Gauer's heath, where *Gaueston* did fall.

28.

They wreake their vengeance in his reeking blood,
My sighes they laugh to scorne, while I lament,
With faire pretence to further common good
They vnderpop their cause, and to preuent
The mischiefe, that may grow from discontent,
    To tracke me step by step in euery thing,
    Whom they do please, they place about their king.

29.

Feeding on griefe for *Gaueston* deceast,
And blushing at such wrong done to my state,
Reuenge doth burne in my distempred brest,
Anger takes hands with griefe, all ioyne with hate,
And to the peeres threaten pernicious fate,
 Who, lest time weaken rage then too too strong,
 Do giue it strength by adding daily wrong.

30.

In this dissension, while on euery hand,
We for our owne destruction do prepare,
Newes from the north giues vs to vnderstand,
How valiant *Brewse* in his successefull warre
Against our powers doth prosperously fare,
 Recouering that from vs againe, with more,
 Which our dread sire had kept from him before.

31.

Beyond the bounds of his owne natiue soile,
He proudly breakes vpon our bordering coast,
None seekes t'oppose, he makes no faint recoile:
The spoile and riches of whole countries lost
Can hardly bound the furie of his host,
 Neuer did bordering foe inuade so far,
 Or wound our kingdome with a greater scar.

32.

Tempestuous tidings borne on Boreas breath
Cooles the hot vengeance of a wrathfull king,
And for a while delaies prepared death
For his proud peeres, feare from the north on wing
Comes flying fast, aud 'bout our eares doth ring,
 Bidding vs haste, and powre our vengeance forth
 Vpon our foes, that brau'd vs in the north.

33.

Mustering vp troopes of foot-men for the field,
To passe in person for this great affaire,
My hopes on number I do vainly build :
Our thoughts made aduerse by the former iar,
Prepare vs mischiefe in the following war :
 Disioyn'd in heart, yet ioyn'd in ranke we goe,
 To giue a famous conquest to the foe.

34.

Stout *Brewse* renownes his sword with *Edward's* flight,
Striuiling, whose siege our rescue crau'd, can tell
England's misfortune in that haplesse fight :
And Banokesborne, who 'boue her bounds did swell
With bodies dead, that in that battell fell,
 Aboue the bordering brookes hath won a name
 Fam'd for this field thus fought vpon the same.

35.

O noble nation, t'whom true fame hath giuen
A glorious name for deeds accomplished,
Equall with any people's vnder heau'n,
Be not dismai'd, 'twas I, 'twas I, that led
To such mishap, on whose vnhappie head
 Heau'n neuer smil'd, but with sterne lookes still frown'd
 Till wearied with mishaps, I was vncrown'd.

36.

O had I perisht by the sword of *Brewse*,
And had not been reseru'd to future daies,
To see my peeres with treason take a truce,
And with their swords by all uniust assaies,
Attempt to hew downe him, whom heau'n did raise :
 I had been blest, and had not liu'd to rue
 The woes yet worse, which after did ensue.

37.

Th'inueterate wounds of wrong infixt so deepe,
Against my barons in my swolne heart,
With drops of blood now made afresh to weepe,
That I from *Brewse* should thus with shame depart,
Did so augment my mind's impatient smart,
    That by my peeres mine ire now new stirr'd vp,
    I with their blood quencht in *Bellonae's* cup.

38.

What they do plot is by my powre controul'd,
What I intend, vnreuerently they crosse:
What they do wish, I will not: what I would,
They do gain-say, though to a publike losse:
Thus vpon mischiefe's racket do we tosse
    The common good, till bandied by vs all
    Into confusion's hazard it do fall.

39.

Both heau'n and earth, as if in mourning clad,
They did bewaile, what they could not preuent,
When on our selues, our selues no pittie had,
Denide those comforts in due season sent,
Which to this nation they before had lent:
    As with their anger they would vs recall
    From running headlong, where we needs must fall.

40.

Towards th'Articke side of heau'n ore Albion's rocks,
A blasing meteor stood in th'vpper aire,
Which with grim looke shaking his dreadfull looks,
Bids earth be barren, and the world despaire:
Then cals the furies with the snakie haire,
    To execute that vengeance to succeed,
    Which fates for wretched England had decreed.

41.

Famine, forerunner to deuouring death,
Haunts euery coast, where food is to be found,
The fruits are blasted by her banefull breath,
She makes the clouds to drop, till that be drown'd,
Which plentie's hand had hidden in the ground :
    Then doth she ransacke both the rich and poore,
    Denouring all, till she can find no more.

42.

If euer pitie moue a stonie eie,
Let her present our age for map of woe,
There see for food, how little infants crie,
Whom, parents wanting, what they would bestow,
With griefe are either forced to forgo,
    Or else with weeping woe to sit them by,
    Till faint for food before their face they die.

43.

The spouse, that wants to feed her fruitfull wombe,
Burying the babe, that neuer came from graue,
Cries, in her deare's deare armes, for death to come,
Who mad with sorrow and in hope to haue
That left of death, which loue desires to saue :
    A horrid thing to tell, to saue his owne,
    Steales other's children for to feed vpon.

44.

When leane-fac'd famine, who with furious thirst
Coasting the countrie, through the land had run,
Began to breath as hauing done their worst,
That other furie pestilence begun
To finish that, which they had left vndone,
    Who 'boue our heads in the infected aire,
    Her poysned shafts for battaile did prepare.

45.

Her angrie arrowes euery way do flie,
Thousands on either hand in death do fall:
But happie they in blessed peace to die,
Not left with vs to liue, when death did call,
To see blood-thirstie warre the worst of all:
    That vniuersall flood of woes powre downe
    In seas of blood, this wretched land to drowne.

46.

In midst of these extreames with griefe cast downe,
The measure of our miserie to fill,
My stubborne peers take armes, and proudly frowne,
Threatning in rage that little left to spill,
If basely I submit not to their will:
    And exile those, whom they themselues did place
    In stead of *Gaueston* t'attend our grace.

47.

He that in bosome of a prince doth dwell,
And by endeuour seekes to gaine his grace,
Though for his seruice he deserue it well:
Yet as the deere pursu'd from place to place,
The enuious dog will haue h m still in chase:
    Danger in chiefest safetie it doth bring,
    To seeme to be familiar with a king.

48.

Spenser, the man, on whom at first I frown'd,
Whom they preferr'd, my *Gaueston* being dead,
Was he, whom they pretend to be the ground
Of all their griefe, gainst him they now made head,
He was of vs too highly fauoured:
    Him must we banish, so they thinke it fit,
    If on our throne in safetie we will sit.

49.

William de Brewse in selling *Gower's* land
To yonger *Spenser* from the other peeres,
Who would haue brought the same at *Brewse's* hand,
First blew the coles, whence now that flame appeares,
· Which had been hid in anger many yeares:
    This is the cause of their conceiued ire,
     For this in armes gainst me they do conspire.

50.

Disloyall *Lancaster*, that did conduct
The rebels to the field, by letters sent
With termes vnfit his soueraigne will instruct,
Assigning daies, within whose termament,
I should reforme such things in gouernment,
    Which he mislikes, thus adding to that fire,
    Which did at length consume him in our ire.

51.

This fire yet burning in our royall brest,
The queene doth with complaint her wrongs prefer,
That in her progresse after long vnrest,
Our late false steward lord *Badelismere*,
Confederate with rebellious *Lancaster*,
    Vnkindly had deni'd in my despight,
     Her lodging in Leeds castle for a night.

52.

To make our furie in reuenge more strong,
Letters from Scotland intercepted were,
Which touch vs neerer then all former wrong,
In number six: the one of which did beare
The armes of *Dowglas*, sent to *Lancaster*,
    In which the *Dowglas* to conceale his name,
     Vnto king *Arthur* doth direct the same.

53.

Prouokt to vengeance for such treacherous spight,
From London with our royall powres we past,
Whose stomackes fill'd with furie for the fight,
I vrged forward with the vtmost hast,
To lay the manours and the lordships wast
  Of our proud barons, promising for pray
  All that was theirs, that came within their way.

54.

Newes of th'vnnaturall deeds which they enact
Vpon the loyall people of our land,
Hasten vs forward with such speed exact,
That ere the *Mortimers*, who both did band
Themselues with *Lancaster*, did vnderstand
  Of our approch our royall armed traine,
  At Shrewsburie did front them on the plaine.

55.

Far from confederates amaz'd with wonder,
At our approch, both daunted to behold
Our frownes of lightning, and our threats of thunder,
Hang downe their heads, scarce daring be so bold
As looke on vs, their fainting hearts wax cold,
  And on their knees they fall, in hope to stay
  Our angrie doome, that threatned their decay.

56.

Yeelding to fate by force of destinie,
Whose foreappointing prouidence hath power
In euery thing t'enforce necessitie,
We grant them life, reseruing in the tower
That *Mortimer* at London for that hower,
  In which by destiny it was set downe,
  That that false lord should ruine my renowne.

57.

Marching more northward from the Cambrian coast,
While vengefull breath the fire of furie fans,
After such good successe to bring our host
To Pomfret, which gainst vs our barons mans:
At last we lite like flockes of snow-white swans
   Fast by the weeping Eye, which runneth downe
   Into the Trent by little Caldwel's towne.

58.

There first did Needwood's echoing forrest tell
The stubborne barons of our whole intent,
There first they seeke our forces to repell,
When with their powers our passage to preuent,
Intended ore the bosome of the Trent,
   They interrupt our purpose with proud braues,
   On Burton bridge ore fishie Trent's blacke waues.

59.

The riuer's watrie wombe did proudly swell,
As if it had turn'd rebell with the foes,
Or as if louing either armie well,
It would preuent poore England of the woes
Which must ensue, if both parts came to bloes:
   Her waters rose beyond their wonted bounds,
   And for three daies deferr'd vnnaturall wounds.

60.

Aquarius with the foot-bands manly fought
Gainst those, that on the bridge at Burton stood,
While with our troopes vnseene we cast about
Vnder the couert of a leauie wood,
Distant three miles from thence, where ore the flood
   Th'whole host did passe by shallowes lately found,
   To meete the barons vpon equall ground.

61.

The deadly drum doth tell the foes from far
The fatall march of their approching king :
Who seeing their weaknesse to sustaine the war
Gainst such a powre, which with vs we do bring,
They turne their backes, swift feare their feet doth wing :
 Yet stubborne men still to prouoke our ire,
 Before they flie, they set the towne on fire.

62.

Horrour pursues them euery way they flie,
Repentance comes too late to calme our frowne,
All former wrongs afresh for vengeance crie,
They, that did whilome wish them all renowne,
By aduerse fortune being thus cast downe,
 Lift vp their hands, yet lower to suppresse them,
 All friends turne foes in pursuite to distresse them.

63.

At Burrough bridge, in their vnluckie flight,
Where for th'encounter death did rendie stand,
They were enforc'd in most vnequall fight,
For loued life to vse defensiue hand
Against the stubborne bands of Cumberland :
 Led by stout *Herckley,* who with bold assay
 Of his drawne sword began a bloodie day.

64.

In mutuall slaughter, both the hosts do stand,
Earth trembling shakes beneath their trampling feet,
The singing shafts thicke loos'd on euery hand,
Flie to and fro, then hand to hand they meet,
And wound for wound each doth the other greet,
 While ouer head the heau'n's remorsefull stood
 Dropping downe teares to see their sides drop blood.

65.

Valiant *Bohume*, Herford's vndanted lord,
That stood in fight by foes besieged round,
His heart not female made to flie as skar'd,
Neuer gaue backe, but brauely kept his ground,
Till life gaue backe from that same deadly wound,
  Giu'n by a stout Welch Britaine, that did stand
  Beneath the bridge with fatall speare in hand.

66.

This lucklesse chance so terrifi'd the foe,
And gaue such strength vnto the northerne bands,
That th'aduerse part their backes began to show,
Clifford, though wounded with a shaft, yet stands
With *Lancaster* in fight, till on all hands,
  Opprest with multitude, themselues they yeeld,
  To conquering *Herckley* victour of the field.

67.

Thus hautie *Lancaster*, that did not feare
To tempt his soueraigne's peace with periur'd hate,
Who in the morning was the mightiest peere
That 'gainst his prince did euer moue debate,
By night was made the meanest in the state:
  In right or wrong, who euer lifts his hand
  Against his prince, his cause doth seldome stand.

68.

Not he alone made forfeit of his head,
Who in this proud rebellion led the ring,
The fatall axe strooke many others dead,
Hewing downe all, that had conspir'd to bring
Their powers for fight against their lawfull king:
  Twice eight great barons and as many knights
  In death paid paines for wrong t'our kingly rites.

69.

O age infortunate, when subiects pride
Did force their soueraigne to such deeds of woe,
That when all men had laid remorse aside,
The sunne in heau'n his griefe in shame to show
Six houres with blood-red cheeks on th'earth below,
    Did blush to see her soile drinke vp their blood,
    Who liuing oft in her defence had stood.

70.

Imprudent prince, since rage did lift thy hand
To lop the pillers of thy kingdome downe,
On whose supportfull powers thy state should stand:
Looke for a ruthlesse ruine of thy crowne,
Looke helplesse now in wretchednesse to drowne:
    The dance vnto destruction they haue led,
    And the same feeting I the king must tread.

71.

When th'hand of Ioue the mightie men shall take
From any state, for their rebellious pride,
By such foresigne this vse we well may make,
Some after-storme of vengeance will betide
That haplesse land, who euer it doth guide:
    The sad effusion of the noble blood,
    Portends confusion to the common good.

72.

With dolefull pen I could bewaile their woe,
Whose wofull wants did after proue me weake:
But far more horrid things we are to show,
To those blacke deeds, of which we now must speake:
They before spoken did that ice but breake,
    At which we falling in did helplesse drowne,
    Once fallen, all do helpe to keepe vs downe.

73:

Not *Herkleye's* treason plotted in that trnce,
Which for aduancement, most ambitious man,
He did intend t'our aduersarie *Breuce*:
Nor the new troubles, which *Valoys* began
In our dominions Guien and Aquitaine,
   Shall be the subiect of our sadder verse:
   Matter of more importance we rehearse.

74.

O *Isabel* my queene, my vnkind queene,
Thy shame must be the subiect of our song,
Had not the weaknesse of thy faith been seene,
When faithlesse thou wast led to do that wrong
To him that liu'd in loue with thee so long:
   That royall blood in Berklie castle spilt,
   Had now not stain'd our storie with thy guilt.

75.

The scene of lust foreruns the act of blood,
Priapus doth his lustfull breath inspire
Into the queene, the ocean's wauie flood
Cannot extinguish fancie's burning fire,
Nor coole the scalding thirst of her desire:
   With heate of lust her inward heart doth gloe,
   T'imprisoned *Mortimer* my mortall foe.

76.

Heere let not any take offensiue spleene,
Or taxe these rimes, for that to light they bring
Th'incontinence of our disloyall queene:
Nor thy muse grieue this argument to sing,
Which is confirmed by the wronged king:
   Foule is the fault, though nere so quaint the skill,
   That conceales truth to lessen any ill.

.77.

Wigmore's false *Mortimer*, (whose fatall name
Vniuocall to him of all his line :
Whether from feare of death we fetch the same,
Or of the dead seas sinke we it define,
The deeds of death t'ensue doth well diuine)
   Reserued was by fate within the tower,
    With time to turne the glasse of my last houre.

78.

On him the queene by loose affection led
Did cast her fancie, burning in the flame
Of priuie lust, which strong desier fed ;
And wanting her delight in wanton game,
To coole her lust-burnt blood with dregs of shame,
   Did cast about how she might him release,
    That he might giue her loue-sicke passions ease.

79.

It is not bands, nor walles, nor thousands spies
That can the woman's wicked will preuent :
Let loue intreate, set shame before her eies,
Let plighted faith, first virgin vow'd consent,
And the wombe's fruit that giues loue most content,
   Perswade with her: yet can they neuer stay
    Her wanton will, if she will go astray.

80.

By sleepie potion of effectuall power
To charme the sense, whether by her conuey'd,
Or by himselfe deuised in the tower,
Segraue the constable was captiue made,
With many more to senselesse sleepe betray'd :
   While *Mortimer*, vnthought vpon, escapes
    And vnto France his prosperous iourney shapes.

81.

Thus far did fortune with my queene conspire,
And after this good hap to giue full ease
Vnto the longing thirst of her desire,
ꝟ Tels her how France inuades beyond the seas,
Which vp in armes she needs must go t'appease:
    When resolution hath prepar'd the will,
    It wants no helpes to further any ill.

82.

Through our neglect of homage to be made,
Constrain'd thereto by our home-bred debate,
Valoys her brother did our lands inuade,
And through late wounds made in our mangled state,
In armes vnable to withstand his hate:
    To treate with him of peace our queene we sent,
    In her vow'd faith being too too confident.

83.

O powre diuine, what mortall wight hath wings
To soare the height of thy vnknowne decree?
Reason, that hath such power in search of things,
Proues then most blind, when most it seemes to see,
In vainly arguing of what must bee:
    When reason bids no danger to suspect,
    Time hastens swift confusion in effect.

84.

The queene effecting that, for which she went,
With these conditions reunites the peace,
That to such couenants I should consent,
Aniou and Aquitaine I should release
Vnto my sonne, my title should surcease:
    And he to France as in times past 't had bin,
    Should do his homage for his right therein.

85.

Pleas'd in this peace, my selfe, or my yong sonne
Inioyn'd in person to confirme these things,
The *Spencers* both being into hatred run,
Not daring be from vnder my safe wings,
So absolute we thinke the power of kings,
 Perswade me heere to stay and send my sonne,
 In hope thereby, what they did feare, to shun.

86.

Thus all hands helping, *Isabel* againe.
To forward that which she on foot had set,
I hauing past my title t'Aquitaine
Vnto the prince my sonne, she sees no let,
But that more easly she the rest may get:
 So large a share cut from vs by her skill,
 She hopes to haue the whole or want her will.

87.

Hauing obtain'd in France what we require,
She call'd vpon to make returue with speed,
Protracts the time, and feasting her desire
So long with *Mortimer*, that she doth need
Excuse to warrant her presumptuous deed:
 Giues flat deniall to her lord's command,
 Not to returne except with force of hand.

88.

Many, that wau'ring wish'd a change in state,
And more, that on reuenge so long had fed
For losse of friends, that fell in that debate
Betwixt vs and our barons, daily fled
Vnto the queene, whose heart being stricken dead,
 As wanting strength to manage her affaire,
 They do reuiue with powre by their repaire.

89.

While in the French court, yet vnfrown'd vpon
By *Charles* her brother king, she did abide,
Our Exceter's true bishop *Stapleton*,
Ioyn'd in commission with her to decide
The iar 'twixt vs and France, now seeing her pride
  Burst out in plaine reuolt, returning ouer
  The seas from her, did all her drifts discouer.

90.

Thus their close treason bare and naked made,
As blushing at their open shame descride,
To cloake the cause of their intent t'inuade,
They vow no more to broqke the *Spencers* pride,
Nor shall the queene vniustly be denide
  The presence of the king, they all will die,
  Or order things that stand in state awrie.

91.

King *Charles* her brother, while they thus deuise,
Whether with our rich gifts or promise won,
Or with respect to his owne royalties,
Or that he would not be a looker on,
While vnto maiestie such wrong was done:
  First wooes our queene for peace, whom wilfull bent,
  He exiles France to frustrate her intent.

92.

Who now would thinke that she should euer find
A hopefull helpe her weaknesse to repaire?
Bewitching beautie, O how dost thou blind
The eyes of man! thy soule is deemed faire,
Thy euill good, thy vice a vertue rare:
  In thy distresse although thy cause be wrong,
  Thou mou'st remorse and mak'st thy partie strong.

93.

Those yonger bloods, *Arthois* and *Beaumont*,
Without respect vnto her cause's right,
Those certaine helpes to her do oft recount
In Heinault to be found, if she excite
The earle thereof to pitie her sad plight:
 Which by a match pretended might be done,
 Betwixt his daughter and the prince our sonne.

94.

As they gaue counsell, so it came to passe,
She t'Heinault goes with *Beaumont* for her guide,
And with kind welcome entertained was:
Where while *Heinault* and she with ioy prouide
To make his daughter our yong *Edward's* bride,
 To England lets turne backe, and see at home
 How we prepare against the storme to come.

95.

To stand vpon our guard against such harme,
And backe our cause against inuading ill,
All castles and strong holds with men we arme,
The coasts are kept, beacons on euery hill
Are set for spies: O had the ioynt good will
 Of subiects loue with me their soueraigne bin,
 Th'inuading foes had found hard entrance in.

96.

In vaine, O wretched king, thy hopes haue trust
On broken faithes of subiects daily fleeting:
Thy lot is cast, from throne thou shalt be thrust,
Thy foes shall of thy subiects at their meeting,
In stead of blowes, be welcom'd with kind greeting:
 Thou only seek'st to keepe out th'vnkind queene,
 While heere at home worse dangers are vnseene.

97.

Whilst now my state begins for to decline,
In whom, alas, should I my trust repose?
My brother *Kent* then resident in Guine
For some displeasure done to him by those
'Bout vs at home, reuolts vnto our foes:
　　O faithlesse *Kent*, thou art the first shalt rue,
　　That euer thou to *Edward* wast vntrue.

98.

Treason transports, what traytors looke for heere,
The queen's stout champion *Iohn* of *Beaumont* comes
With his proud troopes, three thousand men well neere,
Promis'd rich pay in ransacke of our summes,
Who now aboord with trumpets and with drummes,
　　Vrg'd by the hastie queene to launch the deepe
　　With winde-wing'd sailes the seas soft bosome sweepe.

99.

O let the windes their forward course restraine,
Wing not such mischiefe to onr natiue shore,
Let the proud billowes beate them backe againe:
Or if they needs must come, let the seas rore,
Hurle them on rockes that they may neuer more
　　Be seene in England in pretence of good,
　　To bathe their hands in *Edward's* royall blood.

100.

Orwell thy hauen first did let them in,
Harwich with bels did welcome in their fleet:
No sooner did our *Isabel* begin
To presse the sandie shore with wanton feet,
But our earle marshall with his powres did greet
　　Her safe arriue, whose part, false peere, had bin
　　To haue oppos'd her at her entrance in.

101.

The brother to that lord that lost his head,
Leister's great earle did now lift vp his hand,
As in reuenge of *Lancaster* late dead,
T'whom many a peere linckt in rebellious band
Of grudges past, in the queene's cause doth stand:
  And lest they grieue in conscience to betray
  Their lawfull king, the church leads them the way.

102.

Herford's proud prelate, *Torlston*, who before
Conuicted was for treason gainst his king,
When armes gainst vs our stubborne barons bore,
Shrowded till now beneath the churche's wing,
Fled to the foes, and in his heart did bring
  That horrid treason hatcht before in hell,
  Cause of all after mischiefe that befell.

103.

The newes of this new innouation made,
And of the aliens lately set on land,
With terrour doth my fainting heart inuade:
All holds about vs readie open stand,
To yeeld possession ere the foes demand:
  Whose first smal troope now made a mightie force,
  Into the land they take their forward course.

104.

London denies to lend her sou'raigne aid,
To whom inforc'd at length to bid adew,
As doubting there to foes to be betrai'd,
With both the *Spencers* vnto Wales I flew,
There by some powre my hopes yet to renue,
  Hoping amongst the Welch more faith to find,
  T'whom from my youth I had been euer kind.

105.

But thus forsaken, whither shal I run?
Where shall I shadow me with safetie's wing?
Since that a wife, a brother, and a sonne,
Pursues a husband, father and a king:
Pitie, adew, my wrong shall neuer wring
   Remorse from others: Wales conspires my woe,
   And with false England turnes vnto my foe.

106.

Pursu'd on euery hand, and forc'd to flie
My natiue soile to shun death's dangerous dart,
My fortunes on the surging seas to trie
In a poore barke, from England we depart
To th'ile of Lunday with an heauie heart,
   Whom from the maine land Seuerne doth diuide,
   In which we hope in safetie to abide.

107.

But eu'n that little good doth seas denie,
With angrie looke the heau'ns behold the maine,
Gust after gust the winged winds do flie
Vpon the waues, who puft with proud disdaine,
Will vs deuoure or driue vs backe againe:
   As if too much they thought that little land
   For him that late had kingdomes at command.

108.

Remorselesse waues haue we a kingdome lost,
And yet our barke do ye denie to bring
To this small plot of ground two miles at most:
O woe to tell that once so great a king
Should stoope his minde vnto so small a thing,
   Content to share the meanest part of many,
   And yet deni'd to be possest of any.

109.

Long did we wrestle with the waues and winde,
But all in vaine we striue, for neuer more
Shall friendlesse *Edward* any comfort find:
Our barke distrest, her tackle rent and tore,
At length arriues vpon Glamorgan shore,
 Where *Spencer, Baldocke, Reding,* markt for death,
 Go all with me t'a castle called Neath.

110.

With vaine suppose of safetie in that hold,
While there in secret we our selues repose
To the lords *Zouch* and *Leister* we are sold,
Who by rich gifts often corrupting those
That our vnknowne abode could best disclose,
 With violent hands do sease their wished pray,
 And beare vs thence each one a seuerall way.

111.

Leister, thy king is now thy captiue made,
Reuenge is in thy hand, where is thy spleene?
Though vnto thee thy soueraigne was betrai'd:
This be thy praise, thou wouldst not with our queene
In *Edward's* wrongs be any deeper seene:
 While in thy Killingworth thy king remaines,
 Nought doth he want that to a king pertaines.

112.

With a strong guard from starting there kept sure,
Our friends meane time being seas'd on by the foe,
Both *Spencers, Reading, Daniel, Milcheldeure,*
In death do happily shut vp their woe,
As pointing out the way that we must go:
 Baldocke in prison by a milder fate,
 Struck dead with grief preuents their deadly hate.

113.

They, that vnto the king induc'd by reason
Did loyall proue, were traytors to the state:
O impious age, when truth was counted treason,
Heere noble *Arundell* I waile thy fate,
  Whose blood drunke vp by *Mortimer's* sterne hate,
    Did manifest the spleene, on which he fed
    Against his king, for whom thy blood was shed.

114.

Since they by death t'offence haue paid their due,
Who late alone in your displeasure stood,
Whom should your deadly hatred now pursue?
If they were only foes to common good,
  That made you satisfaction with their blood:
    Why is your liege lord as a common foe
    Reseru'd a captiue prince for worser woe?

115.

Bloodie reuenge your hatred cannot bound,
So wilfully to greater mischiefe bent,
The poore imprison'd king must be vncrown'd,
At London by the states in parlament,
  It is decreed by mutuall consent:
    Edward must be depos'd from royall throne,
    Where he had sate now twice ten yeares and one.

116.

O righteous heau'ns, if ye haue powre t'oppose
Fraile man's vnrighteous thoughts in euery thing:
Then suffer not, ah suffer not my foes
Thus to go on, that are about to bring
  Such wofull tidings to a wretched king:
    In thrall though I abide, this grace yet giue,
    That I at least a captiue king may liue.

117.

Strengthned by will, though not by force of lawes,
To Killingworth th'appointed states are come,
Where, as in censure of some weightie cause,
Twentie and foure agreed vpon their doome,
In order sit within a goodly roome,
　And thither do their king to iudgement call,
　Who should haue sate chiefe iudge aboue them all.

118.

From secret closet, though, alas, full loath,
Forth am I brought in mourning weeds, that show
His griefe of mind, whose bodie they do cloath:
And when I would conceale my inward woe,
With head declining downe as I do go,
　The griefe I would not see, I see in teares,
　Which fallen from mine eies the pauement beares.

119.

In presence being come and silence made,
Torleton, whose lookes did wound me with despaire,
A man in tongue most powerfull to perswade,
Stands vp, and as design'd for this affaire,
Doth in few words effectually declare
　The common people's will, the peeres consent
　That I thenceforth resigne my gouernment.

120.

O heere, what tongue can vnto vtterance bring
The inward griefe, which my poore heart did wound?
So far it past all sense in sorrowing,
Passion so powrefully doth sense confound,
That in a swoune I falling on the ground,
　Faine would haue di'd, but *Leister* standing by
　Steps in, and doth that happinesse deny.

121.

Recall'd from death by those that stood about,
When breath through grieued brest found passage free,
In these sad words my woes I breathed out:
" O powrefull God, since 'tis thy will that wee
Do leaue our crowne, I grudge not thy decree:
   Thou art most iust in all, thou gau'st a crowne,
   But ah, mine owne misdeeds haue cast me downe.

122.

To you I yeeld what wrong doth wrest from me,
Since with one voice ye say it must be so,
And beg this mercie in my miserie:
That since your hate hath brought me to this woe,
It heere may end, no further let it goe:
   He whom once king your hate could not forgiue,
   Will be no king so he haue leaue to liue."

123.

Heere teares did choake the end of my sad words,
And while my state in silence I deplore,
Trussell in name of all the English lords
Renouncing th'homage due to me before,
Depriues me of the same for euermore:
   Leauing his liege that was of most command,
   The most deiected subiect of this land.

124.

Blunt, steward of our house in th'open hall,
Protracts no time by any long delay,
But breaking of his rod before them all,
Resignes his office, all depart away,
Many that would in loue, yet dare not stay:
   This was my fate, thus did false fortune frowne,
   Ah God, that euer king was so cast downe!

125.

Yet fortune bath not spent her vtmost hate,
With patience we must arme our selues more strong,
Scarce will fraile eares belieue what we relate,
When now thy muse shall tune her mournefull song,
To sadder times that she may waile that wrong,
   To which with griefe for guide we now proceed,
   Whose woes wil make the hardiest heart to bleed.

126.

Our iealous queen, whom conscience doth torment,
Fearing lest *Leicester* so neare alli'd,
In pitie of our state should now relent,
Tels *Torleton* of her doubts what might betide,
If in his keeping we do still abide,
   Who fearing vengeance for his owne offence,
   Giues her his counsell to remoue me thence.

127.

Leister constrained by expresse command,
To the lord *Berkley* doth his charge restore,
Whence he conueies me with an armed band
Vnto his castle seated neare the shore,
Gainst which great *Seuerne's* raging waues do rore:
   But *Berkley*, thou with *Leister* art too kind,
   Edward with thee doth too much fauour find.

128.

Oh gentle *Berkly*, whither wilt thou go?
Why dost not stand by thy sad sou'raigne's side?
For pitie leaue him not vnto such woe,
Which *Gourney* and *Matreuers* do prouide,
Such woe did neuer any king betide:
   But with command they come, thou must depart,
   And leaue thy king, although with heauie heart.

129.

To *Gourney* and *Matreuers* by decree
In his owne castle he resignes his right :
Who lest that any friend should priuie bee
To my abode, do beare me thence by night
Vnto Corfe castle, whence with more despight
    Through darknesse and blind waies in poore array,
    To Bristow castle they do me conuey.

130.

By night conuey'd thus rudely to and fro,
Lest by my friends from them I rescu'd bee,
At last since none, whom they do feare, do know
Where I am now become, they do agree
To Berkley backe againe to go with mee,
    Staying a time, till night with dewie dampe
    Should choake daie's light and put out Phœbus lampe.

131.

Then do they set me on a beast foreworne
In stead of stately steed, whereon to ride,
And for no crowne I had my head t'adorne,
Bare I do sit, except the heau'n to hide
My woefull head all couering they denide,
    While sharp winds in my face the weather blowes,
    And with their nipping cold augments my woes.

132.

When out of east the day began to peepe,
Who, as if she my ruefull case did mone,
Vpon my head her dewie droppes did weepe,
The right hand way they left, and iourn'ing on,
Where Seuerne's siluer waues doth play vpon
    The marish greene, they forced me to light,
    There to haue slaine my heart with sad despight.

133.

In stead of royall chaire, they set me downe
On a mole-hill (was neuer king so vade)
And *Gourney*, wretched man, in stead of crowne
With wreath of grasse my royall browes abusde,
Patience perforce it might not be refusde:
  Then while in wretched case my hands I wring,
  In scorne the villaines bid auaunt sir king.

134.

While thus I sit all carefull comfortlesse,
With pitious lookes cast vp in wofull wise,
Calling the heau'ns to witnesse my distresse,
In stead of teares, the starres like weeping eies
Drop downe their exhalations from the skies:
  And 'Tithon's bride new rising from her bed,
  Beholds their leaudnesse with a blushing red.

135.

Yet to my plaints no pitie they do yeeld:
But bent to adde more griefe to my disgrace,
In rustie murren with foule water fill'd,
A villaine comes with hands vncleane and base,
To shaue the heare both from my head and face:
  Who, when warme water I desire to haue,
  Replies, that cold will serue his turne to shaue.

136.

With eyes full burthned with a showre of teares,
" Do ye," quoth I, " now helpe me with your might
To waile the sorrowes, which my sad soule beares,
Open your floud-gates wide, and in their sight
Let vs haue water warme in their despight:"
  This said, the teares did downe my cheekes distill,
  As if they stroue t'effect my wofull will.

137.

Hence in this plight to Berkley am I brought,
Where bidding comfort euermore farewell:
And feeding long on care and pensiue thought,
At length I am shut vp in darksome cell,
There to the senselesse walles my griefe to tell,
   Deni'd the comfort of heau'n's common light,
   Bound while I liue to liue in endlesse night.

138.

My sterne tormentors moued with remorse,
Wish death to end my miserable care:
Yet nature will not violently force
Way to a lingring death, they do prepare
By cold, long watching, fast and euill fare:
   But, I euen made insensible in woes,
   Suffer with patience all they can impose.

139.

In hollow vault, through which the channell past
From forth the towne beneath my chamber flore,
Dead carcasses and loathed things they cast,
Whose grieuous stinch did grieue my senses more
Then all the griefe that I endur'd before:
   And forc'd me search the walles for open place,
   To some without to waile my woefull case.

140.

Vpon a time I through a crannie spi'd
Men hewing timber on the greene fast by,
To whom with drearie deadly voice I cri'd,
" O who will helpe me wretch, that heere do lie
In torment worse then death, yet cannot die?
   If any there do mourne man's wretched case,
   Helpe me, ah help me from this loathed place."

141.

The poore men's hearts are pierc'd with point of woe,
And trembling horror doth their hearts appall
For ruth of wronged king cast downe so low,
Vnable t'helpe me, vnto God they call,
That he may yeeld reliefe to wofull thrall:
  Who giuing eare to mine and their request,
  At length in death doth giue my sorrowes rest.

142.

Mischiefe from those that guiltie of offence
Did wish my death in letters sent doth bring
A darke enigma bearing double sense,
Which is vnpointed left a doubtfull thing,
Either to kill or not to kill the king,
  As in such tearmes " king *Edward's* blood to spill
  Refuse ye not to feare I count it ill."

143.

The bloodie villaines construing the same
Vnto that sense, for which it then was sent,
Watch for the night, whose cloudie cloake of shame
With darknesse should conceale their damn'd intent,
Day did abhor the thing 'bout which they went,
  And fled away, grim night on th'earth did frowne,
  And I in carefull bed had laid me downe.

144.

Where for musitian that with sweetest breath,
Had wont to lull my watchfull sense asleepe:
The ghastly owle, the fatall bird of death,
That on my chamber walles her inne did keepe
In my poore trembling heart impressed deepe
  The feare of death with her too deadly note,
  Which oft she shriked through her balefull throte.

145.

The murmuring noise of the rude waters rore
Which not far thence into the seas do fall,
Where Seuerne's billowes do beat vpon the shore,
And bellowing winds which iustling 'gainst the wall
Like death's shrill whistlers at the cranies call,
 Through darknesse and deepe silence of the night,
 Our troubled heart with horror doth affright.

146.

On fearefull things long musing I do lie,
At last with sleepe opprest, in slumber cast,
Vpflew the doores and in the murderers flie,
At which awakt, and suddenly agast,
As from my naked bed I thought t'haue past,
 They with rude hands do hold me downe by force,
 While with vaine words I seeke to moue remorse.

147.

" Ye deadly instruments of other's ill,
Grant one request, which dying I do craue:
Since ye be bent this royall blood to spill,
Send me not hence with torture to the graue:
'Tis life ye seeke, the only thing I haue:
 · Which yet shall vade on wings of willing breath,
 Since better tis to die then liue in death."

148.

By this they with maine strength do me compell,
Strengthlesse for breath to yeeld to their intent:
And then, O horrid, shamefull thing to tell,
By force they thrust an hollow instrument
Much like a trumpe into my fundament,
 By which they do preuent the mone I make
 By sudden death, as thus to them I spake.

149.

" Ah why, why thus torment ye me with smart?
Leaue off to grieue:" not one word more I said,
They had by this time thrust me to the hart
With steele red hot : to sleepe me downe I laid,
And with the pray'rs which godly folke had made,
    When from the castle they did heare my cries,
    My soule on mercie's wings did clime the skies.

150.

Thus hauing heard my lamentable fall
Procur'd by stubborne peeres disloyaltie,
And people's wilfull hate, the spring of all
First flowing from deceitfull flatterie,
That deadly bane t'all princely royaltie:
    Amongst the rest in place with painfull pen
    Insert it for a Mirrour vnto men.

THE LAMENTABLE

Lives and Deaths of the two yong

Princes, Edward the Fifth, and

his Brother Richard Duke of

Yorke.

THE ARGUMENT.

" Th'afflictions, which this wronged king did beare,
He dead," said Memorie, " reuenged were:
Like Vulcan's bride, at Nottingham, his queene
In th'armes of Mars-like *Mortimer* was seene:
He for such deeds, as all true honor staines,
By ignominious death did pay iust paines:
By righteous doome till death she liu'd in thrall,
Within the circuit of a castle's wall:
Her first-borne sonne, the second *Edward's* heire,
(She being to French king *Philip* call'd the faire,
Left liuing of his line) by her made claime
Vnto his right in France, and gain'd the same:
He dead, the second *Richard*, second sonne
To his first-borne, his fatall raigne begonne:
Richard depos'd, *Henrie* ascends the throne,
Heire to duke *Iohn*, king *Edward's* fourth borne sonne,
He disposest lord *Roger Mortimer*,
In *Richard* daies proclaim'd apparant heire,

Who had duke *Lionel's* daughter for his mother,
Edward's third sonne, to *Iohn* the elder brother:
Yet did this *Henrie* after much vnrest
Die in the throne of England's crowne possest:
And to his *Henrie* did bequeath the same,
The fifth and most illustrate of that name:
Who in those few yeares of his happie raigne
Did the French crowne to England's right regaine:
Di'd in his manly prime, left his yong sonne
Henrie the sixth to sit vpon the throne:
Gainst whom *Plantagenet*, Yorke's noble duke
Stood for his right, who his iust title tooke
From *Lionel*, fourth by descent from him:
Yet in his quarrell lost both life and lim:
His sonnes reueng'd his death, put *Henrie* downe,
Edward his eldest did obtaine the crowne:
In peace retain'd it, left it to his heires,
Who are the next, that in their turne appeares:
For they except, heere none exempted be,
Since the sad second *Edward's* tragedie:
Two noble youths are left in yongest yeares
Vnto the guidance of the iarring peeres,
Edward the eldest comes from Ludlowe's towne
To London, with intent to take the crowne,
His vncle *Riuers*, *Vaughan* and lord *Grey*
By *Gloster's* plots, who sought their liues decay,
From him remoued are, yong Yorke his brother
Doth flie to sanctuarie with his mother:
Whom *Richard* his false vncle thence doth bring
Into the tower vnto the vncrown'd king:
Vsurps the crowne, puts both the youths to death,
Who twixt the sheets betrai'd, expire their breath:
The truth of which that we may heere partake,
Their princely ghosts let fame from sleepe awake."

ANOTHER ARGUMENT.

At fame's first call the princes both ascend,
And both by turne do tell their tragicke end.

Richard.

WHAT wit so sharpe is found in age or youth,
That can distinguish trust from treacherie?
Falsehood puts on the face of simple truth,
And maskes in th'habit of plaine honestie,
When she in heart intends most villanie :
　　The panther with sweet sauour of her breath
　　First charmes their sense, whom she hath markt for death.

2.

Of which that future time may mirrours haue
By the fourth *Edward's* murdered progenie,
Vp (brother) vp and let vs leaue our graue
In this night's vision call'd by Memorie,
To tell the truth of our sad tragedie,
　　That princes happily by vs may learne
　　Trust from false treason truly to discerne.

3.

And thou, O mournefull muse, that didst of yore
Th'iniurious wrongs of many a prince complaine,
Helpe two deposed princes to deplore
The wretched fortunes which they did sustaine:
Matter thou hast that fits a ruthfull straine,
   How *Richard's* treason twixt the sheets did smother
   The infant orphants of his kingly brother.

4.

That we may keepe decorum in discourse,
And into order may digest it well,
Let vs alternally succeed in course:
And that we turne by tarne may truly tell
Of euery circumstance, as it befell,
   (Brother) do you begin to mind to call
   Our vncle's treason and our tragicke fall.

Edward.

Must I begin those bloodie pathes to goe,
In which the prints of *Gloster's* steps remaine?
Draw neere then all, that list to heare of woe,
And while our restlesse wrongs I do complaine, ·
If you lament our losse of life and raigne,
   Your sighes soft breathed in still plaints of pitie,
   Be the sad musike to our dolefull dittie.

6.

The sonnes we are of that renowned lord
Edward the fourth, who did the right restore
To *Yorke* againe with his victorious sword:
Which *Lancaster* in three descents that wore,
The royall crowne had kept from vs before,
   Ending those iarres, which *Gaunt's* ambitious son
   With royall *Richard's* blood had first begun.

7.

Three brothers had he, whom by fate's sterne will,
Remorselesse death vntimely did deuoure,
Rutland's yong earle, whom *Clifford's* sword did kill,
Clarence, that duke, who in the fatall tower
In Malmsey But did meet his liue's last houre:
 Richard the yongest, who was stain'd with guilt
 Of *Clarence* blood and ours, both which he spilt.

8.

O that desire of rule so much should blind
The eyes of men, or that to gaine a crowne,
The godlike part of man, th'immortall mind
Of wrathfull heau'n should dare t'incurre the frowne,
And cast it selfe from glorie headlong downe!
 O foule ambition, had thy guilt not stain'd
 This tyrant's deeds, what glorie had he gain'd?

9.

For though he from his mother's painfull throwes,
Mark't for a plague into the world was brought;
Yet with his sword gainst our Lancastrian foes
In many bloodie broiles he manly fought:
And by his courage high achieuements wrought,
 Great *Warwicke*, *Oxford*, *Clifford*, and the rest,
 Did finde a valiant heart in *Richard's* brest.

10.

But where are now those deedes, or who can say
That they with praise doe glorifie his name?
How can he euer hope to wipe away
Those spots of blood vpon the face of fame,
Making his deeds to blush at his owne shame?
 What deedes of fame he did are not his owne,
 His euill deeds remaine to him alone.

11.

With their shed blood thy lines I will not staine,
Whom wrackt by troops to graue his hand did send,
To him in his succeeding tragicke straine,
The sad report thereof I doe commend:
Enongh it is to tell of our owne end,
　To which I will proceede, first setting downe
　The plots our vncle vs'd t'obtaine the crowne.

12.

When on the throne my kingly father sat,
All noise of warre new husht, euen in the greene
Of peace late growne discord did set debate
Betweene the kindred of our mother queene,
And twixt the peeres, who with malignant spleene,
　Did swell to see them fauor'd of the king,
　From whence our future ruine first did spring.

13.

On this, as on a platforme firme and sure,
Gloster did build his hopes for future daies:
Yet England's *Edward* hoping to procure
Peace twixt both parts, did seeke by oft assaies
T'appease the strife, which priuie hate did raise:
　And at his death did cause them each to other
　To giue their faith, as brother vnto brother.

14.

The king scarse dead, from London swift report
With mischiefe at her heeles, or'e hedge and heath
To Ludlowe came, where then we kept our court,
And there with pallid lookes, halfe out of breath,
She tels the tidings of our father's death,
　Bidding me now beware vnhappie fate,
　And looke about in this new change of state.

15.

Though time with so few yeeres my youth had crown'd,
That yet scarse fourteene times the heauenly Ram
Had push't his hornes against the new yeare's bound,
Since first into the world to light I came:
Yet of my father's death, when lucklesse fame
　　Had rung the dolefull knell: then did I know
　　The danger which I was to vndergoe.

16.

Nurst from my cradle in true discipline,
In my weake childhood I had scand this theame,
That if th'ambitious with cleere sighted eyne
Could but discerne what fortune gaue to them,
When they had gain'd a kingdome's diadem,
　　They would account that day their blisse to ende,
　　In which their steps the throne did first ascend.

17.

Our vncle *Riuers*, who my gardian was,
With vs at Ludlowe, then being resident,
Did muster vp his powers with vs to passe
To London by short iournies, with intent
All danger in our passage to preuent:
　　But *Gloster* did intrappe both him and me,
　　And by his plots did frustrate his decree.

18.

By wicked wits, the queene he doth perswade,
To thinke that since by her deceased king,
Betwixt the peeres a vnion had beene made,
With such a power, it were a dangerous thing,
The prince her sonne, to London vp to bring:
　　Distrust might soone disturbe the quiet state,
　　And giue new life to the old dead debate.

19.

Blinded with this deceit, our carefull mother
Directs her letters, bearing such effect
Vnto our vncle *Riuers*, her deare brother,
Who doubting lest his foes might ought obiect
T'haue gone amisse, while he did vs protect,
   Dismist his powers, and only did retaine
   Those, that before were of our daily traine.

20.

All readie now to hoise vp happie saile,
For London we our fatall course do stere,
Our hopes do promise vs a prosperous gale:
But once set forth, clouds thicken in the cleare,
A storme before vs plainly doth appeare,
   And with a gust in gulfe of woe cast downe,
   Vnhappie I made shipwracke of my crowne.

21.

At Stonie-Stratford, being vpon my way,
The bloodie bore, my vncle, that did aime
At England's diadem by our decay,
With that false duke, disloyall *Buckingham*,
With show of humble loue in presence came:
   But after tender of their duties done,
   To put their plot in practise they begun.

22.

They falsely did accuse of treacherie
My two halfe brothers by our mother's side,
Lord *Marquesse* and lord *Grey*, then standing by,
Obiecting gainst them both, that prickt with pride
They sought the realme and me, yet yong, to guide;
   And with our vncle *Riuers*, thought to bring
   The noble peeres in hatred with the king.

23.

Without respect vnto our princely state,
With violent hands they beare them both away,
Too weake were we of power t'auert that fate,
Which in our sight did threaten their decay,
Our words were weaker, *Gloster* bore the sway:
  Riuers my vncle, *Vaughan*, *Grey*, all three,
  After that time I neuer more did see.

24.

Rob'd of my friends, to London we are led,
Vpon the way mourning with sighes and teares,
The wretched fate to fall vpon my head,
Griefe with a multitude of pensiue feares
Sits heauie on my heart: yet in my eares
  Gloster to please me, sings this syren's song,
  " All should be well:" when nought was ment but wrong.

25.

Conuey'd to London, where while I abide
Within the bishop's place, I little knew
Of any tidings, that did then betide,
The tyrant, (brother *Yorke*) then aim'd at you
To hasten that, which after did ensue:
  Then take your turne againe, and briefely tell,
  What in my absence vnto you befell.

Richard.

I shall obey, and truly bring to light
The darke dissembling, and the much vntroth
Of periur'd peeres, to rob vs of our right,
How our queene mother carefull of us both,
With me to holy sanctuarie goth,
  And of our vncle's plots to bring me thence,
  Which was the only bar to his pretence.

27.

When fame with terrour vnto our queene mother,
Then dewing our dead father's cheekes with teares,
Brought the surprise of her two sonnes and brother,
O how those tidings tingled in her eares!
Suspitious thoughts begat a thousand feares,
    Forecasting by that vnexpected harme,
    The greater mischiefe of a following storme.

28.

In this distraction of a doubtfull mind
In change of state, seeing such crosse fortune's frowne,
And doubting in distressefull times to find,
Her friends turn'd foes to helpe to plucke vs downe,
And to bereaue vs of our father's crowne:
    With me to sanctuarie she did goe,
    There to remaine in safetie from our foe.

29.

Of which, when tidings to the tyrant came,
As one depriued of his wished pray,
His wits best engines he begins to frame,
And if they faile, he doth resolue t'assay
With hands prophane to fetch me thence away:
    While from his reach I there did safely won,
    He could not finish what he had begun.

30.

Which our queene mother did presage before,
And thought by force of sanctuarie's right,
Safely to shield vs from the cruell bore,
Who with his tuskes the elder durst not smite,
While I the yonger liu'd in such safe plight:
    By death of th'one, the crowne how could he gaine,
    If th'other after liuing did remaine?

31.

The subtill tyrant to effect his will,
This faire pretence vnto the peeres doth frame,
That for th'auoiding of a generall ill,
Since to the prince and them it was a shame,
That causelesse I should sanctuarie claime,
  Vnto the place he thought it no offence,
  If not by peace, by force to fetch me thence.

32.

Yet to obtaine our mother queene's consent,
Vnto the place before he offer wrong,
The cardinall of Yorke for that intent,
A man graue, sober, subtill, wise, and strong,
To charme an eare with his inchanting tongue,
  He doth select to further this affaire,
  And to his vnknowne plots way to prepare.

33.

When he with many more in presence came,
He with faire speech begins to greet our mother:
Then tels, how to the prince it was a shame,
That she should keepe me there, as if one brother
Did liue in dread of danger by the other,
  What griefe my absence was vnto the king,
  What comfort by my presence I should bring.

34.

Proceeding on vnto the future ill,
Which might ensue by ouer much distrust,
The strengthning of her inconsiderate will,
With sanctuarie's gift by claime vniust,
The priuiledge of the place by them discust,
  Found not of force to her to yeeld the same,
  Who did not truly want, what she did claime.

35.

The queene effectually doth answere all,
He turnes replie, she doth reioyne againe,
And puts such questions to the cardinall,
That at a *non plus* set, he doth remaine
In silent pause, till chaft in tearmes more plaine,
    He threatfully declares the peeres pretence,
    Who had decreed by force to fetch me thence.

36.

With this hard speech, our mother in affright,
Round set with doubts, not knowing when or where,
She safely might conuey me from their sight:
In silence stands, her lookes bewrayes pale feare,
Which she would vtter, yet doth oft forbeare,
    Till taking me by th'hand, sighes forcing teares,
    And teares sad words, no longer she forbeares.

37.

" Behold," said she, " I to your trust commit
This noble impe, whom with the prince his brother,
When in the generall iudgement God shall sit,
I at your hands will aske: feare with the mother,
What may betide him taken to another:
    I make no doubt, but ye will faithfull be,
    Yet others may deceiue both you and me.

38.

Heere I resigne:" and at that word she paus'd,
As loth so soone to part with such a thing:
Then with a sigh, to shew that griefe had caus'd
That silent pause, " to you," quoth she, " I bring
This royall issue of a late dead king:
    Yours be the charge, vnto the child proue true:"
    Which said, she thus gaue me my last adew.

39.

" Farewell my little sonne, God be thy aid :"
With that she turn'd about, and wept for woe :
Then being about to part, she turn'd and said,
" Kisse me my sonne, kisse me before thou go,
When we shall kisse againe, our God doth know :"
    We kist, she sigh'd, I wept and did refuse
    So to depart from her; but could not chuse.

40.

Leauing the queene, I absent, to deplore me,
For that I was an infant then in yeares,
To the Star-chamber in their armes they bore me,
Where our false vncle to delude the peeres,
My pensiuenesse with words of comfort cheeres :
    " Now welcome from my heart, my lord," quoth he,
    Then tooke me in his armes and kissed me.

41.

Thence brother vnto you I was conuey'd
Then in that place, where London's prelats dwell,
Whence like two lambes vnto a wolfe betrai'd,
We to the Tower were led : where what befell,
Since it concernes you most, you best can tell :
    Be it your turne, our sorrowes to deplore,
    For I, alas, for sighes can say no more.

Edward.

If I must tell the horror of that night,
In which by death our soules were set on wing,
Let sorrow lend vs her sad pen t'indite
In lines of woe, what I to light shall bring,
And teach our muse so ruthfully to sing,
    That the sad reader's ruthfull eyes may drop,
    Teares at each point, to teach him where to stop.

43.

Within the Tower, of which my brother spake,
Lockt vp from sight of all our friends we were,
Where while we do expect, when I shall take
The crowne on me, t'whom whilome euery peere,
As to their soueraigne fealtie did sweare:
    At last report these fearefull newes doth bring,
    We were depos'd, *Gloster* was England's king.

44.

Which, when I first did heare, a thrilling feare
Ran through my heart, and sighing thus I spake:
" Alas, that I was borne king *Edward's* heire,
Would God my vncle, though from me he take
My crowne, which willingly I could forsake,
    Would leaue vs that, which none but God can giue,
    And for my kingdome giue vs leaue to liue."

45.

Thenceforth the tower, which late was deem'd my court,
Is made our prison by a tyrant's might :
Farewell the world, our day now waxeth short,
Our gladsome sunne of comfort and delight,
Is ouercast with clouds of enuious night,
    Winter is come euen in our spring of youth,
    Our late sweet smiles are drown'd in teares of ruth.

46.

O noble *Edward*, from whose royall blood
Life to these infant bodies nature drew,
Thy roses both are cropt euen in the bud:
Why didst thou leaue that bore in time t'ensue,
To spoile those plants that in thy garden grew?
    Of all that haruest which thy hand did sow,
    Nought haue we reaped but a crop of woe.

47.

Who now amongst thy peeres of note or name,
The sad mishap of thy deare sonnes doth mone?
Where's *Howard, Louell, Barkley, Buckingham,*
That bound themselues by oath to thee, that none
But thy faire sonnes should sit vpon the throne?
 Woe worth them all, they all do now crie, " downe
 With *Edward's* heires, let *Gloster* haue the crowne."

48.

Ah pitie, in what region didst thou dwell,
Had'st thou been present in those hatefull times,
Then should not I thy shame, O England, tell,
Nor should I seeke to proue thy wicked crimes
Vnto thy face in these impartiall rimes:
 Thy princes, on whose state misfortune frown'd,
 In thy false people pitie seldome found.

49.

Search time's records, there see how poysoned *Iohn*
Stands vp to witnesse thy sterne people's hate,
See how the second *Edward* thrust from throne,
Cries for reuenge on people of that state,
Behold thy shame in *Richard's* wofull fate:
 Gainst whom thy nation vnremorsefull stood,
 Till Pomfret's wals were sprinkled with his blood.

50.

But why seeke I, O England, to reclaime thee,
By sounding former euils in thine eare?
That's yet vntold, the which alone shall shame thee,
As oft of it as any age shall heare,
Tyrants, in whom no pitie doth appeare,
 Shall thee vpbraid, and blushing at thy shame,
 For past compare shall register the same.

51.

When as our vncle had obtain'd his will,
The crowne scarce warme on his vsurping head,
Opprest with care to keepe that gotten ill,
He takes no rest of mind in bowre nor bed,
Suspition with the guilt of conscience fed
  Breeds doubts, distractions, horrors in his brest,
  Which like to hags do haunt him with vnrest.

52.

Each step he treads, by which he climbes his throne,
Is grounded on the death of some great peere:
As he ascends, he sees their blood thereon:
Set in his chaire, shame whispers in his eare
That's not his place, his nephew should be there:
  Doubt askes him, how he hopes t'enioy that long,
  When they do liue, whose right he keepes by wrong.

53.

He that had drunke so oft of murder's cup,
To reach that height to which he did aspire,
Now fils the measure of his mischiefe vp,
And in vaine hope to raise his heart yet higher,
Spares not the blood deduc'd from his owne sire:
  Poore orphanes blood, pris'd at a crowne's rich wealth,
  To his sicke state can only promise health.

54.

Whilst euery where his wandring eye doth range
To find some wretch to put this taske vpon,
All things about vs haue a sudden change,
Vngrac'd, not car'd for, comforted of none,
By our owne seruants we are left alone:
  Those that bemone our fortunes dare not stay,
  By feare constrain'd, with griefe they go their way.

55.

Inconsolatly left in wofull plight,
Each helping other for to waile and weepe,
In dole we spend the day, and in the night
Horror and dread of death doth waking keepe
Our watchfull eyes, and bars them of their sleepe,
    Each little noise, each windie puffe of breath
    Affrights vs infants with th'approch of death.

56.

Thou fatall building stain'd with noble blood,
Thou den where horror and darke treason lies,
Say if thou wast, since thy foundation stood,
More mou'd to pitie humaine miseries,
Hearing the echo of sad sorrowe's cries:
    Then when yong *Yorke* with pitious plaints and mones
    Powr'd forth his sorrowes to thy senselesse stones.

57.

Euen as sometimes we see a silly lambe,
Which for the slaughter in some fold is pent,
There kept from sight of his deare loued damme,
Her absence with faint bleating doth lament,
Whose only sight can giue it safe content:
    So little *Yorke* in vaine lamenting wept,
    That from our mother's presence he was kept.

58.

Oft, wofull child, thus hast thou question'd mee,
" Where is my mother?" and when I for woe,
Haue turn'd my backe and could not answere thee:
With teares againe, thou wouldest aske to know,
Saying, " I would vnto my mother go:"
    But woe, alas, what comfort could I giue thee,
    When of all meanes our vncle did depriue mee?

59.

While thus we waste in woe, the tyrant king
With death to right those, whom he did abuse
With wrong in life, finding a way to wing
Mischiefe deuis'd, a wretched man did chuse
For this affaire, which others did refuse:
 Tirrill by name, a knight decay'd in state,
 Prone t'act this deed in hope of happie fate.

60.

Two desperate villaines, hatefull to those times,
Forrest and *Dighton*, men obscure and base:
Yet to the world notorious for leaud crimes,
For *Tirril's* gold this damned deed embrace,
Who being brought into conuenient place,
 Wait for aduantage of the gloomie night
 To couer that, which did abhorre the light.

61.

The night comes on, and murder doth begin
To act her part within the fatall Tower,
In that dead time of night, the cloake of sinne,
In which the clock chimes twelue, the chiefest houre
When sleepe on man and beast doth vse his powre,
 Both the rude slaues on vs poore infants flie,
 As we together in our bed did lie.

62.

Betwixt the sheets they keepe vs downe by force,
We struggle against death with gasping grones,
They in their hard hearts feeling no remorce,
To heare poore soules powre forth such pitious mones,
As might with pitie moue the ruthlesse stones,
 Holding the pillowes downe do stop our breath,
 Vntill we both giue vp the ghost in death.

63.

Thus hast thou heard, how after all his cares
King *Edward's* fruit did perish in the bud,
By which since we may see how pride prepares
Her passage through the spoile of common good,
Without respect t'affinitie of blood:
   That thou may make a Mirrour of the same,
   A place amongst thy Mirrours we do claime.

THE TRAGICALL LIFE

and Death of King Richard the Third.

THE ARGUMENT.

" The lamentable fall," quoth Memorie,
" Of two such noble youths may Mirrours be,
That man high mounted on ambitious wing,
T'obtaine a crowne attempteth any thing:
They dead, their vncle's tragedie succeeds:
His monstrous birth, his shape, his bloodie deeds:
Horror of conscience haunts him with vnrest,
The mightie *Buckingham's* attempt vnblest:
The tyrant enuying noble *Richmond's* good,
By treason seekes to spill his royall blood,
His strange escape from France to Britanie,
Pursu'd by *Landois* his false enemie,
His safe arriue vpon the English coast,
The skilfull marshalling of either hoast
On Bosworth plaine, the order of the fight:
Stout Norfolke's fall, the king's part put to flight
His desperat valour shew'd on th'aduerse force,
The shamefull vsage of his conquered corse,
Which that we beare, let fame his ghost compe
To leaue his graue, that he the same may tell."

ANOTHER ARGUMENT.

Through night's darke shadowes from the house of bale,
The tyrant's ghost comes vp to tell his tale.

1.

HORROR pursues the homicide's sad soule,
Feare hunts his conscience with an hue and crie,
That drinkes the blood of men in murder's bowle,
Suspitious thoughts do rest in life denie,
Hate seldome suffers him in peace to die,
  By heau'n's inuiolate doome it is decreed,
  Whose hands shed blood, his heart in death should bleed.

2.

I was to noble *Yorke* the yongest sonne
Of foure, which he begot in lawfull bed,
First *Edward* was, the next place *Edmund* wonne,
Rutland's yong earle by *Clifford's* hand strooke dead,
Clarence the third, to death vntimely lead:
  I was the last: of all the foure the worst,
  By heau'n and nature in my birth accurst.

3.

When my sad mother in her fruitfull wombe
Bore me a painfull burthen to and fro,
Then the babe's infant bed had been my tombe,
Had not keene rasors to her paine and woe
Cut me a way, vnto the world to goe:
   Nature did grudge to think, that from her wombe
   A man-like monster to the world should come.

4.

When first I came into this world's huge vast,
My birth was not as others wont to bee:
First did my feet come forth, as if in hast
The child of discord had been then set free,
To cause the wretched world to disagree,
   Heau'n at that time told b'inauspitious starres
   Nations far off of England's ciuil warres.

5.

As hunger-steru'd to flesh my iawes in blood
I readie toothed came, as who would say,
Nature by signes vnto the world hath show'd
How fiercely he shall bite another day,
That in his mother's wombe well toothed lay,
   And maruaile 'twas, seeing viper-like he came,
   He was not borne by death of his owne damme.

6.

If like a cunning painter on a frame
My shape vnto the world I could descrie,
And with a curious pensell paint the same
In perfect colours, each spectatour's eie
Would by my lookes into my manners prie:
   The bodie's ill-shapte limbes are oft defin'd,
   For signes of euill manners in the mind.

7.

Little I was, and of a small compact,
My left side shoulder higher then the right,
Both crooked were, and therewithall contract
Into my backe, so that in all men's sight
I did appeare a most mishapen wight:
　　And hard it was to iudge, if that my soule
　　Or limbes ill fashion'd feature were more foule.

8.

The deeds of noble *Yorke* I not recite,
Done in those fatall daies of miserie,
Nor tell th'euents of euery speciall fight,
As at Saint Albones, Bloreheath, Banburie,
Northhampton, Barnet, Wakefield, Teukesburie,
　　Seeing they are often spoken of before,
　　By those, that heere their wofull falles deplore.

9.

Th'induction to my storie shall begin
Where the sixth *Henrie's Edward* timelesse fell:
Soune to stout *Margaret* that noble queene,
Of whom since heere no poet's pen doth tell:
Though hee a peerelesse prince deserue it well,
　　In breefe we will describe the manner all
　　Of our sterne deede and his vnhappie fall.

10.

His mother queene, the manlike *Margaret*,
After so many a fall in fight cast downe,
With her young *Edward* and stout *Somerset*
Did lastly hazard all for England's crowne
In fight at Teukesburie: but heau'n did frowne,
　　Wenlocke and *Somerset* fled both away,
　　Left vs the field, and lost their queene the day.

11.

The forlorne prince was taken as he fled
By *Richard Crofts*, a knight of Glostershire,
Who hearing of the proclamation spread,
That, who could bring him forth, should, for his hire,
Duely receiue a hundred poundes by yeere:
   The prince he brought to end our ancient strife,
   With promise made, that we should saue his life.

12.

In presence brought, the king to him thus spake:
" Fond wretch," said he, " what did thy thoughts excite
To come within my kingdome's bounds, and take
Rebellious armes t'oppugne thy soueraigne's right,
And traytor-like in field 'gainst me to fight?"
   To which the prince, in whose bold breast did lie
   An inbred courage, made this stout replie:

13.

" I came," said he, " to set my father free,
Whom thou in hold vniustly dost retaine:
I came to reobtaine my dignitie,
And in the throne to seate my sire againe,
In which as king thou wrongfully dost raigne:
   1 am by might enforc'd to stoope to thee,
   Who should by right be subiect vnto mee."

14.

The king being mou'd with this his stout replie,
Thrust him away, in whose heroicke brest
My brother *Clarence*, *Hastings*, *Grey*, and I,
Did sheath our blades, which fact heau'n did detest,
Permitting vs not vnreueng'd to rest:
   For none of vs in peacefull bed did lie,
   When from this world our wretched soules did flie.

15.

He dead, his sire, that poore deposed king,
The aged *Henrie*, sixt of that same name,
Liu'd in the Tower, depriu'd of euery thing
Which to a king pertain'd: yet did he frame
His thoughts with patience to endure the same,
　　Liuing a paterne of a patient spirit,
　　Who for his fame a golden verse doth merit.

16.

I thought, that while this noble king had breath,
His friends my brother's peace would still inuade:
Wherefore I did contriue his sudden death,
And in the Tower the butcher's part I plaide,
For th'hatefull point of that same bloodie blade,
　　Scarce cold with luke-warm blood of his owne sonne,
　　Vnlooked for, I through his sides did runne.

17.

He dead, the battels fought in field before,
Were turn'd to meetings of sweet amitie,
The war-gods thundring cannons dreadfull rore,
And ratling drum-sounds warlike harmonie,
To sweet tun'd noise of pleasing minstralsie,
　　The haile-like shot, to tennis balles were turn'd,
　　And sweet perfumes in stead of smoakes were burn'd.

18.

God Mars laid by his launce and tooke his lute,
And turn'd his rugged frownes to smiling lookes,
In stead of crimson fields, warre's fatall fruits,
He bath'd his limbes in Cypris' warbling brookes,
And set his thoughts vpon her wanton lookes,
　　All noise of warre was husht vpon our coast,
　　Plentie each where in easefull pride did boast.

19.

The king, who swims in streames of court delights,
Plaies like the fish so long with pleasure's bait,
That on her deadly bane he often bites,
Or like the mariner infortunate,
Sayling in seas where syrens lie in wait:
   To please the sense he lends his eare so long,
   Till he be charm'd with their inchanting song.

20.

Meane time not made to feast an amorous eie,
I fox-like lurking lay about the king,
Into the actions of the peeres I prie,
With cautie obseruation of each thing,
While with their wanton sou'raigne reuelling:
   They vainly spend in Venus vassallage
   The tedious houres of that peacefull age.

21.

But clouds do thicken in this peacefull cleere,
Warwicke's faire daughter forc'd by vnkind fate,
Forsakes lord *Clarence* her beloued feere,
Who purposing to take for second mate,
The only heire of some hie towring state,
   Did hope t'espouse with nuptials solemnely,
   Duke *Charles* his daughter, heire of Burgundie.

22.

Which when the queene and her allies doth heare,
At *Clarence* fortunes daily they repine,
And to the king in hast this newes do beare,
Who to their words his will doth so incline,
That *Clarence* match is broke by his designe:
   King *Edward* iealous of his children's fate,
   Gainst *Clarence* in his heart beares secret hate.

23.

This opportunitie I straight do snatch,
Striking the steele while yet the fire is in,
In the king's brest such hatred I do hatch
Against our brother, that his hand I win
To further me in my intended sinne:
　For that blind riddle of the letter *G*,
　George lost his life, it tooke effect in me.

24.

Thus hauing halfe my purpose in my hand
By *Clarence* death, I cast how to confound
The noble queene's neere kinsmen, who would band
Themselues gainst me by law of nature bound,
When *Edward's* bodie should be laid in ground:
　But while the king, my brother did suruiue,
　To worke their woe, nought durst my thoughts contriue.

25.

Yet whom in court I did perceiue, that bore
A grudging heart against their vpstart state:
My brother's death to him I did deplore,
Auouching them with their malignant hate,
T'haue been the authors of his wofull fate,
　Which at such odds the peeres and them did set,
　That neuer age such discord did beget.

26.

Fortune in midst of this their wicked strife,
With pleasing looke so smil'd on my intent,
That by the sudden losse of *Edward's* life,
My kingly brother, she did seeme t'assent
To grant me good successe in the euent:
　The king late sick, leaues heere the peeres at oddes,
　And flies the place of mortall men's abodes.

27.

His corps scarce couered with a clod of clay,
His kingly ghost of heauie newes to tell:
Earle *Riuers, Vaughan,* and lord *Richard Grey,*
The kindred of the queene I did compell
To follow him, amongst the dead to dwell,
  Vnhappie *Hastings, Buckingham* and I
  At Pomfret castle caused them to die.

28.

They dead, protector by consent of peeres
To hold the sterne in state I chosen am:
My nephew yet being in his yongest yeares,
Which once attain'd by helpe of *Buckingham,*
To higher things ambitiously I aime,
  Who for my promise of promotion, gaue
  His minde to mine, in each thing I could craue.

29.

Hastings, whose loyaltie stood in my way,
Vpon his fall to build my future power,
As he at counsell sate vpon a day
With other lordings in the fatall Tower,
By my deceit there met his liue's last houre:
  Where he, fond lord, did think himselfe most sure,
  His best deem'd friends swift death did him procure.

30.

The way made plaine by plucking others downe,
That might withstand in such a generall ill,
With some pretence of title to the crowne,
To win the giddie people to our will,
A man whose tongue could honie drops distill,
  One docter *Shaw,* then deem'd a great diuine,
  To vndertake this taske we did assigne.

31.

He in a sermon fitting mine intent,
Did seeke to proue my brother's progenie
Vnlawfull issue: and with my consent
Chargeth my mother with adulterie,
Of _Edward's_ and lord _Clarence_ bastardie,
  Auouching me to be _Yorke's_ true borne child,
  On whom our house their hopes might only build.

32.

To this his sermon, as it was decreed,
Rushing amongst the people in I came,
Where he most impudent, in hope to breed
Affection in the audience did not shame,
On me with loud applauses to exclame:
  For flying from his text when I came in,
  In praise of me, thus did the wretch begin.

33.

" This is," quoth he, " that very noble duke,
The speciall paterne of true chiualrie,
Who both in fauour and in princely looke,
As well as in the mind's true qualitie,
Doth represent his father's physnomie:"
  Thus did he seeke the people's hearts t'incline,
  But purchas'd nought but his disgrace and mine.

34.

For after, when disloyall _Buckingham_
Vnto the commons that set speech did make,
Which with inuectiue scandall he did frame
Against the late dead king: when much he spake
To moue them, me for lawfull prince to take:
  Strooke dumbe with shame, of so abhorr'd a thing,
  Not one amongst them crie, " God saue the king."

35.

After I had obtain'd by tyrannie,
The fancied blisse of empire and renowne:
I thought so long as *Edward's* progenie
Did breath on earth, fortune did seeme to frowne,
Threatning to cast my new got glorie downe:
   Wherefore, betwixt the sheets with cruell paine,
   Vnhappie I did cause them to be slaine.

36.

Thinking thenceforth to enioy all worldly blisse,
And with my crowne's delight my soule to feast:
What I expect, I do not only misse,
But am depriued eu'n of that small rest,
Of which before that time I was possest:
   Conscience my former deeds in question brings,
   And frights my guiltie soule with fearefull things.

37.

Each night, when quiet sleepe should close mine eies,
Long waking on my pallat I do lie,
And if by chance sleepe doth my sense surprise,
Then doth illusion set before mine eie
My murthered nephewes, who aloud do crie,
   Calling for vengeance for that bloodie sinne,
   In strangling them the diadem to winne.

38.

Then starting vp from forth my naked bed,
With sword in hand I frantike-like would flie
About my chamber, and orecome with dread,
Vnto my guard I oftentimes would crie,
That treason in my chamber hid did lie:
   Thus the remembrance of my wicked deed,
   In me euen sleeping, did strange horror breed.

39.

In day time wheresoeuer I did go,
My watchfull eyes I whirled round about,
Fearing the onset of some sudden foe,
And to be out of dreadfull danger's doubt,
My bodie priuily was fenc'd about:
  Vpon my dagger still I kept my hand,
  Readie to stab those that by me did stand.

40.

After the murther of my nephewes twaine,
Not long it was ere *Buckingham* and I
Began to iarre, for which my lawlesse raigne
Not long did last, his last conspiracie
Did end his owne life and my royaltie:
  Who gag'd his honor t'helpe me to the crowne,
  With his owne death did help to bring me downe.

41.

Of Hereford the dukedome he did claime,
Which was the chiefest cause of our debate:
For his pretended title to the same
Did touch the kingly title of our state,
For which his sute I spurn'd in spitefull hate,
  And rated him with speeches minatorie,
  Which was the fall of my vsurped glorie.

42.

When thus the wrathfull duke did plainly see
His sute reiected, and himselfe despis'd,
He cast how to auenge himselfe on mee,
And in his thoughts my ruine he deuis'd:
In which a bold attempt he enterpris'd,
  For he in battell bold himselfe did band,
  Against me for to fight with force of hand.

43.

Many with him against me did accord,
For when the sudden fame abroad was spread,
How noble *Richmond* that Lancastrian lord,
My brother's heire, *Elizabeth* should wed,
Many that were that often wisht me dead:
  Vowing to spend their blood in *Richmond's* right,
  And to assist the duke with all their might.

44.

Then were commotions raised euery day,
The duke in Shropshire hard by Shrewsburie,
The proud wilde Welchmen troopt in battell ray,
Who vainly vaunted on their chiualrie,
As in the sequell they did testifie:
  Yet their example many did excite,
  To moue rebellion to my heart's despight.

45.

In Yorke-shire marquesse *Dorset* with his crew,
Gainst me in field to fight were boldly bent,
In Deuonshire both the *Courtnies* did pursue
Those that my cause did fauour, and in Kent
The *Guilfords* were in armes for that intent:
  Thus I in euery corner of this land,
  Was round beset with force of foe-men's hand.

46.

Yet from my youth in warre affaires being bred,
I knew that if in this conspiracie
I did without delay cut off the head,
The rest being stricken with timiditie,
Would soone be quell'd by force or pollicie:
  Wherefore with all my power I did pursue
  The duke of *Buckingham* and his Welch crue.

47.

He towards Glocester his way did take,
There to haue ioyned with the westerne powre,
But as in safetie passage for to make,
He with his host by Seuerne's coast did scowre,
Heau'ns cloudie mountaines brake, and many a showre
  Through darksome aire, from heau'ns wide floud-gates fel,
  Which made the wombe of raging Seuerne swel.

48.

The shores did shrinke, the lustie waues did grow,
Trees hid their heads, dumbe beasts on hilles were drown'd,
Infants in cradles wandred to and fro:
Yea those that of the floud stroue to win ground,
Both men and horse the waters did confound:
  And to this day the Seuerne men by name,
  Stout *Buckingham's* great water call the same.

49.

Thus the bold duke was of his purpose crost,
Who of my swift approch, when he did heare:.
In good array did range his warlike host.
But they, before in field we did appeare,
Turning their backes put on the wings of feare,
  Leading their duke the way, who thus distrest
  Durst not abide, but fled amongst the rest.

50.

Who tooke himselfe in his vnhappie flight,
Vnto his seruant's house vpon the way,
Hight *Humfrey Banester*, a wicked wight,
Who fosterd by this duke did yet betray
His lord and master, to his liue's decay:
  By him descri'd he in disguise was taken,
  In a darke wood, of all his friends forsaken.

51.

He dead, the rest of his conspiracie
Dispers'd their powers, and each one fled his way,
Some fled to *Richmond*, then in Britannie,
And others here in England lurking lay,
Expecting the approch of that wish'd day,
　When *Richmond* should on England's coast arriue,
　Mee of my crowne and kingdome to depriue.

52.

But I, not slacking opportunitie
In this beginning of my good successe,
Did studdie both by strength and policie,
Richmond's increasing powers to suppresse,
Although in vaine; for heauen, his cause did blesse:
　The people's loue did towards him incline,
　Wishing in hart, that he might victor shine.

53.

To giue content vnto my carefull minde,
One *Peter Landois*, cheefe of Britannie
Vnder the duke, with gold I did so blinde,
That hee did promise mee by policie
To bring the earle into my custodie:
　The Britaine duke his friend did only stand,
　To whom my subiects dayly fled the land.

54.

This *Peter* was th'earle's onelie seeming frend,
And in pretence of loue, a warlike band
Of men at his owne cost he did commend
Vnto the earle, to be at his command,
When hee should purpose to inuade this land:
　But when towards England hee was in his way,
　His purpose was that they should him betray.

55.

The earle reseru'd vnto more happie fate,
Informed was of this false treacherie,
Wherefore t'escape their hands, that lay in wait,
To take away his life, he priuilie
Did into Aniou flie from Britannie,
  To which as hee did flie in speedie hast
  With greedie pursuit hee was follow'd fast.

56.

But in a thick wood standing by the way,
He in his seruant's weedes himselfe did clad,
And caused him the master's part to play,
While hee himselfe fast by his side full glad
On foote did runne like a young lustie lad,
  Whereby at length hee past without mischance
  The British confines to the realme of France.

57.

Thither stout *Oxford*, his old hate to show
Vnto our house of Yorke, repaire did make,
To ioyne with *Richmond* my Lancastrian foe:
Then *Brandon*, *Blunt* and *Cheynie* did forsake
Me and my part, with *Richmond* part to take,
  Which newes my daylie dread doth so increase
  That I no houre can liue in restfull peace.

58.

To whom I might giue trust, I did not know,
Since seeming friends from mee do daylie flie,
In court each one doth wish my ouertbrow,
In towne and citie euery one doth crie
Shame on my deedes of death and tyrannie:
  Thus in my rule I liue belou'd of none,
  Dreaded of many, hated of euerie one.

59.

To my distresse some comfort to applie,
And that I may remoue the onely thing,
On which earle *Richmond's* hopes doe most relie :
Now such strange mischiefe I doe set on wing,
That neuer age the like to light did bring :
   Through blood to incest I intend to swim,
   To breake the match betwixt my neece and him.

60.

For *Anne* my queene, great *Warwicke's* daughter deere,
By poyson's force I sent vnto the dead :
Which done, my troubled thoughts I vp did cheere,
In hope I might my brother's daughter wed,
And bring her vnto mine incestuous bed :
   Foule sinne I now do feare in no degree,
   That I from feare of *Richmond* may be free.

61.

Her mother queene (strange that it should bee so)
Wonne with faire words consents vnto the same :
Who forc'd by feare, or by distresse brought low,
In hope to raise her state againe (fond dame)
In vaine doth wooe her daughter in my name :
   Which heau'n abhorring hastens on my end,
   And by my death preuents what I pretend.

62.

The royall virgin doth so much detest
My damn'd intent that I no grace can finde,
And daily newes my thoughts doe so molest
With foes inuasion, that my troubled minde
Is altogether vnto care inclinde :
   Gainst those abrode that doe intend t'inuade,
   While I prepare, at home I am betrai'd.

63.

At Nottingham, where then in court I lay,
Inform'd I was, that th'hated enemie
Had taken land, at which in much dismaie,
Turning my feare to rage, at last I crie
For vengeance on my subiects treacherie,
    And forc'd to trie my cause by bloodie blowes,
    I mustred vp my men to meete my foes.

64.

When that I heard where *Richmond* did ariue,
I did digest my bands in battel ray :
In ranke forth marcht my footemen fiue and fiue,
Who in that order kept the readie way,
That led directly where earle *Richmond* lay :
    Then wings of horsemen coasting euerie side,
    Did vnto bloodie battell boldly ride.

65.

In midst of whom, vpon a tall white steede
Mounted I sat with cruell countenance,
Still crying out, march on, march on with speede:
And in this sort without incumberance,
To Lecester we forward did aduance :
    Through which we past to Bosworthe's ample plaine,
    Where I did end my wreched life and reigne.

66.

And there vpon an hill, *Anne Beame* by name,
I downe did pight my standerd, and fast by
My campe in martiall order I did frame:
Richmond fast by vs on the plaine did lie,
Next morne the chance of battell for to trie :
    For it was euening ere we could attaine
    To meete each other vpon Bosworth plains.

67.

The sad night's cold forerunner Vesper faire,
Dispreades her golden lockes in easterne skie:
Then courts of guard are set with speciall care,
Lest that our foes aduantage to espie,
In ambuskado neere should lurking lie:
 And euery one with hearts to heau'n did pray
 To scape the horror of th'approching day.

68.

The heau'ns that in eternall booke do keepe
The register, for life or deathe's decree,
By vision strange did shew to me in sleepe,
That next daie's cheerefull light the last should be,
That in this world I euermore should see:
 As in my tent, on bed I slumbring lie,
 Horrid aspects appear'd vnto mine eye.

69.

I thought that all those murthered ghosts, whom I
By death had sent to their vntimely graue,
With baleful noise about my tent did crie,
And of the heau'ns with sad complaint did craue,
That they on guiltie wretch might vengeance haue:
 To whom I thought the Iudge of heau'n gaue eare,
 And gainst me gaue a iudgement full of feare.

70.

For loe, eftsoones, a thousand hellish hags
Leauing th'abode of their infernall cell,
Seasing on me, my hatefull bodie drags
From forth my bed into a place like hell,
Where feends did naught but bellow, howle and yell,
 Who in sterne strife stood gainst each other bent,
 Who should my hatefull bodie most torment.

71.

Tormented in such trance long did I lie,
Till extreame feare did rouze me where I lay,
And caus'd me from my naked bed to flie:
Alone within my tent I durst not stay,
This dreadfull dreame my soule did so affray:
     When wakte I was from sleepe, I for a space
     Thought I had been in some infernall place.

72.

About mine eares a buzzing feare still flew,
My fainting knees languish for want of might,
Vpon my bodie stands an icie dew:
My heart is dead within, and with affright
The haire vpon my head doth stand vpright:
     Each limbe about me quaking, doth resemble
     A riuer's rush, that with the wind doth tremble.

73.

Thus with my guiltie soule's sad torture torne,
The darke night's dismall houres I past away,
But at cocke's crow the message of the morne,
My feare I did conceale, lest men should say
Our foes approch my courage did dismay:
     And as dire need did me thereto constraine,
     My troopes of men I marshall'd on the plaine.

74.

Who with swift concurse fill'd the smothred ground,
And did enranke themselues in braue array,
The foreward with bold bowmen did abound,
Commixt with pikes to beare the violent sway,
When on our front the foe should giue th'assay,
     And to their forme in fight good heed to take,
     Iohn duke of *Northfolke* chieftaine I did make.

75.

After this vantguard I my selfe did goe,
And round about me chosen men of might
Did range themselues to shield me from the foe,
Our skirts were lin'd with horse, and fit for fight,
Each place was stuft with men in armes well dight:
  In this array I troopt my armed traine,
  To meete earle *Richmond* on the equall plaine.

76.

Who wisely did his folke to fight instruct,
Iohn earle of *Oxford* did the vaward lead,
The right wing *Gilbert Talbot* did conduct,
The left wing sir *Iohn Sauage*, one that fled
From me to *Richmond* for to saue his head:
  Richmond himselfe with *Pembrooke* that stout knight,
  The middle ward did lead vnto the fight.

77.

As thus both hosts stood each in other's sight,
Expecting when the trumpe, whose blast doth breed
Courage in men, would call them forth to fight,
Arm'd in bright steele vpon a stately steed,
From ranke to ranke 1 rode about with speed,
  And fit for fight my souldiers hearts to make,
  Hie, and with courage thus to them I spake.

78.

" Fellowes in armes, and my aduenturous friends,
Giue heedfull eare to that which I shall say:
Be valiant hearted, thinke vpon the ends
Of fight or flight, of triumph or decay,
Both which the battell doth propose this day,
  Th'one of which doth bring eternall fame,
  The other ignomie and dastard shame.

79.

O thinke vpon the matchlesse valiancie
Of our forefathers deeds in former daies,
And let vs counterchecke the memorie
Of their stout acts by that immortall praise,
To which our deeds our names this day may raise:
　　Yea, let vs thinke gainst whom we come to fight,
　　The thought of which might cowards harts excite.

80.

First with our foe-men's captaine to begin,
A weake Welch milke-sop, one that I do know
Was nere before for fight in battle seene,
Not able of himselfe as guide to goe
In marshall discipline against his foe:
　　But backt by his consorts, a sort of slaues,
　　Against his will vs now in field he braues.

81.

And for his company, a sort they bee
Of rascall French and British runawaies,
People far more couragious for to flee,
Then stand in fight, whose faint hearts former daies
Could witnesse to our land and their dispraise:
　　Who doubtlesse now shall by your valours die,
　　Or else at least from battell wounded flie.

82.

That bearing wounds vnto their natiue home,
Their fellowes may be strucke with heartlesse dread,
Fearing in future times againe to come
Into our kingdome with bold banners spred,
Gainst souldiers that in England's bounds are bred:
　　Then courage, friends, think on renowne and fame
　　For which we fight, let cowards flie with shame.

83.

And as for me, assure your selues this day
I will triumph by glorious victorie,
Or win a lasting name for liue's decay :
Take then example by my valiancie,
And boldly fight against your enemie :
   · You for your wiues and goods, I for my crowne,
   Both for our countrie's good, all for renowne.

84.

Aduance them captaines, forward to the fight,
Draw forth your swords, each man addresse his sheeld,
Hence faint conceites, die thoughts of coward flight,
To heauen your hearts, to fight your valours yeeld :
Behold our foes do braue vs in the field,
   Vpon them friends, the cause is yours and mine,
   Saint *George* and conquest on our helmes doth shine."

85.

This said, the dreadfull trumpet loudlie blowes,
To bring them forward to the furious fight,
Then did the bowmen bend their stift string'd bowes;
The souldiers buckled on their helmets bright;
The bilmen shooke their bils, and euerie wight
   Did proue his fatall weapon on the ground,
   Ready prepar'd his foemen to confound.

86.

The archers drew, the fatall fight began,
Thick flew the shafts, many to death were done :
Which once being spent, close ioyn'd they man to man :
Then did sterne slaughter through the battell runne; .
Not any one at first his foe did shunne :
   But equallie their heads they vp did beare
   In fight, not stooping vnto seruile feare.

87.

Stout *Norfolke* in the forefront boldlie stood,
Imploying deeds of death against the foe;
Not fear'd, in midst of dust, of death and blood,
Th'extreamest of his vtmost strength to show,
To winne his soueraigne's weale by his owne woe:
  Where he, braue lord, by friends vnkindlie left,
  In manlie fight was of his life bereft.

88.

For in my cheefest hope to winne the day,
Appointed by the heauen's most iust decree,
My souldiers in the forefront shranke away,
Which heauie newes declared was to mee
By one that counsel'd mee away to flee:
  But I his counsell rashly did forsake,
  And vnto him in furie thus I spake:

89.

" Curst be thy coward thoughts that thinke on flight,
And curst those traytors that are fled away :
I am resolu'd in this daie's dreadfull fight,
To lose my life, or win a glorious day:
Flie those that will, for I am bent to stay:"
  This said, my plum'd deckt helme I downe did close,
  And with my eager launce made toward my foes.

90.

Hie was the furie of my desperate fight,
And like a tempest in a stormie day,
When I did see vnto my heart's despight,
Where *Richmond's* standard stood without delay :
Through th'armed men to it I made my way,
  The which, with *William Brandon* that bold knight,
  To ground I downe did cast in *Richmond's* sight.

91.

Many beneath my conquering strokes did fall,
Each one did flie from me with coward shame,
But one whom sir *Iohn Cheynie* men did call,
Who for huge swinge of strength did beare the name
Of all the captaines that with *Richmond* came,
   Who single did my charge at first repell,
   Though in the end beneath my sword he fell.

92.

But as with him alone in fight I stood,
Behold with foes I was incircled round,
Who did imbrue their swords in my deare blood,
Where mastered with the smart of many a woond,
I bleeding fell vnto the dustie ground :
   Where cursing *Richmond* and his conquering crue,
   Thence in disdainfull sort my sad soule flew.

93.

I being slaine, those that for me did fight,
Turning their backes, away forthwith did flie,
In field my slaughtered bodie in despight,
Drag'd from the place where it did bleeding lie,
Was naked made to euery vassals eye,
   Despoil'd of all those kingly robes I wore:
   Thus they to Leicester my bodie bore.

94.

Behind a slaue vpon a halting iade
All naked as I was, hog-like I lay:
And in that sort with blood and dust array'd,
To Leicester they bore me; whence that day
To field I came in pompe and rich aray:

Where to the graue my bodie they commend:
Thus had my bloodie life a bloodie end.

95.

Th'ambitious prince, whose hand vniustly gripes
Another's right to make himselfe a king,
Suffers the smart of many furies stripes:
Th'internall worme his conscience still doth sting,
His soule t'a fearefull iudgement death doth bring:
　　Of which let my vsurped royaltie,
　　Remaine a Mirrour in this historie.

96.

My storie told, I may no longer stay,
My grieued ghost doth smell the morning's aire:
The night on sable wings flies fast away,
The honres in east expecting daies repaire,
On cloudie hill sets vp her siluer chaire?
　　My guiltie ghost her light may not behold,
　　Adew, remember well what I haue told.

　　" Our night is at an end," quoth Memorie,
　　" With which we heere will end our historie:
After this tyrant's fall, that dismall night,
　Which did obscure this kingdome's faire day-light,
Did take an end: heere some auspitious star
Twixt *Yorke* and *Lancaster* did end the iar,
Appointing *Richmond* that Lancastrian knight,
T'inoculate his *Red Rose* with the *White*:
Heere therefore with this blissefull vnitie,
We will shut vp our tragicke historie,

And thou, whose pen we do appoint to write
Those Mirrours past, which thou hast heard this night;
Awake from sleepe, and let thy willing pen
Set forth this dreame vnto the view of men."
This said, with fame she vanisht from my sight,
This was the vision of a winter's night.

FINIS.

END OF PART IV.

[THE
Mirrour for Magistrates,
AS]
E N G L A N D S
E L I Z A :
or
The Victoriovs and Trivmphant Reigne
of that Virgin Empresse of
sacred memorie,
E L I Z A B E T H,
Queene of England, France and Ireland, &c.

P A R T V.

By RICHARD NICCOLS,
Oxon. Mag. Hall.

From the edition imprinted by Felix
Kyngston, 1610.

ENGLANDS

ELIZA:

OR

THE VICTORIOVS AND

TRIVMPHANT REIGNE OF THAT

VIRGIN EMPRESSE OF SACRED

memorie, ELIZABETH, Queene of

England, France and Ireland,

&c.

AT LONDON

Imprinted by FELIX KYNGSTON.

1610.

TO THE VERTVOVS

Ladie, the Ladie Elizabeth Clere,

Wife to the Right Worshipfull

Sir Francis Clere, Knight.

My muse, that whilome wail'd those Briton kings,
Who vnto her in vision did appeare,
Craues leaue to strengthen her night-weathered wings,
In the warm sun-shine of your golden *Clere:*
Where she (faire ladie) tuning her chast layes
Of England's empresse to her hymnicke string,
For your affect, to heare that virgin's praise,
Makes choice of your chast selfe to heare her sing:
Whose royall worth (true vertue's paragon)
Heere made me dare t'ingraue your worthie name;
In hope, that vnto you the same alone
Will so excuse me of presumptuous blame,
That gracefull entertaine my muse may find,
And euer beare such grace in thankfull mind.

Your Ladiship's euer humblie
at command,

RICHARD NICCOLS.

TO THE READER.

GENTLE Reader, when I first writ this poem, I had thought for the length therof to haue distinguished it by section into cantoes or bookes; but since perswaded by the printer to publish it with this worke: it being, though no fall, yet a worthie Mirrour answerable to that of the empresse Helena in the first part of this volume: I present it in one whole entire hymne, distinguishing it only by succession of yeares, which I haue margented through the whole storie, and by an analysis of euery chiefe exploit inserted in their proper places. For my quotation of authors, I heere vse it not for singularitie, it being a thing not customarie to writers in this kind, but to confirme the truth of that which is written, as not being ignorant that I shall be bitten by those mongrill English (1 can terme them no other) that barke at the maiestie of that most noble princesse, against whose railing, an inseperable propertie to their profession, I only arme my selfe with this confidence, that the fame of her royalties mounting aloft like the sun verticall, shall in the height of all true borne English estimation, abate the shadowes of their enuie.

Farewell.

THE INDVCTION.

In that sad month, whose name at first begun
From Rome's *Augustus*, great *Octauius* son,
When heau'ns fierce dog, sterne Albahor did rise
To bait the lion in th'Olympian skies ;
Whose hot fier-breathing influence did cracke
Our thirstie grandame Terrae's aged backe :
By wrathfull Ioue, thicke darted from the skie
The thunder shafts of pestilence did flie :
In top of heau'n he tooke his wreakfull stand
Ore that great towne vpon the northerne strand.
Of siluer Thamisis, vpon whose towres
Downe dropt his shafts, as thicke as winter's showres,
Which daily did his indignation show
In euery place, dispersing worlds of woe :
Witnesse ye ghosts and spirits dolefull drerie,
Vntimely sent by troopes to Charon's ferrie,
Leauing your limbes wrapt vp in sheets of clay,
As dustie reliques of your liues decay :
Yea, thou sweet genius of that ancient towne,
Thou ladie of great Albion's chiefe renowne;
Of that sad time a witnesse maist thou bee,
When death did take so many sonnes from thee;
Whose funerall rites inconsolate alone,
When thou vnkindly left, didst kindly mone,
Who staid with thee, alas, to helpe thee mourne,
And fled not from thee, leauing thee forlorne ?
Mongst whom, though I, strooke terror-sicke with dread
Of heau'n's hot plague, was one that from thee fled :

Yet of thy sight I daily did partake,
Which of thy woes a partner did me make:
Not far from off that slimie southerne strand,
By which with Isis, Thames runnes hand in hand,
In that high mountaine countrie's fruitfull soile,
That nere in fight of forren foes tooke foile,
Where those same famous stout men-mouing wood,
Against the Norman conqueror boldly stood,
Was my abode: when foule infection's breath
In Troynouant imploy'd the workes of death.
There in this wofull time vpon a day,
So soone as Tython's loue-lasse gan display
Her opall colours in her easterne throne;
It was my chance in walking all alone,
That ancient castle-crowned hill to scale,
Which proudly ouerlookes the lowly vale,
Where great *Elizae's* birth-blest palace stands,
Gainst which great Thames cast vp his golden sands.
There when I came, from thence I might descrie
The sweetest prospects, that the curious eie
Of any one did euer elsewhere see,
So pleasant at that time they seem'd to mee:
It is a choice selected plot of land,
In which this ayrie mount doth towring stand;
As if that nature's cunning for the best,
Had choicely pickt it out from all the rest:
Beneath this loftie hill shot vp on high,
A pleasant parke impaled round doth lie,
In which the plaine so open lies to sight,
That on this hill oft times with great delight
That heau'nly queene, *Plantagenet's* great blood,
The faire *Elizae's* selfe hath often stood,
And seene the swift-foot dogs in eager chace
Pursue the gentle hinde from place to place.

From hence recalling my weake wandring eye,
I gan behold that kingly palace by,
Whose loftie towres built vp of ancient time
By worthie princes, to the stars do clime;
Proud, that so many a prince to do them grace,
Beneath their roofe had made their resting place.
Fast by this princely house, afront before
Thames gliding waues do wash the sandie shore,
Whose fruitfull streames with winding in and out,
Forcing their way through hollow lands about,
From th'occidentall with swift course do run,
Where Hesper bright brings vp the golden sun :
And on the siluer brest of this great lord
Of all the deepes, that Albion's wombe doth hoard,
Downe from the easterne seas I might descrie
Many swift-winged barkes, that seem'd to flie,
Cutting their passage through the threatning waue,
That 'bout their sides in vaine did rore and raue;
With swelling sailes, not fearing sad mischance,
Each after other came in stately dance,
And nimblie capring on the purple waue,
With loftie foretops did the welkin braue,
Vutill they came vnto that stately place
Fam'd for the birth of great *Elizae's* grace :
To which they vail'd their towring tops before,
And from their sides the thundring cannons rore
Flew as a witnesse of their loyaltie
And loue vnto that house of maiestie;
From thence full fraught with many a precious prise
They sail'd along, whereas the passage lies
To Troynouant, whose pride of youthfull lust
The hand of death had smothered in the dust;
The smiling heau'ns, that with sweet sunshine howres
Did once vouchsafe t'adorne her hie topt towres,

Now with grim lookes, which did my heart appall,
Did seeme to threaten her approching fall:
Downe from their cloudie browes in threatning pride,
Death-darting pestilence did seeme to slide:
Grim-visag'd-like the grizly dreaded night,
In noysome fumes and mistie fogs bedight:
The aire once pure and thin, now wing'd with death
Grewe gloomie thick, being poyson'd by her breath,
In which, I thought, she took her horrid stand,
And with fierce look and stiff-bent bowe in haud,
She drew her shafts, impatient in her minde,
From forth her quiuer at her back behinde:
Then did I thinke vpon the shreekes and cries
Of dying soules, that did ascend the skies
By thousands sent vnto the gaping graue,
On whom no mercie pestilence would haue:
Yea then (thou glorie of great Albion)
Thy sad distresse I gan to thinke vpon,
Thy mournefull widowes groueling in sad swound
On their dead husbands, on the ashie ground,
Thy husbands striuing to preserue the breath
Of their deare spouse from vnrelenting death;
Thy orphans left poore, parentlesse, alone
The future time's sad miserie to mone :
The thought of which, in that vnhappie season
With woefull passion did so maister reason,
That as I stood vpon that pleasant hill
To fancie sweet delight I had no will;
But seeking for some groue or gloomie wood,
Where I might feede my melancholie mood:
Vpon this hil's south side at last I found
Fitting my thoughts a pleasing plot of ground;
It was to wit, that wel knowne happie shade,
Which for delight the royall Britaine maid

Did oft frequent, as former times can tell,
When her sweet soule in mortall mould did dwell:
It is a walke thicke set with manie a tree;
Whose arched bowes ore hed combined bee,
That nor the golden eye of heauen can peepe
Into that place, ne yet, when heauen doth weepe,
Can the thin drops of drizeling raine offend
Him, that for succour to that place doth wend.
Where, when alone I first did enter in,
And call to minde how that truth-shielding queene,
In former times the same did beautifie
With presence of her princelie maiestie;
O how the place did seeme to mourne to mee,
That she should thence for euer absent bee!
In this sad passion, which did still abound,
I sat me downe vpon the grassie ground,
Wishing that heau'n into my infant muse
That antique poet's spirit would infuse,
Who, when in Thracian land hee did rebearse
Ianthee's wofull end in tragick verse,
Did make men, birds, beasts, trees and rockes of stone
That virgin's timelesse tragedie to mone:
For then I thought, that to that mournefull place,
I might haue sung my verse with lesse disgrace
To great *Elizae's* worth: for who doth bring
Her deeds to light, or who her worth doth singe?
O, did that Fairie Queene's sweet singer liue,
That to the dead eternitie could giue,
Or if, that heauen by influence would infuse
His heauenlie spirit on mine earth-borne muse,
Her name ere this a mirror should haue been
Lim'd out in golden verse to th'eyes of men:
But my sad muse, though willing, yet too weak
In her rude rymes *Elizae's* worth to speak,

Must yeeld to those, whose muse can mount on high,
And with braue plumes can clime the loftie skie.
As thus I sat all sad vpon the greene
In contemplation of that royall queene,
And thinking, what a Mirrour she might be
Vnto all future time's posteritie,
Inclining downe my hed, soft fingered sleepe
With pleasing touch throughout my limbes did creepe,
Who hauing seas'd vpon mee with strong hands,
Bound vp my thoughts in soporiferous bands,
And held mee captiue, while his seruant slie
A vision strange did vnto mee descrie:
For vp from Morpheus den a vision came,
Which were it sent in mightie loue's own name,
Or by some other power, I wot not well:
But as I slept, I say, thus it befell:
As at that time in walking to and fro,
I 'bout this pleasant place alone did goe,
Each obiect of the same all suddenlie
Seemd strangelie metamorphiz'd to myne eye;
The Helliconian spring, that did proceed
From th'hoofe of Pegasus that heauenlie steed,
And those pure streames of virgin Castalie,
The place of loue's nine daughters nurserie,
Did seeme to haue resign'd their proper place,
Transported thither to that land's disgrace:
Where, as I thought, I heard an heauenlie sound,
Of which the place did euerie where redound:
Vnto the which as I attentiue stood,
Descending downe from out a neighbouring wood,
I might behold the sacred sisters nine,
Whether from heauen or other place diuine,
I am vncertaine; but their way they made
Where as I stood beneath the leauie shade:

Before them all a goodlie ladie came
In stately portance like Ioue's braine-borne dame,
To wit, that virgin queene, the faire *Elize,*
That whilom was our England's richest prize;
In princelie station with great Iunoe's grace
(Me seem'd) she came in her maiesticke pace,
Grac'd with the lookes of daunting maiestie,
Mixt with the meekenesse of milde clemencie;
Such haue I seene her, when in princely state
She goddesse-like in chariot high hath sate,
When troopes of people with loud shouts and cries,
Haue sounded out their auies in the skies:
And rid each other in the present place
With great desire to see her heau'nly face:
Mongst whom she came, as if Aurora faire
Out of the east had newly made repaire,
Making a sun-like light with golden shine
Of her bright beauty in the gazer's eine.
Approching neere the place where I did stand,
With gratious beckning of her princely hand,
She seem'd to call to me; but sillie I,
Daunted with presence of such maiestie,
Fell prostrate downe, debasht with reuerent shame
At sudden sight of so diuine a dame;
Till she with gentle speech thus mildely said:
" Stand vp," quoth she, " and be no whit dismaid;
Let loyall loue and zeale to me inflame
Thy muse to sing the praises of my name;
And let not thoughts of want, of worth, and skill,
Impeach the purpose of thy forward quill;
For though thy homely stile and slender verse
Too humble seeme my praises to rehearse:
Yet to the world, that I a Mirrour bee
Amongst those many Mirrours writ by thee;

Feare neither bite of dogged *Theon's* tooth,
Nor soone-shot bolts of giddie headed youth;
For th'awfull power of my sole dreaded name,
Shall from thy verse auert all foule defame:
And lest in any point thou chance to faile,
Which may my name's great glorie ought auaile;
Loe here the cheefest of the daughters nine
Of sacred Memorie and Ioue diuine,
Great Clioe's selfe, in order shall rehearse
My storie to thee in her stately verse."
This said, more swift then lightening from the skie,
She on the suddaine vanisht from mine eye
With all her nymphes, for none of all her traine
Excepting Clio did with mee remaine,
Who being the first borne childe of Memorie,
The ladie was of noble historie,
A peerelesse dame past al compare to sing
The deeds, that vertue vnto light doth bring:
In comelie garments, like some virgin maid
Of Dian's troope, shee trimlie was arraid,
Saue goddesse-like her globe-like head around
With verdant wreath of sacred bay was crownd;
From which downe either side her comelie face,
Her golden lockes did flow with goodlie grace,
And in her hand a lute diuinelie strung
She held, to which oft times she sweetlie sung;
With this she sat her downe vpon the ground,
And with her fingers made the strings to sound,
Vnto the which her sweet voice she did frame
To sing the praises of *Elisae's* name.
Which hauing done, shee thus did silence break;
" Would God," quoth shee, " her prayses I could speak,
Who claimes a greater power her praise to sound,
Then Phœbus self, if greater could be found:

Yet will I triall make with all my might,
With her great fame the golden starres to smite :
Which while I sing, heark thou with heedful eare,
And in thy mind the same hereafter beare :"
This said, she lightlie toucht each trembling string,
And with sweet voice did thus diuinelie sing.

ENGLAND'S ELIZA.

1.

.WHEN England's Phœbus *Henrie's* hopefull sonne
The world's rare Phœnix, princely *Edward* hight,
To death did yeeld, his glasee of life outrun,
And Phœbus-like no more could lend his light:
Then men did walke in shades of darkesome night,
    Whose feeble sight with errors blacke strooke blind,
    Could in no place time's faire *Fidessa* find.

2.

That blind borne monster, truthe's sterne opposite,
Begotten first in Demogorgon's hall,
Twixt vglie Erebus and grizlie night,
The sonnes of truth did horriblie appall
With her approch, much dreaded of them all:
    Who euer came in reach of her foule pawes,
    She in their blood imbru'd her thirstie iawes.

3.

Witnesse may bee the manie a burning flame,
Made with the limbes of saints to mount on high,
Whose constant soules without the least exclaime,
In midst of death downe patientlie did lie,
And in bright flames did clime the clow'd-brow'd skie:
    Yea, let *Elizae's* woes in that blind age,
    A witnesse bee of bloodie error's rage.

4.

Whose deepe distresse and dolefull miserie,
I not assay to sing, but leaue the same
To our deare sister sad Melpomene,
That she her sweet patheticke voice may frame
In dolefull dittie to condole the same:
   I onely here in high heroick streine,
   Do striue to sing of her triumphant reigne.

5.

Ioue looking downe, from his celestiall throne
With eies of pitie on poore England's woes,
Did lend her helpe, when hope of helpe was none,
And in his mercy did his power oppose
Gainst error's night-borne children, her cheife foes,
   Who sought t'obscure with cloudes of enuious night,
   Her Cynthia's shine, the lampe of all her light.

6.

But he disperst those cloudes, and droue away
The lowring stormes, that ouercast our skie,
And made our glorious Cynthia to display
Her heauenlie shine, to giue them light thereby,
Who long before in darknesse bound did lie:
   For she it was, who with her sweet repaire
   From th'hearts of men did banish black despaire.

7.

Euen as that morning starre that doth display
Her golden tresses in th'orientall skie,
Brings happie tidings of approching day
To them, that long in bed do restlesse lie,
Expecting comfort from the sun's bright eye:
   So our *Eliza* did blest tidings bring
   Of ioy to those, whom sad distresse did sting.

8.

No sooner did this empire's royall crowne
Begirt the temples of her princelie hed;
But that Ioue-borne Astrea straight camè downe
From highest heauen againe, to which in dread
Of earth's impietie before shee fled:
   Well did shee know, *Elizae's* happie reigne
   Would then renew the golden age againe.

9.

The heau'ns did smile on her with sweet delight,
And thundering Ioue did laugh her foes to scorne,
The god of warre did cease from bloodie fight,
And fruitfull plentie did her land adorne
With richest gifts, powr'd from her plenteous horne,
   The happie seedes, which th'hands of peace did sow
   In euerie place with goodlie fruit did grow.

10.

Deuouring Mulciber, whose flames before
With blood of holy men were heard to hisse,
Of England's happie sonnes were seene no more:
But truth and mercie did each other kisse,
And brought sweet tidings of their heauenly blisse:
   All which by powerfull loue haue granted been
   For loue t'*Eliza*, Albion's matchlesse queene.

11.

Matchlesse for all the gifts of heauenly grace,
For nature's good and happie destinie,
All which, in one sole subiect hauing place,
If they a mortall wight may beautifie,
And giue a prince earth's true felicitie,
   She truly did enioy, while she did liue,
   That *summum bonum*, which this life could giue.

12.

In th'happie horoscope of her sweet birth,
Both heauen and nature seemed to consent
With fortune's selfe t'augment their fame on earth,
Each one in hope to perfect their intent,
By this queene virgin and her gouernment,
　And 'mongst themselues, they seemed to contend,
　Who should to her the greatest gifts extend.

13.

For when from *Annae's* wombe, she came to light,
Th'whole aggregate of heau'n from Ioue's high throne,
Vnto the lowest orbe lookt blithe and bright,
And in the same, each constellation
Vnited was in sweet coniunction,
　Powring their influence of felicitie
　Vpon the virgin's blest natiuitie.

14.

Nor can I tell the gifts of grace exact,
With which heau'n did enrich her royall mind,
Had I a brazen throat or voice infract,
A thousand tongues, and rarest words refin'd,
With vtterance swifter, then the swiftest winde;
　Yet were they all too weake at large to tell
　The gifts of grace, that in her soule did dwell.

15.

Her setled faith, fixt in the highest heau'n,
Remained firme vnto her liue's last date,
Nor her vndanted spirit could be driuen
·At any time one iot thereof t'abate
By Spaine's sterne threats, and Rome's pernitious hate,
　The ankor of the same, her hope, aboue
　Stood fixt vpon the promise of great Ioue.

16.

Her deeds of mercie, not in hope to merit,
Were true ostents of her fidelitie,
For which a name on earth she shall inherit
Which shall outliue the vading memorie
Of spitefull Rome's defaming forgerie;
    For not alone did we her bountie know,
    But forren shores the same likewise can show.

. 17.

Heau'n hauing dignifi'd her soule diuine,
With rarest gifts of goodly qualitie,
Dame nature's selfe, as seeming to refine
The common mixture of mortalitie,
Into a matter of more puritie,
    Made for her soule a mansion house so faire,
    That few with it for beautie might compare.

18.

And though her beautie were exceeding rare,
Yet Rome's Lucretia for a sober eie
So far renown'd, with her might not compare,
Nor the Greekes constant queene Penelope,
Might match this maiden queene for modestie :
    For Phœbe's selfe did want her gouernance
    In modest gesture and chaste countenance.

. 19.

Thus heau'n and nature hauing shew'd their skill
In perfecting a creature so diuine,
Fortune, as loth so rare a worke to spill,
At our Great Britaine maid did not repine,
But did to her all happinesse assigne,
    Whereby no prince on earth yet euer was,
    That for rare gifts *Eliza* did surpasse.

20.

Cease then, yee black-mouth'd brood of enuie's race,
Men monsters like, or monsters like to men,
Whose tongues with scandall tipt, seeke to disgrace
Our royall soueraigne, loue's anoynted queene,
Whose like in any age hath seldome been:
   Cease vipers, cease I say, from your offence,
   In spitting poyson at such excellence.

21.

Yet, if your English Romanized hearts,
Gainst nature's custome swell with foule defame,
Brandish your stings, and cast your vtmost darts
Against the greatnesse of her glorious name,
Yet shall it liue to your eternall shame;
   Yea, though Rome, Spaine, and hell it selfe repine,
   Her fame on earth with sun-bright light shal shine.

22.

And while that we, the brood of Phœbus wit
In golden verse her deeds to light can bring,
On mount Parnassus, as we safely sit,
In such high straine her worth we all will sing,
That earth's whole round of her great fame shall ring:
   For endlesse praise to her well may we giue,
   That did protect our cause, while she did liue.

23.

O, how the wreath of Phœbus flowring bay,
The victor's due desert, and learning's meed,
Did flourish in her time without decay!
Which to obtaine, each one did striue t'exceed
In high atchieuement of some glorious deed:
   Though now, alas, such custome is forgot,
   And loue of ease great Albion's sonnes doth blot.

24.

Lull'd in the bosome of securitie,
Vpon th'ignoble bed of idle ease,
Foully defacing true nobilitie,
Few now do care, but how they best may please
The hungrie fancie of sweet loue's disease,
   That pitie 'tis so many a worthie wight,
   Let's honor flie for fancie's fond delight.

25.

But wake, yee honor'd impes of noble race;
Rouze vp the dying sparkes of courage bold,
'Tis Clyo speakes to you, that she may place
Your lasting praises writ with lines of gold,
In flying fame's great booke to be inrol'd,
   Yea let your father's late done deeds inflame
   Your sleeping thoughts to gaine a glorious name:

26.

Who thought it not true honor's glorious prize
By nimblie capring in a daintie dance,
To win th'affects of women's wanton eies,
Ne yet did seeke their glorie to aduance
By only tilting with a rush-like lance,
   But did in dreadfull death themselues oppose,
   To winne renowne against *Elizae's* foes.

27.

How stoutly did they march in honor's field,
In stately station like the sonnes of fame,
Led by renowne, who nere did let them yeeld,
Though drown'd in death in midst of martiall game,
Till by their deeds they gain'd a glorious name,
   Whose valour still *Eliza* did direct
   Each where to beat downe wrong and right erect:

28.

When England's Scotland in distresse did stand,
Ambitious *Guise* intending her decay,
England's faire virgin lent her helping hand,
And soone did chace th'insulting French away,
That proudly did their ensignes there display:
  For that braue lord great *Grey* of Wilton hight,
  Did force them thence by warre's impulsiue might.

An. Reg. 2.

29.

When France within it selfe diuided stood,
Th'aspiring *Guise* in hostile furie bent
Against braue *Condie*, prince of royall blood,
Then our faire queene all danger to preuent,
Great *Warwicke* ore the seas broad bosome sent,
  Whose dreaded powers our Calice losse had quited,
  Had heau'n not sicknesse through his host excited.

An. Reg. 4.

30.

When Ireland's great *Oneale*, first that did moue
The Kernes and Gallowglasses, men of might,
Vnto their soueraigne to renounce their loue,
Hight *Henrie Sidnie* that heroick knight,
Did oft times turne him to inglorious flight,
  Till traytor-like mongst friends he found his fall,
  Who hew'd his bodie into pieces small.

Anno Reg. 9.

31.

Nor heere renowned *Randol* braue esquire
Can I forget to giue to thee thy right,
When with thine owne few troopes, whose hearts on fire
Thy valour set, thou put'st to shamefull flight
This *Shane Oneale,* and all his host in fight:
  Where though thou fell in venturing past the rest,
  Thy name shall liue in fame's great booke exprest.

An. Reg. 8.

32.

An. Reg. 12. And heere at home, when in the north did rise
The louring stormes stirr'd vp by discontent
Of peace-disturbers, who did enterprize · · · · .
By force of hand their soueraigne's right to rent,
And take from her this kingdome's gouernment,
    Then stood vp many a loyall hearted peere,
    To shield her safe from threatning foe-men's feare.

33.

For well they knew, with right it could not stand,
That any one their soueraigne might displace,
And take the scepter from the prince's hand:
The rule of many is absurd and base,
One prince must sit inthron'd in iustice place;
    For many heads, what bodie euer bare,
    That was not monster like and out of square?

34.

Which little did those iarring members know,
When with their banner of the fiue wounds spread,
And holy-seeming crosse, a fained show
Of their vngodly zeale, they first made head
At Durham's towne against their soueraigne dread,
    Where their first outrage men did vnderstand,
    In tearing th'holy writs of God's owne hand.

35.

Gainst whom, these great *Heroes* vp did stand,
Renowned *Sussex,* th'eldest sonne of fame,
Great *Warwicke, Rutland,* and stout *Cumberland,*
Bold *Deuorax, Howard* lord of Effingham,
Braue lord of Perham *Willowby* by name,
    Scroope, Euers, Knoles, all men of famous might,
    From whom their foes to Scotland tooke their flight.

36.

And thou braue *Hunsdon* borne of prince's blood,
Though last in place yet not the least in name,
When a disloyall lord vndaunted stood,
To bid thee battell, to thy endlesse fame,
Thou mad'st him flie the bounded field with shame:
  'Gainst whom with thy few troopes, thou didst aduance
  And authoriz'd high seruice with thy lance.

L. [eonard]
D. [acre]

37.

Vpon the bankes, where siluer Chelt doth glide,
With his three thousand men in armes well dight,
He stoutly stood and did thy charge abide,
Gainst whom with fifteene hundred thou didst fight,
And forc'd him yeeld vnto thy powerfull might:
  For heartlesse from the field away he fled
  To Scotland by, to hide his shamefull hed.

38.

And as the lordly lion, king of beasts,
When he by chance hath lost his wished prey,
Runs roring through the wood, and neuer rests
Till he haue truly tract the readie way,
Where he may follow his escaped prey:
  So noble *Hunsdon* with his conquering crew,
  His flying foe to Scotland did pursue.

39.

With that stout sonne of Mars, great *Sussex* bent,
T'inferre reuenge vpon the borderers by
For misdemeanor done, much time he spent
In making hostile spoile on th'enemie,
That sought to succour rebels treacherie:
  Which done, loden with honor and rich spoile,
  They made returne vnto their natiue soile.

Anno eodem
12.

40.

Thus did these lords to their faire virgin queene,
Returne with glorie got from euery place,
Though at her greatnesse with malignant spleene,
Many leaud sonnes of enuie's hellish race,
Did much repine, and sought her name's disgrace :
 For spitefull enuie neuer doth repine,
 But where true vertue's glorie most doth shine.

41.

Downe in the deepes of earth's profunditie
Her dwelling is in dungeons darksome blind,
Where she nere sees the bright sunne's cheerefull eie,
Ne comfort of the wholesome aire doth finde,
Tost to and fro by gentle breathing winde ;
 But with the furies of the Stygian flood,
 Sits low in hell in hate of humane good.

42.

The restlesse griefe, which carking care doth breed,
Her thoughts with endlesse torment doth oppresse,
Her woes of other's welfare do proceed,
Ne euer is she seene to laugh, vnlesse
At lucklesse hap of other's ill successe;
 For other's happinesse her woe doth bring,
 And all her ill from other's good doth spring.

43.

To this foule helhound from that blood built towne,
Which Tybur's siluer armes doe round imbrace,
Blind error came, where truth was troden downe,
Since bloodie *Phocas* to the world's disgrace,
Did seat the first false priest in *Cæsar's* place ;
 And thence did error take her speedie flight
 To enuie's caue to worke the world despight.

44.

Where when she came before the hags foule sight,
Elizae's glorie she did oft propose,
And more to whet her forward to despight,
She shew'd how truth and loue their two chiefe foes,
On that faire virgin only did repose,
 Which enuie's malice did so much augment,
 That she throughout the world with error went.

45.

Blinde error bore foule enuie on her backe,
And ouer many kingdoms tooke their flight,
Where enuie's poison mixt with errors blacke,
In scalding drops, as they did flie, did light
Vpon the limbes of many a wretched wight,
 Which through their veins diffus'd did swiftly run,
 Choaking that loue, that in their hearts did won.

46.

At length to Rome with error, enuie came,
Where gorg'd with fulnesse of excessiue feast,
Finding proud *Pius*, fift of that false name,
Laid on soft couch his heauie head to rest,
She laid her scuruie fist vpon his brest,
 And from his feet, euen to his sleepie head,
 She made her poison canker-like to spread.

47.

And with more malice to augment his hate,
She did propose vnto his enuious eye,
Th'admired glorie of *Elizae's* state,
And his lost priuiledge and dignitie
In this her kingdome of great Britanie;
 Which did so vex great *Pius*, that on nought,
 But mischiefe gainst our queene thenceforth he thought.

48.

His threatning bull, whose rore in ages past,
The superstitious world did terrifie,
Amongst *Elizae's* subiects he did cast,
Thereby to alienate their loyaltie,
And dutie vow'd to her soueraigntie ;
 Yea pardon in it he did denounce to all,
 That from our queene their dutie would recall.

49.

An. Reg. 12. Which bull, fond *Felton*, thy vnhappie hand
Did fixe vpon that prelate's palace gate,
Which doth by Paule's high towering temple stand ;
Where thou didst iustly meete thy wretched fate,
The meed that traytors steps doth still await ;
 Nor could that priest remit thy foule offence,
 Though with large sinne his bull did then dispence.

50.

And though he did denounce both pardon and curse,
Yet by the one small comfort didst thou find,
Ne yet was England's happie state the worse ;
But as in gloomie caues and corners blinde,
The sun's bright blazing beames most cleare we finde ;
 So did the virgin's glorie shine most brim,
 When her proud foes did seeke the same to dim.

51.

An. Reg. 15. For hereupon, when with rebellious sword,
Those stout strength-breathing Irish vp did stand,
Walter Deu, Renowned *Deuorax* vicount Hereford,
Earle of Es- That most illustrate lord of high command,
sex. No sooner did approch with powerfull band,
 But that the rebels daunted with his name,
 Armes laid aside, in humble manner came.

52.

Brian *Mac-Phelin*, that much scath had done,
With *Ferdorough Macgillastick*, that bold knight,
By some surnam'd the blind Scot's valiant sonne,
With *Odonel*, *Rose*, *Oge* and *Macknel* hight,
Did yeeld themselues to famous *Deuorax* might,
　Which shewes, that he of heau'n beloued was,
　That without blood could bring such things to passe.

53.

And heau'n, the more to blesse our happie queene,
After this Romish buls loud bellowing rore,
Three times the famous *Frobisher* was seene,
In winged barkes full fraught with golden ore,
Dancing ore Neptune's backe to England's shore:
　For *Iason*-like to his eternall fame,
　Thrice from Catay with golden fleece he came.

Anno Reg. 18, 19, 20.

54.

To adde more fame to this for future time,
Great *Drake* to quell their pride that had set downe,
Their *ne plus vltra* in the farthest clime
By seas, sands, rocks and many a sea-sieg'd towne,
Did compasse earth in spight of Neptune's frowne:
　For which his name with fame for aye is crown'd,
　Whose barke still sailes about the world's whole round.

An. Reg. 21.

55.

And thee braue *Holstock* may I not forget,
Whose conquering sword on Neptune's high command
Elizae's haplesse foes hath often met,
And brought them captiue with victorious hand,
Rich fraught with spoile to *Albion's* rockie strand,
　Whereby the greatnesse of *Elizae's* name
　A terror both by land and seas became.

Anno Reg. 11, 15, 21.

56.

O what a princely charge did she maintaine
Of men, munition and artillirie
In flying castles on the purple maine,
Which on the clowds of Thetis liquid skie,
Seeming to frisk about for iollitie,
 Stood like safe centinels 'bout England's shore
 Making seas tremble at their cannons rore.

57.

Thus did the heau'ns showre downe felicitie
In ample manner on *Elizae's* state,
At which Rome's holie sire did still enuie,
Who failing in our English home-bred bate,
In foraine shoares shew'd his malignant hate:
 For by false *Desmond's* meanes he made great show
 · Gainst our *Elizae's* weale to worke much woe.

58.

Anno Reg. 22. But heau'n did soone oppose against his might
Th'heroick spirit, that burned in the hart
Of noble *Grey* of *Wilton*, that bold knight,
Who vnto wounds did challenge th'aduerse part
In manie a field, who hauing felt the smart
 Of his keene sword, the stoutest hid his hed,
 And from his furie to the wilde woods fled.

59.

And when th'Iberian troopes did there display
Rome's ensigne, in that castle hight Del Ore,
In *Desmond's* cause against our queene, great *Grey*
Did thunder gainst their walls with cannons rore,
Ne would from fierce assault desist before
 Vnto his furie passage he had made
 In Spanish blood to bathe·his conquering blade. ·

60.

Thus all his plots still failing in th'euent,
Preuented by heau'n's all foreseeing eye,
A thousand mischiefes now he. gan inuent,
Inuasion, outrage, murder, treacherie,
Sounding the depths of all iniquitie;
 For all blacke deedes his vice-blackt thoughts could find,
 He turn'd and return'd in his vengefull minde.

61.

Vpon his furrowed front, the signes of ire,
Furie and rage, did sit like lowring night,
And both his burning eyes like glowing fire
Beneath his bended browes did sparkle bright,
As irefull lightnings of his heart's despight,
 Yea nought could mollifie his raging teene,
 But blood and vengeance gainst our royall queene.

62.

Amongst his holie sonnes he cald a quest,
Whose counsell to his mischiefe might giue way,
And to his raging thoughts at length giue rest,
Setting his wrath on wing against that day,
Wherein he purpos'd England's swift decay;
 For by them all in counsell 'twas decreed,
 England should fall, *Elizae's* hart should bleed.

63.

The time was set by stratagems deuise,
And force of hands to worke their wicked hate,
The persons chosen for that enterprise,
All bent to tread downe England's happie state
Beneath the feete of some disaster sate,
 Bosting abroad before the deed was done,
 By their firme valor, what rich prize was wone.

64.

The conquerd nations of the Indian soyle,
At whose huge wealth the world is made to wonder,
Their mother's wombe were forced to dispoyle,
And rudely rend her golden ribs in sunder,
Thereby to set on wing warre's roring thunder:
　For souldiers thoughts on golden wings flie far,
　And earth's rich spoiles are sinewes of the war.

65.

Manie tall pines were leueld with the plaine
By the confederates of the Latin shore,
Being taught to flie vpon the purple maine
By force of winde and strength of sable oare,
That on the solid ground stood firme before,
　Whose hugenesse mightie mountaines did resemble,
　Making the monsters of the deepe to tremble.

66.

The famous artizans, that by their art
Do imitate the thunder of the skie,
And digging downe into the earth's black hart,
With that salt humor, that doth hidden lie,
Into the ayre make fierie lightnings flie,
　Were all imploy'd by Spaine's supreme command
　To hurle their thunder gainst our sea-sieg'd land.

67.

All warre habiliments they did prepare
To set sterne Mars vpon his conquering feete,
Their farre-fetcht Indian gold they did not spare,
That nothing might be wanting, that was meet
To furnish out their most vnconquered fleet;
　Before all which was consummate and done,
　Bright Phœbus oft his yearely race had runne.

68.

Meane time Rome's dragon reasde his bloodie crest,
And wau'd his wings, from whence that rabble rout,
That hell-batch'd brood, who, fed on error's brest
And suck'd her poysonous dugs, came crawling out
As was their woont, to flie the world about:
 For those he hatch'd beneath his shadie wings,
 T'imploy 'gainst potentates and mightiest kings.

69.

Manie of these to England's shores he sent,
All diuerslie attir'd in strange array,
Closely thereby to worke his foule intent,
And by their presence to prepare a way
Against the enterprize of that great day;
 In which Spaine's potent fleete the world's great wonder,
 With hidious horror should gainst vs enthunder.

Anno.

70.

Most of the which (O that time's swan-white wings
Could sweepe away record of such foule shame)
Where home-borne impes, vntimely shot vp, springs
Of Britaine brood, Britaine's alone by name,
By nature monsters borne of foule defame,
 That sought the ruine, shame, decay and death
 Of their deare dam, from whom they took their breath.

71.

Vnkindly impes, euen from your birth accurst,
Detested stock of viper's bloodie brood,
That sought to satisfie your burning thirst
By drinking vp your dying mother's blood,
Making her death your life, her hurt your good;
 Your deeds are sunke to Plutoe's darksome den,
 Shame is your portion mongst the sonnes of men.

73.

Mee seemes, I see them walk about the brim
Of black Styx dangerous flood, where Dis doth wonne,
Prince of dead night and darknesse gloomie grim,
Howling for passage, where deep Styx doth run,
Although in vaine, their funerall rites not done:
   For hatefull fowles of heau'n being their best graue,
   No passage to Elyzium can they haue.

73.

Alas, how error, enuie and despaire
Did troope them vp to leade them on the way,
Error orecast their skie, darkened their ayre,
Obscur'd their sight, then enuie did assay
To make them seeke truth's ruine and decay;
   Which hauing faild, despaire to them did bring
   Confusion, shame, and conscience griping sting.

74.

In fatall barkes fast flying ore the maine,
They daylie came with doctrine seeming sound,
In which as meritorious they maintaine
The bloodie hand that should his prince confound,
If good thereby to holy church redoun'd,
   Aboue all whom the self-conceited *Campian*
   Past all compare, was reckn'd Rome's arch champian.

75.

This English Romane wretch with manie more
Did spred themselues disguis'd about the land,
Seducing daylie both the rich and poore
Against their prince to lift rebellious hand,
Renouncing as vniust her dread command,
   And 'gainst the time appointed to prouide
   With forren force to set vp Romane pride.

76.

And then with dread and horror to dismay.
Their wauering thoughts, they set before their eyes
The generall slaughter of that dismall day,
When Spaine's black fleet on Neptune's liquid skies
Should woefull England suddenlie surprise;
   Wishing them craue the pope's protection
   T''escape such horror and confusion.

77.

But as the wolfe disguis'd with fleecie skin
Of sillie sheep, the shepheard long did blinde,
And 'mongst the flock thereby did credit win,
Till he at length, did by his bloodie minde
Bewray himselfe to be a wolfe by kinde:
   So they, though making manie saint-like showes
   Did by their deeds themselues at length disclose.

78.

With shamefull death, their shamefull liues took end,
Leauing on earth for signes of infamie
Their totter'd carcases, to which no friend
At anie time, could giue due obsequie,
Or scarse bewaile their woefull destinie;
   But left they were for prey, both daies and nights
   To black night rauens and to hungrie kites.

79.

Which might haue been a terror vnto those,
That after sought the faire *Elizae's* fall,
And in their harts did wickedlie suppose
To England's bounds againe back to recall
The popish pride and Romane slauish thrall:
   But after this did manie vndergoe
   Dire death and shame, to worke *Elizae's* woe.

Anno

80.

Anno Reg. 26. First furious *Sommeruile*, that posting came
With his owne hands to act his soueraigne's death,
Preuented in the way, to shun such shame
As might ensue, did stop his owne deare breath,
Thinking the same a far more glorious death;
But simple man with far more shame thereby,
Thy trembling ghost vnto the dead did flie.

81.

An. eodem.
F. [rancis]
T [hrogmor-
ton] The next, whose shame no time away shall sweepe,
Was he, who by the helpe of traytor's hand,
Searching the mighty Neptune's waterie deepe,
Vs'd all his art and skill to vnderstand
The depth of euery hauen in this land;
Thereby to giue safe conduct to the foe,
And bring them in to worke his countrie's woe.

82.

He went to that great God's dread kingdome's bounds,
Who often chargeth on the clouds in skie,
Who cuffes the seas, who by his power confounds
High hils and mountaines, who doth terrifie
Euen the sad ghosts of Plutoe's emperie;
He went to know what winde the fleet should wing,
That should confusion vnto England bring.

83.

O, vnremorsefull man! O, wretched wight!
Shame to thy selfe and thy posteritie,
Nor friends nor countrie's good, to whom of right
Thy care was due, nor loue of loyaltie
To thy dread queene thy heart might mollifie,
But wing'd with mischiefe, hauing once begun,
Thou to vntimely death didst head-long run.

84.

Whose wretched steps, in that same fatall way·
That leads to house of death, loe many more
Had follow'd fast in giuing like assay,
Had not our queene, whose virgin bosome bore
A melting heart admir'd for mercie store,
   In pitie far excell'd th'impietie
   Of their false treason 'gainst her maiestie.

An. eodem.

85.

Out of her bountious grace and princely mind,
She gaue them passage at her owne expence,
Seldome on earth such mercie shall we find,
For which strooke blind with shame of their offence,
Against a person of such excellence,
   They sent their owne hand writs to testifie
   This worthie deed to all posteritie.

Read the certificat of the prince's mercie written by their owne hands. *Ralph Hol.* p. 1413.

86.

Yet that vngratefull man, to whom before
Iustly conuicted for foule felonie,
Renown'd *Eliza* did lost life restore,
Sought to enact a bloodie tragedie
Vpon the person of her maiestie,
   To wit that boaster who did beare the name
   Of doctor *Parrie* to increase his fame.

An. Reg. 27.

87.

The Babylonian bawd, whose strumpet-breath
Giues life to treason, did with him conspire
To end their vengeance in the virgin's death;
And lest his heart should faile and he retire
From his intent, to wing him with desire,
   His soule from sin, from death, and hell was freed,
   With impious hands to act this tragicke deed.

88.

The foolish man with resolution came,
As sent from heau'n, yet did it nought auaile :
For getting licence to this royall dame
With her to talke alone, his heart did faile,
Her lookes alone his height of sprite did quaile ;
  For daunted with her sight, he did repent,
  And closely sought to colour his intent.

89.

He did declare to her, how he had taken
A solemne oath to take her life away,
And how her soueraigntie he had forsaken,
The Romish beast as supreame head t'obay,
Who by his hands expected her decay,
  To which, he said, he did but seeme t'agree,
  That so it might by him detected bee.

90.

The royall virgin, when as she did heare
The wicked purpose of her treacherous foe,
To shew how little she the same did feare,
Pardon'd him in secret, that no peere might know
His leaud intent, and so might worke him woe :
  O height of princely spirit, past humane sence !
  O mercie past compare, for such offence !

91.

Yet this false wretch, in whose obdurate heart
No loyall loue did dwell, persisted still
In his blacke treason, and did vse all art
Oft times with dagger, dag or any ill,
T'effect the purpose of his bloodie will :
  Which once being brought to light for such offence,
  His grudging ghost with shame was posted hence.

92.

Thus Rome's blood-thirsting wolues with cruell pawes,
Sought daily to deuoure our virgin lambe,
And plunge poore England in death's yawning iawes,
Hiding for aye the glorie of her name,
Rakte vp in cinders of a ruthlesse flame:
   Thereby t'extinguish that celestiall light,
    Which Rome's red dragon did so sore affright.

93.

They knew for certaine, while our glorious lampe,
Our maiden queene did liue to lead vs light,
She would disperse foule errors dismall dampe,
Which suffocates the soule, and choakes the sight
With fearefull shadowes of eternall night;
   Yea much they fear'd pure truth's true light diuine,
    Which then in forren shores began to shine.

94.

The sea-diuided seuenteene lands great nation,
The Belgick borderers by the bankes of Rheine,
Cast off Rome's yoke, and left their blind deuotion,
With one consent beginning to incline
Vnto a truth more perfect, more diuine;
   Which they with martyr'd blood did long maintaine,
    Gainst th'inquisition of Rome-wronged Spaine.

95.

But at the last, when with warre's dreadfull thunder,
Don Iohn of Austria and his warlike band,
Began to shake the Belgicke state in sunder,
To tyrannize and bring them with strong hand
Beneath the yoke of *Philip's* sterne command,
   The great *Eliza* they did humblie craue,
    Their Belgick state from hostile spoile to saue.

An. eodem. **27.**

96.

The Briton maid, remorsefull of their woes,
In their defence did lift her royall hand,
Against the threats of their inuading foes,
And sent in safe conduct a warlike band,
With fame-grac'd *Norrice* to the Belgicke strand;
　　Which with his valiant crew he did maintaine,
　　Against the incursions of the power of Spaine.

97.

As. eodem.
Drake's voy-
age to Cartha-
gena and Do-
mingo.

Meane time th' vndaunted *Drake* no time did sleepe,
Vpon the maine king *Philip's* powers to sease,
Who thought himselfe the Neptune of the deepe;
But of such yoke, the sea-gods sounes to ease,
Drake tooke from him the scepter of the seas,
　　And put the same in his faire soueraigne's hand,
　　Teaching the deepe to know her milde command.

98.

Her winged barkes, like sea-nymphes in their flight,
The aged sea-god's daughter safely bore,
Whose nimble dance the deepe did so delight,
That 'bout their bosomes sweeping by the shore
The siluer waues did play with wanton rore,
　　Thinking themselues releas'd from yoke of Spaine,
　　Whose gold-heap'd mountaines did oppresse the maine.

99.

With these vpon the seas, the noble *Drake*
Did saile as lord of th'ocean emperie,
At whose dread name th'Iberians hearts did quake,
Who left the rule of Neptune's moistned skie
To *Drake's* command, and to the shores did flie,
　　Whom now for ancient wrongs done long before,
　　He with swift vengeance follow'd to the shore.

100.

Braue *Carlile, Winter, Frobisher* and *Knoles,*
With many more of Neptune's noble race,
Made peopled cities place for beasts and fowles,
Burnt bowers, sackt towers, raz'd townes before the face
Of their base foes, who fled with foule disgrace,
 Leauing wife, children, gold and goods for pray,
 By stranger people to be borne away.

101.

Foure townes in this their voyage they did foile,
First did Saint Iago by their power decline,
That done, then Saint Domingo did they spoile,
Next towring Carthagena, and in fine
In Terra Florida, Saint Augustine:
 Thus fortune with rich spoile their deeds did crowne,
 And home they came with glorie and renowne.

102.

And while these valiant men, true sonnes of fame,
In forren shores our foe-mens force did quell,
And by their deeds made knowne *Elisae's* name,
The stif-neckt Irish proudly did rebell,
Whose hearts with stubborne pride did euer swell:
 But noble *Bingham,* that illustrate knight,
 Did bring them downe and tame their towring might.

103.

When that false traytor, *Mahowne Obrian*
To Rome's proud strumpet bound his loue to show,
In Thomond with rebellious hand began,
To stirre vp strife, and worke his countrie's woe,
In hope to haue been backt by forren foe,
 In warre affaires this *Bingham* far renown'd,
 In castle Clanowen did him confound.

An. Reg. 28. Taken from a note confirmed vnder the hands of diuers gentlemen imployed in this action.

104.

And when the *Burkes*, who did false rumours noise
Of wrong intended gainst their countries good,
With *Clangibbons*, with *Clandonnels* and *Ioyes*,
Themselues in armes did bound and proudly stood
On daring tearmes in field to spend their blood,
    Renowned *Bingham* with his valiant crew,
    Did them through woods from caue to caue pursue.

105.

And when the Redshankes on the borders by
Incursions made, and rang'd in battell stood
To beare his charge, from field he made them flie,
Where fishie Moine did blush with crimson blood
Of thousand foes, that perisht in the flood,
    For which braue *Bingham* crown'd with endlesse fame,
    Enioyes on earth a neuer dying name.

106.

Sixtus Quin-
tus Pope.

Although these ciuill warres of home-bred hate,
First hatcht at Rome by England' ancient foe,
Did much disturbe *Elizae's* blessed state,
Yet did the royall virgin not forgoe
Th'afflicted Belgians drencht in depth of woe:
    But to support them gainst all foes annoy,

Earle of Leic.
    For that designe, she *Dudley* did employ.

107.

Anno eodem
28.

Who, Iason-like to Colchos iland bound
To fetch the golden fleece by force of hand,
With many great Heroes far renown'd,
Past with triumphant sailes ore seas and sand,
From England's shores vnto the Belgicke strand,
    Where after all their high atchieuements done,
    Their fleece was fame, their gold was glorie won.

108.

O, noble virgin! O, victorious dame,
England's Bellona, nurse of chiualrie!
What age brought forth so many sonnes of fame,
In all the world's thrice-changed monarchie,
As in the time of thy great emperie?
   Whose deeds from England's bounds did beare thy name,
   As far as Phœbus spreads his golden flame.

109.

Who now arriuing on the Belgian coast
With fatall steele did deepe ingraue thy name,
Vpon the proudest crests in that great host
That with the valiant prince of Parma came,
Enacting wonders for immortall fame;
   Witnesse those famous deeds by Zutphen done,
   Where many high exploits were vndergone.

110.

When both the aduerse powres afront did meet,
Although the foe farre more in number were;
Yet did our men with Mars swift-winged feet,
Charge on their troopes, whose hearts strooke dead with feare,
Vnable to resist, they backe did beare,
   T'whom valiant *Audlie* in their faint recoyle,
   With his foot-bands alone did giue the foyle.

Recorded at large by *I. Stow*, in his Ann. pag. 1233, taken out of *H. Archer.*

111.

Then th'Albanois vnto the rescue came
With their horse troopes, amongst whom stout *Norris* went,
And boldly singl'd out a man of fame,
Gainst whom his pistoll with full charge he bent
To act his fall; but failing in th'euent,
   His foe-man's head he with the same did greet,
   And made him fall at his victorious feet.

112.

Lo. *Will.* of
Eresbeie.

Next noble *Willoughby* with lance in rest,
Arm'd like the god of warre on winged horse,
Met captaine *George,* opposing brest to brest,
Whom from his steed halfe dead with furious force,
He downe did beare in his winde-winged course,

This he spake
in French.

 Who falling said : " I yeeld me to thy might,
 In that I see thou art a seemely knight."

113.

Rob. Earle of
Essex.

Then noble *Deuorax,* Mars his yongest sonne,
Chear'd vp his troope, " Fellowes in armes," quoth he,
" The honorable prease let vs not shunne,
Ne with the dread of death dismaied be,
But for your countrie's glorie follow me:"
 Which said, he fiercely charg'd on th'enemie,
 And shew'd high proofe of his stout valiancie.

114.

Sir *William
Russell.*

To second him, *Russell* that martiall knight,
Like feathered shaft sent from a stiffe-bent bow,
Or boysterous Boreas in his nimble flight,
With weightie lance did charge vpon the foe,
And horse and man to ground did ouerthrow,
 Who with affright did from his furie runne,
 As braying goats the king of beasts doth shunne.

115.

Amongst them all, that impe of honor's bed,
That worthie of the world, that hardie knight,
The noble *Sidnie* to aduentures led
With glory-thirsting zeale in death's despight
Vpon his foes himselfe did noblie quight :
 For in one skirmish with high valiancie,
 Thrice did he charge vpon the enemie.

116.

But cursed fortune, foe to famous men,
Beholding *Sidnie's* deeds with enuious eie,
Turning her malice into raging teene,
With deadly shot did wound him on the thigh,
Which from a foe-man's fatall peece did flie:
   Whose timelesse end, if time did serue thereto,
   I should bewaile in lines of lasting woe.

117.

Many more sonnes of Mars his noble race,
In this daie's fight great fame with perill wonne,
Yea many high exploits each breathing space,
By many a worthie wight were vndergone;
Mongst whom that deed with resolution done,
   By valiant *Williams*, and the Belgian *Skinke*,
   Downe to obliuion's den shall neuer sinke.

118.

For when that well wall'd towne, which Venlo hight,
Was round about begirted by the foe,
Huge spirit and high conceit did so excite
Stout *Williams'* mightie mind, to vndergoe
Some great attempt, that he full bent to show
   Proofe of his valour by some famous act,
   With hardie *Skinke* this wonder did enact:

Anno eodem
28.
H. Archer,
Author.

119.

When grizly night her iron carre had driuen
From her darke mansion house, that hidden lies
In Plutoe's kingdome, to the top of heau'n,
And with black cloake of clouds muffling the skies,
With sable wings shut vp all wakefull eies,
   Obscur'd with darknesse grim they both did go,
   To act this stratagem vpon the foe:

120.

Husht were the winds, the aire all silent was,
Sad was the night, in skies appear'd no starre;
Yet through darke horror dreadlesse did they passe,
And listning vnto euery breach of aire,
With stealing steps this dangerous worke did dare,
 Whom at the length the dark night's shadie wing,
 Into the foe-men's campe did closely bring.

121.

Where, when they came, the vtmost watch they found
Vpon the ground all carelessely dispread,
Who tir'd with toile, lay in deepe sleepe fast drown'd,
And as they slept, each one secure of dread,
His weapon had fast fixed at his head,
 Mongst whom, like hungrie wolues on flockes vnkept,
 Stout *Skinke* and worthie *Williams* boldly stept.

122.

Then death triumpht in slaughter of the slaine,
Soules strugling in the pangs of many a wound,
Departs in griefe and makes aire sigh againe,
Swords blusht with blood, grim horror did abound,
A crimson dew stood on the grassie ground;
 Disorder, dread, death, noise and darknesse grim,
 In blood and gore of slaughtred foes did swim.

123.

By the still watch and two strong courts of gard,
Through death, through blood and armes they boldly went,
Vntill they came, where horriblie they scar'd
The prince himselfe sweet sleeping in his tent,
Whom in their power they long'd to circumuent,
 Where many a noble wight fast snoring drown'd,
 In deepest sleepe with death they did confound.

The Prince
of Parma.

124.

But as their swords they in their foes did sheath,
At last, through massacres, through shrikes and cries
Of sad soules groning in the pangs of death,
On euery side the startled foes did rise,
And shrikt out thicke alarmes to shun surprise,
   Crying arme, arme, whereby appall'd with feare,
   Th'whole host in sudden throngs all gathered were.

125.

Then fled the valiant *Skinke*, blacke death to shun,
But hardie *Williams* in contention stood
With his great mind, if he more fame t'haue won,
Should stoutly stay, and hazard his owne good,
With slaughtering swotd to shed more foe-men's blood:
   Whereby at length in depth of danger drown'd,
   By armed foes, he was incircled round.

126.

But by aduantage of the gloomie night
Amongst the foe-men's troopes, vnknowne he goes,
And cri'd: " Where's *Williams?* where is *Williams* hight?"
To whom againe one answer'd amongst the foes,
" Pursue, pursue with speed, before he goes:"
   Thus cloudie night this worthie wight did saue,
   Who shun'd his foes, and fled his darksome graue.

127.

These were the foster children of that nurse,
England's Minerua, queene of glorie bright,
Who through the paths of warre their way did force,
In armes to get true honor's meed by might,
And grace their name with title of true knight:
   Which honor'd order only vertue's meed,
   Each one then purchas'd by some glorious deed.

128.

But while these captaines wedded to renowne,
True loyall sublects of a royall queene,
On Belgian shores their soueraigne's head did crowne,
With conquering wreath of neuer vading greene,
In spight of spight for aye fresh to be seene,
   Rome's raging Python full of furious wrath,
   Did once againe belch vp his poisoned froth.

129.

Anno eodem 28.

Foureteene false traytors from darke treason's den
He vp did call, foule elues of enuious night,
Rebels accurst, monsters abhorr'd of men,
Who for the black fleet now alreadie dight,
To passe th'vnfruitfull deepe with all her might,
   Should make fit passage gainst that dreadfull day,
   By their sweet prince and countrie's swift decay.

130.

Ballard, first author in this villanie,
Sent from the triple-crowned sonne of night,
To put in practise this their treacherie,
Proud *Babington* and *Sauage* did excite,
With vnremorsefull hands of violent might,
   To spoile and ruinate their countrie's good,
   And bathe their swords in their deare soueraigne's blood.

131.

Babington made choice of the six.

Six resolute and bloodie minded mates,
Should haue been actors in her tragedie,
Then the graue peeres and honorable states,
Had been the slaughter of their butcherie,
And thou, O, glorie of this emperie!
   Thy loftie towers been leuell'd with the plaine,
   Thy nauie burnt, and many a thousand slaine.

132.

Such dismall deeds and blacke confusion,
By proud Rome's twice-seuen sonnes intended were
Against the time of that inuasion,
Report whereof with terror and with feare,
Swift-winged fame about the world did beare;
   But high heau'n's King, who for his seruant chose
   Our virgin queene, their drifts did soone disclose.

133.

Their plot bewray'd, each one did seeke t'escape,
Vengeance pursuing them from place to place,
Hight *Babington* attir'd in rusticke shape,
With walnut-leaues discolouring his face,
Did seeke t'escape sad death and foule disgrace:
   And all the rest being clad in strange disguise,
   With trembling feare did seeke to shun surprise.

134.

As guiltie homicides, that in dead night
Pursu'd for tragick deeds of dismall death,
To woods and groues disperst, do take their flight,
Whose gloomie shade they trembling stand beneath,
With fainting knees, cold spirit and panting breath,
   With feare, expecting at their backes behinde,
   The pursuit made at euery puffe of winde:

135.

Euen so these wretched men, whose selfe-doom'd soules,
Now prickt with deepe remorse, did daily looke
To be the spoile and prey of hungrie fowles,
From place to place their couert passage tooke,
Whose hearts the thought of death with horror shooke,
   Vntill surpriz'd at length, vntimely death
   To end this feare expir'd their fainting breath.

136.

Of whose surprise, when as the trumpe of fame
Had blowen the blast, the subiect euer giuen
To blesse the fate of so diuine a dame,
For this so strange escape did morne and euen,
With praises magnifie the King of heau'n,
  Imploring still his gratious hands for helpes,
  Against the danger of that dragon's whelpes.

137.

That day was held diuine, and all the night
Consum'd in pæans to th'Olympian king,
Then crown'd they cups of wine, and with delight
At sumptuous feasts did sit, while belles did ring,
And sweet voic'd minstrels round about did sing,
  Whose suppers sauour wrapt in clouds on high,
  The friendly winds blew vp into the skie.

138.

And as the siluer moone in calmest night,
When she in shining coach the skies doth scale,
As golden starres, that in the heau'ns shine bright,
When gentle Auster blowes a pleasing gale,
Do glad the shepheards in the lowly vaile:
  So many thousand flames, that glaz'd the skies,
  Did at that time glad all true English eies.

139.

But most of all, that plentious peopled towne,
Elixae's best belou'd, faire London hight,
Her mistresse rare escape with ioy did crowne,
Whose loftie towers thrust vp themselues in sight,
And ioy'd to glitter in the golden light,
  Affrighting sore sad night's black drowzie dame,
  With splendor of huge fires refulgent flame.

140.

This ioy once past t'auènge that villanie,
Which Rome did by this bloodie plot pretend,
Against *Elizae's* sacred maiestie,
The aged sea-god's backe, *Drake* did ascend,
And towards the foes wing'd with reuenge did wend,
 Mongst whom his name had been the gastly bug,
 T'affright yong infants at the mother's dug.

An. Reg. 29.
Drake's voy-
age to East
Cales. Out
of the second
part of the se-
cond volume
of Nauiga-
tions, p. 121.
Hakluit.

141.

His fleet transferr'd, with prosperous gale did sweepe
'Through parted waues of 'Thetis waterie skie,
Vnto the shores of the Castilian deepe,
In whose proud billowes he did wafting lie,
Vntill for truth he heard by his espie,
 Of that prepare, that in Cales harbor lay,
 For Spaine's Armada gainst th'appointed day.

142.

Then gaue he order for the nauall fight,
And in the euening tide, when setting sun
Leaues steepe Olympus to the darkesome night,
The pine-plough'd seas with black clouds ouerrun,
To giue the onset valiant *Drake* begun :
 Hurling forth burning flames with hidious rore,
 Of brazen cannon on th'Iberian shore.

143.

And as, when Boreas in a tempest raues,
Leaping with wings of lightning from the skie,
Makes clouds to crack and cuffes the swelling waues,
Who from the storme of his fierce furie flie,
In roling billowes on the bankes fast by ;
 So wrapt in clouds of smoake and lightning pale,
 With dreadfull fight, *Drake* did his foes assaile.

144.

Six gallies thwart the towne at first did stand
The violent onset, which the English gaue;
But had they with strong oares and readie hand,
Not made swift speed themselues and fleet to saue,
They with the same had perisht in the waue;
   For *Drake* with fire in hand without delay,
   Had burnt their ships and sunke them in the sea.

145.

But loe a richer prize, he soone had wonne,
Which did repay that losse with trebble gaine,
Three barkes, of which each bore a thousand tunne,
And in the deepe such compasse did containe,
Seeming like floting mountaines on the maine,
   With cannons wounding shot he did intombe,
   With all their men in Thetis watrie wombe.

146.

Nor yet could this his noble heart suffice,
But with more conquest to renowne his name,
Thirtie eight ships his valour did surprise,
Of which most part with fire he did enflame,
The rest he kept for trophies of his fame,
   Which in the sight of *Cales* that loftie towne,
   He brought away in triumph and renowne.

147.

And as a bellowing bull, that doth disdaine,
Amongst an heard of cattell grazing by,
That any other bull in all the plaine,
Should proudly beare his curled head on high,
But makes him basely yeeld, or fainting flie:
   So did great *Drake*, as lord of all the deepe,
   His foes on th'ocean in subiection keepe.

148.

And when of all great *Philip's* nauall might,
On the seas wildernesse none durst appeare,
Drake to prouoke his heartlesse foes to fight,
With his whole fleet vnto the shore did beare,
Where three strong holds by him assaulted were,
  With that faire castle of Cape Sacre hight,
  All which did fall beneath his nauall might.

149.

From thence to seas with his triumphant sailes
He did returne, wafting vpon the waues
Before hight Lisbone, neere to easterne Cales,
Where of th'Iberians he the combate craues,
Though none amongst them durst interrupt his braues,
  But fled into the ports and harbours by,
  Where out of danger they might hidden lie.

150.

Yet thence he rouz'd them, while that heartlesse knight,
The marques of Saint Cruz lay wafting by
In his swift sayling gallies, in whose sight
Drake burnt and spoil'd his ships and made them flie,
Who to his care for helpe did seeme to crie:
  Yet durst he not come forth in their defence,
  But suffred *Drake* to lead them captiue thence.

151.

A hundred ships with furniture full fraught
For Spaine's Armada, that world-wondred fleet,
He did dispoile, and some away he brought
As signes of victorie, which as most meet
He did subiect at faire *Elizae's* feet;
  The praise of which with humble zeale and loue,
  She offred vp to heau'n as due to Ioue.

152.

Such humble thoughts in such a noble mind,
Do beat downe pride in chiefe felicitie:
And such a noble mind in kingly kind,
With best aduice, doth teach true maiestie,
To shew it selfe in milde humilitie,
    Such humble thoughts, such noble minde had she,
    Which in her heart, heart-searching loue did see.

153.

For which in spight of her death-threatning foes,
As high as heau'n, he did exalt her name,
And did his blacke death-darting hand oppose
Against her brauing foes, that proudly came
With all their power gainst such a royall dame,
    Whose mightie fleete, fifteene yeares worke of wonder,
    Now launcht into the seas began to thunder.

154.

An. Reg. 30.
1588.

For now loue's helm'd-deckt sonne, the god of warre,
Rouz'd from his rest with cannons dreadfull rore,
Leapt on the earth from out his iron carre,
Shooke his strong lance, steept in black blood and gore,
Whose brazen feet did thunder on the shore,
    The noise of which that from the earth did bound,
    Made all the world to tremble at the sound.

155.

And vp from darkesome lymboe's dismall stage,
Ore Stygian bridge from Plutoe's emperie,
Came night's blacke brood, Disorder, Ruine, Rage,
Rape, Discord, Dread, Despaire, Impietie,
Horror, swift Vengeance, Murder, Crueltie,
    All which together on th'Iberian strand,
    With Spaine's great host troopt vp did ready stand.

156.

Fame downe descending from her siluer bower,
On duke *Medinæ's* huge black barke did stand,
The generall of all the Spanish power,
Whence looking round ore seas, and sea-sieg'd land,
Holding her siluer trumpet in her hand,
　The same she sounded loud, whose echo shrill,
　With sound thereof the wide world's round did fill.

157.

Then all th'Iberian kings stout men of warre,
Renown'd for those replendent armes they bore,
Marching beneath his ensignes heard from farre,
Who vowing England spoil'd of all her store,
Should stoope her pride, and them outface no more;
　Made swift repaire in concourse and thick crow'd,
　To Spaine's black fleet t'effect what they had vow'd.

158.

The sun-burnt Spaniards from that Indian shore,
Subdu'd by *Ferdinandoe's* bloodie hand,
Where Perue's streames casts vp her golden ore,
And Zenewe's waues bring to the slimie strand,
Pure graines of gold amongst the ruddie sand,
　Like Cadmus bone-bred brood came thicke in swarmes,
　As newly borne from top to toe in armes.

Ferdinando
Cortez.

159.

The captiu'd nations of the Castile king,
Luxurious Naples and proud Lombardie,
Their troopes in faire refulgent armes did bring,
And those of Portugale and Soicilie,
With slick-hair'd youth of wanton Italie,
　T'auenge faire England's foule supposed wrong,
　To Spaine's Armada in thicke troopes did throng.

160.

Readie t'imbarke vpon the shores they stood,
Like flowers in spring, that beautifie the plaine,
Or like May flies orewhelmed by the flood,
As infinite, as leaues or drops of raine,
Powr'd from the heau'ns vpon the liquid maine,
   That with their weight, dame Terrae's aged backe
   Beneath the sway of horse and foot did cracke.

161.

And as blacke swarmes of ants with loaden thies,
Hauing vpon the flowrie spring made pray,
In number numberlesse with fresh supplies,
Climbes some steepe hillock, and through all the day
By thousands in thick flockes do fill the way;
   So Spaine's great host from trampled shores did wend,
   In thronging troopes, their mountaine ships t'ascend.

162.

And such a blustring as against the shore,
When as the swelling seas the welkin braues,
Or storme-driuen billowes on the bankes do rore,
Or such a noise as in earth's hollow caues
We often beare, when stormie Boreas raues:
   Such clamorous noise out of the tumult sprong,
   When they from shores vnto their ships did throng.

163.

Hous'd in their fleet, their ankors vp they weigh'd,
Hoisted their top-masts with their sailes on high,
The misens then with winged winds displaid
Before their hollow keeles, that low did lie
Within the deepe, made parted billowes flie;
   Their huge big bulks made Neptune's back to bow,
   And waues to swell vpon his waterie brow.

164.

Their towring heads, the heau'ns blacke clouds did kisse,
Borne by the winde-driuen stormie wanes on high,
Their hollow bosomes in the deepe abysse
Amongst the surges of the fish-full skie,
Like mightie rockes from sight did hidden lie,
 Whose brasse-arm'd sides such compasse did containe,
 They seem'd to couer acres on the maine.

165.

Whoso had seene them on the gulphie flood,
He would haue thought some Delos now againe,
Some towne, some citie, or some desert wood,
Or some uew vnkowne world from shores of Spaine
Launcht off to seas, had wandred on the maine,
 Peopled with those, that like quicke sprites in skie,
 By little hold-fast all about could flie.

166.

Each barke, whose bulke was proofe against the wound
Of common shot, besides those buls of brasse,
Whose bellowing rore did equall thunders sound,
Of such great thicknesse and high building was,
That like large towers they on the deepe did passe;
 For scarce could brazen cannons banefull thunder,
 With battering bullet beat their sides asunder.

Musket shot could not pierce them. *Emanuel Van-Metran,* in his 15 booke of his historie.

167.

Their vpper deckes, all trim'd and garnisht out
With sterne designes for bloodie warre at hand,
With crimson fights were armed all about,
And on the hatche many a goodly band
Deckt in braue armes, together thicke did stand,
 Whose plume-deckt heads themselues aloft did show,
 And seem'd to dance, with windes wau'd to and fro.

168.

With glittering shields their bosomes they did bar,
Each one well brandishing his fatall blade, ·
And from their bright habiliments of war,
Such blazing shine, as in the gloomie shade,
We often see by Phœbus beames displaid,
　A splendor vp into the aire did throw,
　And glittered on the glistning waues below.

169.

Their top sailes, sprit sailes, and their misens all,
Their crooked sternes, and tackle euery where　·
Adorned were with pennons tragicall,
Which in their silken reds did pictur'd beare
The sad ostents of death and dismall feare,
　Who while their keeles through seas did cut their way,
　In wanton wauing with the winde did play.

170.

The clangor of shrill trumpes triumphant sound
And clattering horror of their clashing armes,
Vpon the bordering shores did so redound,
That euen the deepe of their intended harmes
On England's coasts did sound out thicke alarmes,
　Which strooke a terror to the heart of him
　Who then did border about Neptune's brim.

171.

So great a fleet, since that same god so old,
Grim-bearded Neptune bore the sea-gods name,
The golden eye of heau'n did nere behold,
Nor Agamemnon's thousand ships, that came
To sacke proud Troy, and all her towers enflame,
　Nor that Eoan monarche's fleet, that scar'd
　The sonnes of Tyre, with this might be compar'd.

172.

But while this mightie fleet did proudly boast
Her matchlesse might on Neptune's high command,
Braue *Parma*, lord of all th'Iberian host,
Both of the horse and foot, that came by land,
Did troope them vp vpon the Belgicke strand,
   To whom th'assistants of the Castile king,
   Their seuerall troopes of men did daily bring.

173.

Beneath the bird of Ioue the prince of ayre,
Which th'house of Austria in their ensignes bore,
The proud Burgundian marcht in armour faire,
Th'Italian, Germaine, Dutch, and many more
Of other lands and language, who before
   Had often been renown'd in many a fight,
   For their high valour, and approued might.

174.

Such, and so mightie bands of famous men,
Adorn'd in richest armes of purest gold,
Vpon those coasts before had neuer been,
Nor any Belgian euer did behold·
Such martiall troopes vpon that trampled mold,
   So skill'd in habit of all fights in warre,
   And for fights true direction past compare.

175.

Both horse and foot of Spaine's impetuous might,
And of the auxil'arie bands, that came
As mercenaries for the bloodie fight,
Distinguisht vnder guides of speciall name,
Whom hope of spoile did to this warre inflame,
   Drew towards the shores of Neptune there to meet
   And ioyne their forces with the nauall fleet.

176.

Which being titled long before in Spaine,
The fleet Inuincible by all consents,
In all her pride now floted on the maine,
Readie prepar'd t'effect those blacke euents,
Presag'd before by proud Spaine's sad ostents;
    Who by report through all the world had won
    The name of conquest ere the fight begun.

177.

The threatfull subiects of the Castile king,
In this huge fleet did such firme hope repose,
That all their sun-burnt brats they taught to sing,
Triumph and conquest, which they did suppose
Their very threats would purchase gainst their foes,
    Who like braue lords, their valour to renowne,
    Did cast the dice for faire *Elizae's* crowne.

178.

Much like the vanting French, when *Iohn* of France
In Poyctiers battell with his mightie host,
Not pondering in his mind warres doubtfull chance,
The gotten victorie did vainely boast,
Before that either part had won or lost,
    Where braue prince *Edward* with his troope so small,
    Renown'd his sword with *Iohn* of France' his fall.

179.

Euen so this brauing fleet, whose dreaded name,
Ineuitable ruine did foretell,
Thought, that the faire *Eliza*, who did frame
Her life in happie daies of peace to dwell,
Vnfurnisht was such forces to repell,
    And therefore sent as from king *Philip's* hand,
    A sterne inscription with this proud command :

180.

" With auxil'arie bands she should no more
Vphold the Belgian gainst king *Philip's* frowne,
All Spanish prizes back againe restore,
Build vp religious houses beaten downe,
And vnto Rome subiect her selfe and crowne;
 All which to do, if that she did withstand,
 Her imminent blacke end was now at hand."

This was sent
written in
Latin.

181.

The noble queene, who in her royall hand
Did beare the state and stay of *Britanie*,
In deepe contempt of such a basse command,
With spirit of princely magnanimitie,
Did briefely answere this proud ambasie:
 For in prouerbiall words her answere was,
 " *Ist hæc ad Græcas fient mandata Kalendas.*"

182.

An answere worthie, for the grace it bore,
The virgin spring of old *Plantagenet*,
Who from the foes to shield her natiue shore,
Her subiects hearts for fight on fire did set,
And their bold stomackes did with courage whet,
 Who fir'd with loue of their *Elisae's* good,
 In her defence did thirst to spend their blood.

183.

For when for certaine, fame th'intended harmes
Of *Spaine's* blacke fleet to *England's* shores did bring,
How gladly did her people flocke to armes,
And when the trumpe warre's scathfull song did sing,
About their eares how pleasing did it ring?
 Whose hearts with furie fed, to battell giuen,
 With braue conceits did leape as high as heau'n.

184.

All townes did ring with sudden cri'd alarmes,
Whence with loud clamour to the marine shore,
The armed people clustred in thicke swarmes,
Where red-ey'd Eris warre's blacke ensigne bore,
And mongst their troops did sprinkle blood and gore;
  Stirring them vp with eager minds to wade
  Through seas of blood, the aduerse fleet t'inuade.

185.

And as the golden swarmes of black-backt bees,
Their thighes full loaden from the flowrie field,
With humming noise flie to the hollow trees,
Where they with busie paine fit shelter build,
Their treasure and themselues from harme to shield ;
  So thicke in armes, th'alarum once begun,
  Vnto their ships with shouting they did run:

186.

Where with their mutuall strengths they did assay,
To hale *Elizae's* fleet from off the shore,
Some pumpt, some cleans'd, some drew the stockes away,
Some hoist the top-masts, some great burthens bore,
The nauie's want with furniture to store:
  And with their vtmost diligence all wrought,
  Till to perfection they their worke had brought.

187.

Which from the shores, once launcht into the maine,
Not all the world a fairer fleet could show:
For though in hugenesse, that black fleet of Spaine
Did farre surpasse; yet was it farre more slow
In nimble stirrage wafting to and fro:
  For England's fleet through seas swift passage won
  With gentle gale, though th'ocean smooth did run.

188.

To shun their foes, each like a nimble hinde
In Neptune's forrest, on the watrie greene,
Haue skipt from waue to waue, and with the winde,
When they list turne againe; they haue been seene
Like raging lions in their heate of spleene,
   Flie on the Castile fleet to bring them vnder,
   And with fell rore to teare their sides in sunder.

189.

All readie furnisht wafting to and fro,
Ouer the narrow seas deepe sandie beds,
They 'bout the coasts themselues did daily show,
In th'huffing winds wauing their silken reds,
And crimson crosses on their loftie heads:
   Those ancient badges, through the world renown'd,
   Which with high conquest fortune oft hath crown'd.

190.

Their braue demeanor did so much delight
The people, that beheld them on the maine,
That many more all readie for the fight,
Did make repaire, t'oppugne the fleet of Spaine;
Then all that royall nauie could containe:
   Such feruent loue vnto their soueraigne's name,
   With fierie courage did their hearts enflame.

191.

Those stout sea-searchers of the stormie flood,
The sonnes of Nereus broad sea-sayling race,
And the braue offspring of Prometheus brood,
That with loud thunder-claps their foe-men chace,
Who in *Elizae's* royall fleet had place,
   Made solemne vowes, backe to returne no more,
   Except with conquest to their natiue shore.

192.

Mongst whom the noblest obiect of them all,
That in the fleete did hold supreamest sway
Went honor'd *Howard,* as chiefe admirall,
Who by his stout demeanor did assay,
With courage bold to lead them on the way,
  And euery heart did fill with hautie spirit,
  By glorious deeds immortall fame to merit.

Now Earle of
Nottingham.

193.

Vpon th'Eolian gods supportfull wings,
With chearefull shouts, they parted from the shore,
While heau'n and earth and all the ocean rings
With sounds, which on her wings loud echo bore,
Of trumpets, drums, shrill fifes and cannons rore,
  To which the people's shouts on shores fast by,
  Reecho'd in the rockes with loud replie.

194.

While they aboord at sea, so heere at home
T'auert all harmes, all subiects did prepare,
In mightie tumult to the murmuring drumme,
The multitude did make repaire from farre,
To trie their valour in th'approching warre
  Thirsting to meete their foes on equall ground,
  All hoping in their fall to be renown'd.

195.

With ornaments of warre, the earth did flow,
Glazing the skies with armes resplendent light,
And euery place in aire, shot vp did show
The blood-red crosse, which did conduct to fight
Many faire bands, all men of powerfull might;
  For both of horse and foot, from euery shiere,
  Thicke squadrons daily did in field appeare.

196.

Th'appointed place of generall meeting was
In Essex, on the coast at Tilburie,
To which the people in such troopes did passe,
That with their traine the shores they multiplie
Like Palamedes birds that forme the Y,
 When cloud-like in thicke flockes their flight they take
 Ore Thracian woods, to Strymon's seuen-fold lake.

197.

There pight they downe their tents t'oppose all harmes,
Set vp the royall standards all about,
The faire supporters of *Elizae's* armes,
The rampant lion, and the dragon stout,
And th'ensigne of Saint George, which many a rout
 Of Mars his noble race with conquering hand
 Hath famous made, in many a forren land.

198.

Vnder whose colours like a leauie wood,
The host in seuerall bands digested all
Inrankt about with shot and pike-men stood,
As firme for battell, as a brazen wall,
Who to the workes of death did thirst to fall,
 Inflam'd in heart with burning fire to fight
 For England's virgin, and their countrie's right.

199.

Well did each horse-man teach his horse to run,
To stoope, to stop, to turne, to breake the field,
Well each bold musketier did vse his gun,
Each launceer well his weightie launce did wield,
Each drew his sword and well addrest his shield,
 Teaching each other by this braue array,
 How on their foes they best might giue th'assay.

200.

The sound of fifes, of drums, and trumpets shrill,
And mutuall exhortations for the warre,
All fainting hearts with manly sprite did fill,
And th'armed horse, that smell the fight from farre,
Inraged that the curbing bit should barre
　　Their forwardnesse, with neighing loud did crie
　　For present combat gainst the enemie.

201.

Thus in the field the royall host did stand,
None fainting vnder base timiditie,
But readie bent to vse their running hand
Against the force of forren enemie,
If they should chance t'arriue at Tilburie :

Earle of Lei-
cester.
　　Mongst whom great *Dudlie* bore supreamest sway,
　　Against their foes to lead them on the way.

202.

And as the daughter of the mightie Ioue,
When from the browes of heau'n she takes her flight
Downe to those sonnes of Mars, whom she doth loue,
In her celestiall armes with glorie dight,
To bring them dreadlesse to th'approching fight ;

Rich. Hakluit,
and Stow in
his Annals.
　　So England's empresse, that vndaunted dame,
　　Vnto the campe in glorious triumph came.

203.

Like noble Tomyris, that queene of Thrace,
Deckt in rich vestiments of shining gold,
Vpon a snow-white steed of stately pace,
Mounted aloft she sate, with courage bold,
And in her hand a martiall staffe did hold,
　　Riding from ranke to ranke, and troope to troope,
　　To whom with reuerence all the host did stoope.

204:

Her comely gesture, and her angel's face,
The lodge of pleasure, and of sweet delight,
Did make the souldiers thinke some heauenly grace
Had left Olympus, and with powerfull might
Had come from Ioue, to cheare them vp for fight,
  Her presence did with such high spirit inspire
  Their manly brests, and set their hearts on fire.

205.

And as *Bunduca*, that bold Britaine dame,
When ore this land proud Rome did tyrannize,
Her Britaine's heart with courage to enflame,
Amidst their troopes all arm'd in seemely wise,
Did Pallas-like a pythie speech deuise:
  So our faire queene, bold spirit to infuse
  Through all the host, these princely words did vse:

206.

" Captaines and souldiers, men of worthie fame,
And most admitted to our princely lone,
Thinke, what it is, to win a souldier's name,
And fight the battels of the mightie Ioue,
With safe protection from his power abone,
  Faint thoughts from your stout hearts be farre expell'd,
  And feare of foes with courage bold be quell'd.

207.

If that the foe dare set his foot on land,
We with the best all danger will out dare,
And step by step with you in person stand,
To be a partner with you, in that share,
Which God shall giue vs, be it foule or faire:
  Then by my side like loyall subiects stand,
  And Ioue assist vs with his powerfull hand."

208.

This said from ranke to ranke, she rode about,
Enabling their endeuours for the fight,
And with sweet words from their bold brests blew out
All fainting spirit, and did their hearts excite
With ready hands, to vse their vtmost might:
 Which royall gesture of so faire a queene,
 Would haue inspir'd a coward's heart with spleene.

209.

Thus hauing chear'd the common soulderie,
The cloudie euen began to shut vp day:
Wherefore she backe return'd from Tilburie,
And towards that martiall field did take her way,
Where as that other royall armie lay,
 In which did march the nobles of the land,
 In rich array, each with his seuerall band.

210.

Troopt vp there were in that same strong-arm'd host,
Fortie three thousand perfect in the frame
Of euery fight, who of that time may boast,
And craue inscription in the booke of fame,
T'haue been the guard of so diuine a dame,
 Who for her person only chosen were,
 Martiall'd by *Hunsdon* that true hearted peere.

211.

But while the noble queene her selfe appli'd
T'oppugne the foe, that should her state assaile,
Loe, from the Groyne the blacke fleet was descri'd,
Who now befriended with a gentle gale,
For England's rockie bounds did make full saile,
 Of whom hight captaine *Flemming* first had sight,
 And fled before them with industrious flight.

M. Thomas Flemming.

212.

At Plimmouth port where th'English fleet did lie,
He with full saile came in, and cri'd amaine:
" Weigh vp your ankors, hoise your sailes on high;
For like *Ortigian . Delos* on the maine,
Behold, th'Iberian fleet from shores of Spaine
   Comes hard at hand, and threatens our decay;
   Then arme, aboord with speed, make no delay."

213.

This said, confusedly the souldiers ran
To ships from shore, earth flew about their feet,
Then weigh'd they vp their ankors, and each man
Put to his helping hand, to bring their fleet
Into the seas, the aduerse foes to meet,
   And though the froward winds did them withstand,
   They warped out their ships by force of hand.

214.

Then might they see from farre vpon the maine,
Like a blacke wood approching more and more,
Their foe-men's tragicke fleet, which in disdaine
With sound of trumpets, drums, and cannons rore,
Came proudly thundring by the rockie shore,
   And with amazement th'English to affright,
   Their souldiers with loud shouts the heau'ns did smite.

215.

They sayling came in order for the fight,
In such a forme on Thetis siluer brest,
As bright-cheekt Cinthia shewes in darkest night,
When stretching out her hornes into the east,
She shewes but halfe her face, and hides the rest,
   Which made a crescent moone vpon the maine,
   Whose hornes eight miles in compasse did containe.

Stow
Ann.

216.

The royall English fleet, which did behold
The martiall order of their nauall traine,
Came sayling forward, and with courage bold,
For England's queene did waue their fleet amaine,
Who in contempt soone waued them againe,
    Whereby defiance with vndaunted pride,
    By cannons cuffe was giuen from either side.

217.

Then bloodie Ennyon thundring out aloud,
Made each one thirst in fight his foe t'offend,
And as fierce fire wrapt vp in dampish cloud,
With violent force the sides thereof doth rend,
And with pale lightning thunder downe doth send;
    So England's warlike fleet wing'd with swift gale,
    Broke through the waues th'Iberians to assaile.

218.

The drums did beat, the trumpets shrill did sound,
Each aduerse force began the furious fight;
Then in the aire the fierce claps did redound
Of cannons hidious rore, and with affright,

The first fight before Plimmouth.

Fire flashing leapt about and maz'd their sight;
    And thus in furie did the fight begin
    With darknesse, horror, death and dreadfull din.

219.

The seas did boile, the buxome aire did swell,
A cloake of clouds did ouercast the skie,
The echoing rockes the fight farre off did tell,
The bullets thicke as haile from clouds on high,
From either side in gloomie smoake did flie,
    And pale-fac'd death vnseene of all the throng,
    Aboue their heads in thicke fumes houering hung.

220.

The fight grew fell, and of ·disaster haps
In each blacke barke reports loud trumpet sings,
While heau'n records the cannons roring claps,
And the darke aire with·grumbling murmurings
Of whistling bullets, borne on fiery wings,
    Whose horrid thunder drown'd the volleies hot
    And lesser noise of many a thousand shot.

221.

Oft did the English with·the winde and weather,
Charge on their foe-men's ships with hot assay,
Who for their safegard bound round vp together,
Pluckt in their hornes and in a roundell lay,
While on their sides the cannon still did play,
    Not daring fight, except to rescue those,
    That beaten were by their bold Britaine foes.

222.

Both the bold *Howards* and lord *Sheffield* hight,
With *Hawkins, Frobisher*, and famous *Drake*,
Braue *Barker, Crosse*, and *Southwell* that stout knight,
There, where the foes the fight most hot did make,
Through danger, dread and death their way did take,
    And gainst their foes did fierie vengeance spit,
    Which did their barks great bulkes in sunder split.

Lord *Thomas Howard* now Earle of Suffolke.

223.

They brake into the midst of Spaine's blacke fleet,
Opposing dreadfull death to win renowne,
As when in skies the earth-bred brothers meet,
When Boreas flying about with·stormie frowne,
Doth cuff the clouds, and brings his brothers downe;
    For with high spirit, heau'n did their hearts inspire,
    T'assaile the foes and burne their fleet with fire.

224.

Renowned *Howard*, England's admirall,
Longing to see the Castile king's disgrace,
Their stoutest hearts with terror did appall,
Who meeting with his foe-men face to face,
Vnto his furie made them all giue place,
   Breaking so farre into the fleet alone,
   That from the aduerse foes he scarce was knowne.

225.

Where in the midst of danger vncontrol'd,
Vpon the vpper decke he stood on high,
From whence, when as from far he did behold
One of his captaines, who did wafting lie
Without the danger of the enemie,
   Out of a cloud of smoake he loud did call,
   Aboue his head wauing his sword withall.

226.

M. George Fenner, This was in the second fight before Portland. *Rich. Hak.* in the end of his 1. volume.

"O *George,*" quoth he, " why dost thou shun the presse?
Report renownes thy name for valiancie;
Then leaue me not alone in this distresse;
But with vndaunted spirit follow me
To gaine the palme of glorious victorie;
   So shall that hope, which I conceiue of thee,
   In this daie's bloodie fight not frustrate bee."

227.

The captaine heard, and like a stormie puffe,
That stoopes from clouds and beats the billowes vnder,
He brake into the fight with cannons cuffe,
And came in height of spirit importing wonder
In clouds of smoake, in fierie flames and thunder,
   With whom did many others giue th'assay,
   And through Spaine's fleet did furrow vp their way.

228.

The foes turn'd head, and made a violent stand,
Both parts stood bent each other to confound;
The cannons thicke discharg'd on either hand
Wrapt clouds in clouds of smoake, which did abound,
And hurl'd their horrid thunder forth to wound;
  But fortune on the foes in fight did frowne,
  And in her ballance, Spaine's hard lot sunke downe.

229.

With fruits of death the fruitlesse waues did flow,
The seas did blush with blood, the ayrie skie
Did swell with grones, and wandring to and fro,
In clouds of smoake the grudging soules did flie
Of slaughtred bodies, that did floting lie
  About the ocean, seeking for their tombes
  In hollow rockes and monsters hungrie wombes.

230.

And in the fight, t'increase the foe-men's harmes,
A ruddie flame from th'English fleet did flie,
Which swiftly seased in his spoilefull armes
The stout viceadmirall of th'enemie,
Who proudly bore her loftie head on high,
  And with the violence of his shamefull flashes,
  Did quickly burne her vpper workes to ashes.

This happened in the third conflict before the Ile of Wight. It was fired by a shot.

231.

A golden bonfire on the siluer waues
Did flote about, whose flame did reach the skies,
While the poore Spaniard and his captiue slaues,
Seeing their tragicke fall before their eies,
Amids t he fire in vaine shriekt out shrill cries;
  For th'horrid fire all mercilesse did choake,
  The scorched wretches with infestiue smoake.

232.

Many tall ships, that did in greatnesse passe
The greatest of our fleet, did fall in fight,
Mongst whom, that faire galeon surprised was,
In which renowned *Valdes*, that stout knight,
With other captaines of approoued might,
　　Did yeeld themselues and all their golden treasure
　　To noble *Drake*, to be at his good pleasure.

233.

Three famous conflicts, in three seuerall daies,
Elizae's hardie captaines did maintaine,
And by their valour won eternall praise,
Oft turning into flight the fleet of Spaine,
With dreadfull fire, and cannon's deadly bane,
　　Who now t'effect what they did vainely boast
　　Houer'd twixt Calice and the English coast.

234.

There cast they ankor, and conuei'd with speed
Swift notice to the prince of Parma hight,
Who thither should repaire, as was decreed,
And while each aduerse fleet stood hot in fight,
For England he should passe with all his might,
　　For which intent he had prepar'd before,
　　Foure hundred ships vpon the Belgicke shore.

235.

But noble *Seimer* in the foe-men's sight,
With *Iustin* of Nassau, that Belgian bold,
And worthie *Winter*, that vndaunted knight,
With their tall ships on th'ocean vncontrol'd,
About the Belgicke strand strong gard did hold,
　　Whose proud afront the foes did daunt so sore,
　　That not a ship durst launch from off the shore.

236.

Yet the stout prince of Parma fondly led
With hope, that *Allen*, that false fugitiue,
Sent from proud *Sixtus* to adorne his head
With faire *Elizae's* crowne, in vaine did striue
With all his power, his purpose to atchieue;
  And vnto Dunkirk came with all his force,
  To put in practise his intended course.

Allen was made Cardinall for that purpose.

237.

Meane time the fleet, that did expect his aide,
Before French Calice did at ankor lie,
And now the chearefull day began to vade,
And Vulcan's louely Venus mounting high,
Appear'd for euening starre in easterne skie,
  Whereby both aduerse fleets did cease from fight,
  And rendred place vnto th'approching night.

238.

But when soft sleepe, the carelesse thoughts did bind
Of others, that secure in cabbins lay,
Each English leader in his labouring mind
Did fashion counsels, how to giue th'assay,
And driue from thence their foe-men's fleet away,
  Who there did purpose by the shore to lie,
  That from the prince they might haue fresh supplie.

239.

Amongst themselues our captaines did agree,
That eight small ships with artificiall fire,
Amidst the Spanish fleet should driuen bee
In dead of night, to execute their ire
Vpon the foes, that did sweet sleepe desire:
  Which dreadfull stratagem against the foe,
  Stout *Yong* and valiant *Prowse* did vndergoe.

240.

The time came on, the drowzie night did frowne,
Who clasping th'earth's wide bounds with sable wings,
Vpon the seas did powre grim darknesse downe,
. While sleepe, that vnto care sweet comfort brings,
· In quiet slumber, husht all watchfull things;
   And then the ships all fir'd for the euent,
   Amongst the foes with winde and tide were sent.

241.

Through foggie clouds of night's Cymmerian blacke,
A glimmering light the watch did first espie,
Which drifting fast vpon the sea-god's backe,
And to the Spanish fleete approching nigh,
Burst out in flames into the darkesome skie,
   Glazing the heau'ns and chasing gloomie night,
   From off the seas with admirable light.

242.

A sudden puffe with force of powder driuen,
Oft blew vp sulphurie flames, in aire on high,
From whence, as if that starres did drop from heau'n,
The liuely sparkes on wings of winde did flie,
Threatning confusion to the enemie;
   Who startled from their sleepe, shriekt out th'alarme
   To euery ship, to shun such dismall harme.

243.

Th'Iberians drown'd before in sweet repose,
With feare affrighted from their naked rest,
Their eye-lids wanting weight one winke to close,
Beheld the fire on Neptune's burning brest,
Which trembling horror in their hearts imprest;
   For floting towards them with fearefull flashes,
   It threatned sore to burne their ships to ashes. .

244.

Then with disorder euery one did cut
Their blacke pitch'd cables, hoysing sailes with speed,
And from the shore to the maine seas did put,
In hope from present danger to be freed,
That did such terror in their bosomes breed,
  While on the waues the burning ships bright light,
  Did make a sun-shine in the midst of night.

245.

Who being disperst amongst their nauie came,
And like fire-spitting monsters on the maine,
In sable clouds of smoake and threataing flame,
Did fiercely bellow out their deadly bane;
Which horror th'English nauie did maintaine,
  Discharging all their thundring shot together
  Vpon th'Iberian foes with winde and weather.

246.

The horrid noise amaz'd the silent night,
Repowring downe blacke darknesse from the skie,
Through which th'affrighted Spaniard with blind flight,
His friends from foes not able to descrie,
Vpon the darkesome waues did scattered flie;
  In which disturbance driuen with winde and weather,
  Spaine's chiefe galiasse fell foule vpon another.

247.

Which all vnable to escape with flight,
The startled fleet did leaue alone forlorne,
Keeping aloofe at sea, all that sad night;
But when from th'east the opall-coloured morne
With golden light the ocean did adorne,
  The English fleet Spaine's great galliasse did spie,
  Which cast vpon a sandie shoale did lie.

248.

Whom captaine *Preston* valiantly did bord,
Sent from the fleet in his long boat well man'd,
Which with an hundred hardie men was stor'd,
Who to the face of death oppos'd did stand,
About the ship vsing their readie hand,
  Gainst whose assault at first th'Iberian foes,
  With proud resistance did themselues oppose.

249.

For *Hugo de Moncada*, valiant man
With noble courage did the fight maintaine,
Till through his wounded forebead's hardned pan,
A fatall shot with bullets deadly bane,
Made open passage to the liuely braine,
  Who being slaine, to shun the slaughtering sword,
  Most of the residue leapt ouer bord.

250.

Thus great king *Philip's* mountaine-like galliasse,
In which three hundred slaues lug'd at the oare,
And twice two hundred armed men did passe,
Was soone despoil'd of all her golden store
By a small band of men on Calice shore,
  Which fiftie thousand duckets did containe,
  Of the rich treasure of the king of Spaine.

251.

Meane time the blacke fleet floting on the maine,
The night before disperst with foule affright,
In hope her former purpose to obtaine,
Return'd againe from base inglorious flight,
Arang'd in order for the nauall fight,
  Which in diuided squadrons th'Englishfleet,
  With hot incounter furiously did meet.

252.

Who bound vp round together in a ring,
Lay close in their defence against their foe;
But as the southerne blasts in budding spring,
When Auster's swelling cheekes do ouerflow
In handfuls thicke the blossomes downe to blow;
   So thicke and dreadfully did slaughter flie
   From th'English fleet amongst the enemie.

This conflict being the fourth and last, was before Greueling.

253.

Then had th'Iberians dread, their pride did bow,
Their foes by valour brake their nauall round,
And as a torrent from an hil's steepe brow,
Clad in fresh showers and thunder's fearefull sound,
Beares all before it in the plaine land ground;
   So did they beat from off their natiue bounds,
   Spain's mighty fleet with cannons scathful wounds.

254.

And where the skirmish was propos'd most hot,
Their valiant *Drake* did breake into the fight,
And though his ship were pierc'd with wounding shot
Twice twentie times; yet with vndaunted might
He horriblie did plie their sudden fright,
   And with wide wounds the hollow keeles did batter
   Of three tall ships betwixt the winde and water.

255.

Then in despaire with hands and weeping eies,
To heau'n the wretches prai'd for their escape,
And to some saint of heau'n with open cries,
Each one in blind deuotion prayers did shape;
But all in vaine, the gulfie flood did gape,
   And in the deepe of his deuouring wombe,
   Both men and ships did suddenly intombe.

256.

The rest all daunted with such vncouth sight,
From spoile to saue their fleet no time did spare,
But hoysing saile betooke themselues to flight,
Cursing sterne fate, that brought their fleet so farre,
To be despoil'd in such successelesse warre;
    And after all their boasting backe recoile,
    With emptie hands vnto their natiue soyle.

257.

They heartlesse fled, but in their hastie flight,
Two great galeons of captiu'd Portugale,
The huge Saint *Philip*, and Saint *Matthew* hight,
Great *Seymer* and stout *Winter* did so gall
With wounding cuffe of cannons fierie ball,
    That on the Belgian coast by friends forsaken,
    They with their captaines by their foes were taken.

258.

Meane time the English with full saile did plie
The manage of the foes inglorious flight,
And as high stomack'd hounds, that with full crie
Pursue the fearefull game, do take delight
To pinch the haunch behind with eager bite;
    So did *Elizae's* fleet pursue the foes
    With shouts of men, and bullets banefull blowes.

259.

They all array'd in warre's vermillion,
Did chace them to those seas of stormes and thunder,
Ouer whose waues in heau'ns pauillion,
Amongst those many golden workes of wonder,
A dragon keepes two wrathfull beares asunder,
    And there they left them, in those seas to drowne,
    Returning backe with conquest and renowne.

260.

They gone, the wretched foes in wofull case
Helplesse, perceiuing by sterne fortune's doome,
Their action ended in extreame disgrace,
And in fame' stead, for which they forth did come,
Finding but wounds to cure when they came home,
  Did curse the ordinance of mightie Ioue,
  Gainst whom with their huge strength in vaine they strowe.

261.

But while at sea, all were to labour giuen,
Securely rigging vp their crazed ships,
Al-seeing loue' did worke their banes in heau'n;
For in an instant from his heau'nly lips,
From pole to pole a winged message skips,
  And posting round about the earth's great ball,
  From th'house of stormes th'Eolian slaues did call.

262.

Then furious Auster, Ioue's command once giuen;
With Eurus', Zephirus, and Boreas ruffe,
Stoopt from the cloudie corners of the beau'n
Vpon those seas, and with a violent puffe,
The tumbling billowes all on heapes did cuffe;
  And raving gainst the rookes with hidious rore,
  Wrapt waues in waues, and hurl'd them on the shore.

263.

Meane while night's curtaines steept in Stygian blacke,
The crystall battlements of heau'n did hide;
Then Ioue did thunder, and the heau'ns did cracke,
Pale lightning leapt about on euery side,
The clouds inconstant flood-gates opened wide,
  And nought, but mists, baile, raine, dark stormes and thunder,
  Did fall from heau'n vpon the salt seas vnder.

264.

The white froth-foaming flood began to rane,
And enter combate with the fleet of Spaine,
Hurring it head-long on the mountaine-wane,
Now from the shores into the roring maine,
And now from thence vnto the shores againe,
  While all the stoutest sea-men quake and quiuer,
  Lest winde-driuen waues their ships in sunder shiuer:

265.

" Heere strike, strike, sirs, the top mast:" one doth crie,
Another saies : " Vale misene and sprit saile:"
And heere a third bids : " Let the maine sheate flie:"
All fall to worke themselves from death to baile,
Some cut the saile-cloaths, some againe do haile
  The saile yards downe, while others pumpe with paine,
  Sending the seas into the seas againe.

266.

Heere one vp lifted on a mountaine steepe,
By dreadfull flashing of heau'ns lightning bright,
With pallid feare lookes downe vpon the deepe
Into a pit, as deepe and blacke in sight,
As Tartarus the lothsome brood of night,
  In whose wide gulfie mouth he thinkes to drowne,
  Seeing the ship all topsie turning downe:

267.

Another heere in sandie shoale doth lie,
With mountaine waues on all sides walled round,
And seemes from hell to see the loftie skie,
Looking, when wallowing waues with windie bound,
In that deepe pit the vessell would confound,
  Till with the lustie waue, the mounting ship
  From thence to heau'n doth in a moment skip.

268.

The poore sad sailers beaten out of .breath
With toilesome paine, and with long watching worne,
Through feare, the feeble consort of cold death,
Not knowing, alas, which way themselues to turne,
With wofull cries their fatall fall did mourne,
  And cast their eyes to heau'n, where, what was seene,
  Was blacke as hell, as if no heau'n had been.

269.

Heere the greene billowes bounding gainst a ship,
Vncaukes the keele, and with continuall waste,
Washing the pitch away, the seames vnrip,
While th'angrie tempest, with a boistrous blast,
Beares the false stem away, springs the maine mast,
  And breaking downe the decke, doth passage win
  For the next surging sea to enter in.

270.

Then all amaz'd shriekes out confused cries,
While the seas rote doth ring their dolefull knell,
Some call to heau'n for helpe with weeping eies,
Some moane themselues, some bid their friends farewell,
Some idols-like in horrors senselesse dwell,
  Heere in sad silence one his faint heart showes,
  Another there doth thus his feare disclose:

271.

" Thrice happie they, whose hap it was in fight
Against the foes to fall, when others stood :
Ye conquering English, causers of our flight,
Why were your swords not bath'd in my deare blood;
And why did I not perish in the flood?
  Where braue *Moncada* di'd with many more,
  Whose bodies now do swim about the shore."

272.

This said, a waue, that neuer brake asunder,
But mounting vp, as if with loftie frowne
It view'd the working of the waters vnder,
Came like a ruin'd mountaine falling downe,
And with his weight the wretched ship did drowne,
   Which sinking, in the gulfe, did seeke her graue
   And neuer more appear'd aboue the waue.

273.

Many more ships did perish in the deepe,
Some downe from top of waues to sandie ground,
All rent and torne the angrie surge did sweepe,
Some the winde-turned water whirling round,
In the blacke whirle-poole helplesse did confound,
   And some with boystrous billowes bruz'd and battred,
   In sunder split, aboue the waues were scattred.

274.

The other ships, that huge of building were,
Whose bulkes the billow could not beat asunder,
And whom the furious storme perforce did beare
Amongst the raging seas, now vp, now vnder,
Though through the waues, they wrought it out with wonder,
   Yet many gainst the rockes the surge did beare,
   And with the fruitlesse sands some couered were.

275.

Heere fiue at once round set with surging waters,
Sticke fast in quick-sands, sinking more and more,
There fiue againe the furious billow batters,
Being hurried head-long with the south-west blore,
In thousand pieces gainst great Albion's shore,
   Whereby the fruitlesse waues tost to and fro,
   With fruits of ship-wracke euery where did flow.

276.

Here one fast holding by the broken shiuers
Of some wrackt ship, to heau'n lifts vp his eies,
There drifting on the mast, one quakes and quiuers,
Another heere his outstretcht armes applies
By slight of swimming on the waues to rise;
　But all in vaine, the billowes breake in sunder
　Aboue their heads, and beate their bodies vnder.

277.

Heere with sustentiue palmes themselaes to saue,
Two crawling vp a cliffe, one backe is borne
By the next surge in seas to seeke his graue,
The other by the billow rent and torne
Vpon the ragged rocke, is left forlorne,
　Where in his luke-warme blood he sprawling lies,
　And th'haplesse food of hungrie fowles he dies.

278.

The rest, that did the Irish coast obtaine,
And had escap'd the furie of the flood,
By those wilde people wofully were slaine,
The Irish swift of feete, and flesht in blood,
Who thicke vpon the shore together stood
　With deadly darts, to strike each foe-man dead;
　That 'boue the waue did beare his fainting head.

279.

Great loue's command, perform'd vpon the foes,
Th'Eolian king call'd home his windes againe;
Then ceast the storme ; then did the seas disclose
The armes, the painted robes, and spoiles of Spaine,
Which heere and there did flote vpon the maine,
　By England, Ireland, Norway, Normandie,
　Where Ioue did act their fleet's blacke tragedie.

280.

For of one hundred thirtie foure faire keele,
But fiftie three did greet their natiue soile,
Of thirtie thousand men arm'd with bright steele,
The greatest number after all their toile,
Did perish in great Neptune's wrackfull spoile,
  And all the prince of Parmae's mightie bands
  Return'd with shame, disgrace and emptie hands.

281.

Thus our *Elizae's* boasting enemie,
Who in vaine pride did blacke their tragicke fleet,
And brought ostents of threatning destinie,
In top of all their hope with shame did meet,
And fell beneath the conquering virgin's feet;
  Vnable many yeares to cure againe
  The wounds, which in this warre they did sustaine.

282.

A million of gold, one halfe paid in readie money, the other halfe to be paid when any famous port was taken in England.

Thus Rome's proud *Sixtus*, England's mortall foe,
Who towards the conquest of this emperie,
A million with his blessing did bestow,
And did presage vndoubted victorie
With seeming future searching prophesie,
  Nor with his holy blessing, nor his gold
  This mightie fleet from falling could vphold.

283.

But while Rome's *Sixtus*, twixt foule shame and feare,
For such great losse gainst fortune did exclaime,
Fame through the world triumphantly did beare
This glorious act in our *Elizae's* name,
Who glorifying not in her foe-men's shame,
  With bounteous grace did vse the victorie
  To her proud foes in their captiuitie.

284.

The baser sort, though made her people's scorne,
Yet of her bountie she from death did spare,
The better sort as her owne liege-men borne,
All common benefits did freely share,
And tooke the solace of the open aire,
   Whom she, though subiects of a mightie foe,
   To his disgrace triumphing did not show.

285.

Vnder a canopie of gold wide spread
In chariot throne, like warre's triumphant dame,
With crowne imperiall on her princely head,
Borne by two milke-white steeds in state she came
To Paul's high temple, while with loud exclaime,
   The people in her passage all about
   From loyall hearts their auies loud did shout.

286.

Where round about the temple's battlements
Hung th'ensignes of her vanquisht enemie,
As gracefull trophies, and fit ornaments,
T'adorne with state and greater maiestie,
The triumph of her noble victorie,
   Which in the people's sight made pleasing showes,
   Who laugh'd to scorne the threatning of her foes.

287.

But she meeke prince dismounting from her throne,
With iuorie-fingered-hands vplifted high,
On humble knees, ascribed vnto none
The honor of this great deed's dignitie,
But to th'Olympian king's great deitie,
   Who 'boue the rest, that scepter's states did weeld
   Her as his chosen, did from danger sheeld.

When many were brought out of Ireland and other parts with halters about their neckes, she sent them into Spaine at her owne charge.

An. Reg. 31

288.

O matchlesse prince; though thy pure maiden breast
Retain'd that spirit of magnanimitie,
That only brau'd proud Rome's world-brauing beast,
Yet didst thou not with vaunting vanitie
Abuse the glorie of thy victorie:
  But after all thy high atchieuements wonne,
  To heau'ns great King gau'st praise, of what was done.

289.

Which he accepting as an humble show
Of her milde meeknesse, did so glorifie
The fame of this high conquest gainst the foe,
That her great name, since that great victorie,
Yet liues a staine vnto her enemie;
  Yea many that beneath his yoke did grone,
  Then su'd for succour at her princely throne.

290.

Prince *Don Antonio*, heire suppos'd by right
Of all consents to *Don Sabastian*, slaine
Against the barbarous Moore in bloodie fight,
Exil'd his countrie by the power of Spaine,
Of his hard hap did vnto her complaine,
  Imploring aid at her assistant hands,
  To free his countrie from Iberian bands.

291.

The noble virgin with remorsefull eyne,
Viewing that wretched state all rent asunder,
To pitie did her princely heart inclíne,
And to the seas sent those two sonnes of thunder,
That in the world had wrought so many a wonder,
  Renowned *Drake*, and *Norrice*, worthie wight,
  With *Don Antonio* to obtaine his right.

292.

With many a worthie souldier shipt from shore,
The stormie seas wilde wildernesse they plow'd,
And though the wrinckled waues rouz'd in rough rore,
Began to bandie billowes, waxing proud;
Yet th'English nauie, through tumultuous crowd
  Of darksome surges, did swift passage sweepe
  Vnto the shores of the Galician deepe.

293.

Where taking land, as bees from craníed rockes
Breake through the clefts, and to increase their store,
About the fields flie euery way in flockes:
So from their ships the souldiers more and more
In mightie tumult multipli'd the shore,
  Where vncontrol'd themselues they did conioyne
  In martiall troopes, and marched towards the Groyne.

294.

Which to defend from spoile the fainting foes
By need constrain'd, at first forth boldly came,
And in the field our forces did oppose;
But being with furie charg'd by men of fame,
Vnto the towne they backe retir'd with shame,
  Whom to the gates the English did pursue,
  And with smart stripes did reach them as they flew.

295.

Nor could their strong erected walles withstand
The fierce assaylants, who with nimble sprite
Did scale their bulwarkes, and by force of hand
Did turne th'Iberians into shamefull flight,
Although with most aduantage they did fight,
  Of whom fiue hundred on the dust fell dead,
  The rest to th'vpper towne amazed fled.

An. eodem.
31. Portugale voyage, taken out of the discourse written by *Colonel Anthonie Winkefield,* imployed in the same voyage.

296.

The towne surpris'd, stor'd in the same were found
The sterne designes of *Philip's* raging teene;
For euery place with shipping did abound,
Which for another fleet prepar'd had beene,
Intended once againe against our queene;
　　But by despoiling of this conquered towne,
　　King *Philip's* hopes they in despaire did drowne.

297.

From hence the victors, in *battalia* led
To th'vpper Groyne by *Norrice* noble knight,
To which the foes had for their safegard fled,
Did march with speed, and in their foes despight
Before the towne their warlike tents did pight,
　　Where in strong battery many daies they lay,
　　And to remoue them none durst giue th'assay.

298.

Yet by the towne six miles from off the coast,
The count *D'Andrada* with his armie lay,
Betwixt Petrance and the English hoast,
Who boasting with his powers to driue away
The foes from Groyne; yet durst not giue th'assay;
　　But kept aloofe intrencht within the ground,
　　With strong built barracadoes fenced round.

299.

Which, when braue *Norrice* heard, with *Darke's* consent
Nine regiments amongst the rest he chose,
And whirlewinde-like with furie forth he went,
Marching with winged pace vpon the foes,
On their owne ground with them to bandie blowes,
　　On whom hight *Edward Norrice*, lion like,
　　Gaue the first charge with his sharpe pointed pike.

300.

Which with such furious force he did pursue,
That ouer thrusting downe he fell to ground,
At which aduantage in the foe-men flew,
And in the head the valiant knight did wound,
Whom in extremitie begirted round
  By eager foes, his brother with strong hands
  Rescu'd from danger, death, or captiue bands.

301.

Then noble *Sidnie*, *Wingfield*, *Middleton*,
Each with his band made in vpon the foes,
Then *Hinder*, *Fulford*, and stout *Erington*,
Stood firme in fight, and in the violent close
Amongst th'Iberians dealt such martiall blowes,
  That their chiefe leaders in the field were slaine,
  Or wounded, could no more the fight maintaine.

302.

The other fled, and th'English did pursue
With speedie haste, a number fell in chace,
Three miles the dust, with blood they did imbrue,
Some downewards groueling did the ground embrace,
Some vpwards spread, did shew death's gastly face,
  Three mi les in compasse on that haplesse soile,
  Did flow with fruits of blood, of death, and spoile.

303.

The valiant victors, that did backe returne,
Loaded with golden bootie from the chace,
The fruitfull countrie round about did burne
With wastfull fire, which did in euery place
Townes, towers, woods, groues with hungrie flames embrace,
  Whose people did from farre behold the flame
  With teare-torne eyes; yet could not helpe the same.

304.

Thus fam'd-grac'd *Norrice* crown'd with victorie,
Vnto the Groyne returned backe againe,
And with more worth his deed to amplifie,
King *Philip's* standard with the armes of Spaine,
Which from his foes in fight he did constraine,
  Before him in his march aduanced was,
  As with his troopes he towards the Groyne did passe.

305.

Where he not long the voyage did delay
For Portugale in *Don Antonioe's* right;
But left the Groyne and lanched off to sea,
Where with that noble earle great *Essex* hight,
His brother, and stout *Williams* that bold knight,
  He happily did meet, who with full gale
  To Portugale together forth did saile.

306.

And in a storme, as people sent from heau'n,
That nation vnto freedome to restore,
They by the tempest gainst Peniche driuen,
Vp to the waste in waters raging sore,
Through death and danger waded to the shore;
  Where when they came vpon the marine-sands,
  In spight of foes they martiall'd vp their bands.

307.

For when the *Conde De Fuentes* came
With his proud troopes t'afront them in the fight,
The valiant *Deuorax* in *Elizae's* name
Before the castle, and the towne in sight,
Did charge vpon them with such violent might,
  That horror spread, through each Iberian troope,
  To seruile feare made stoutest hearts to stoope.

308.

None durst abide, with foule retreat all fled,
Free passage to the victors open lay,
Who towards the towne did march, from whence, in dread
Of their approch, the people fled away,
And left the towne vnto their foes for prey,
  Whereby the castle taken with the same,
  They did possesse in *Don Antonioe's* name.

309.

From hence towards Lisbon they did march forthright,
And in the way the noble generall
Did enter Torres Vedras, in despight
Of that vaine boast of the proud cardinall,
Who gaue his faith to them of Portugale
  T'oppose him in the field, though with delay,
  He kept aloofe, and durst not giue th'assay.

310.

To Lisbon gates, troopt vp in martiall pace
The English went, and in the suburbs pight
Elizae's ensignes in the foes disgrace,
In hope that *Don Antonio* would excite
The people to his aide, and in his right
  Shake off the bondage which they did sustaine,
  Thereby their late-lost freedome to regaine.

311.

But they ignoble kind of dunghill brood,
With female hearts, more cold in valiancie
Then naked Indians, who with losse of blood
Haue often sought in midst of miserie,
To free themselues from seruile slauerie;
  When such stout champions in their cause did stand,
  Durst not appeare to vse their helping hand.

312.

The sweets of libertie, for which the Iew
Withstood stout *Titus*, mightie *Cæsar's* sonne,
The loyall loue, that th'ancient Britaine drew
To those great deeds for *Caratacous* donne,
When Rome's *Ostorius* did this land orerun,
   The heartlesse Portugale could not excite,
   To hazard fortune gainst the foes in fight.

313.

For many daies the English with renowne,
Gainst death and danger did themselues oppose,
And gaue assault vnto the chiefest towne,
By their high fortitude t'imbolden those,
That liu'd in dread of their insulting foes;
   And to performe their promis'd force for fight
   Against the foes, in *Don Antonio's* right.

314.

Yet at their hands no helpe to this assay
Elizae's famous captaines could obtaine,
Who wanting power their valour to display,
When the sad prince *Antonio* all in vaine
The people's helpe had sought, and none could gaine,
   Remou'd their martiall power gainst Lisbon bent,
   And towards Cascais vnto their nauie went.

315.

Where valiant *Drake* with his triumphant fleet,
Came vp the riuer as it was decreed,
And with the armie at Cascais did meet,
Whose meeting to the foes such feare did breed,
That at their first approch, the towne with speed
   And castle both without long batterie,
   Did stoope their pride to th'English valianoie.

316.

And where the foes that proudly ranged were
Fast by Saint Iulian's, readie arm'd for fight,
Had broadly misreported, that with feare
Of their approch their foes with foule affright,
Themselues had taken to inglorious flight,
 Vndaunted *Norrice* with his martiall traine,
 Did towards Saint Iulian's backe returne againe.

317.

And valiant *Essex* this bold challenge sent,
As combatant in his great soueraigne's name,
To know, who durst of noble borne descent,
Stand forth amongst the rest to fight for fame,
And trie by blowes the cause, for which they came;
 Or if that eight to eight, or ten to ten,
 Durst tempt their fate in fight like valiant men.

In *Colonel
Wingfield's*
discourse, pag.
148, in the se-
cond volume
of *R. Hak.*
Nauigations.

318.

But through th'Iberian armie not a man
Stood forth as combatant in single fight;
For when the generall with his troops began
T'approch their campe, before he came in sight,
They fled away befriended by the night,
 Nor stai'd they till they made great Lisbon gate,
 Their safe asylum gainst all aduerse fate.

319.

Meane time, that sea-fam'd captaine worthie *Drake*,
Twice fortie martiall ships well man'd for fight,
In seas did sinke, did burne, did spoile and take;
Mongst whom Saint *Iohn de Colerado* hight,
Third vnto none in building and in might,
 He burnt with raging fire of flaming brand,
 And sunk her bulke in shoales of swallowing sand.

320.

Thus though the English disappointed were
Of seating *Don Antonio* in the throne,
Through that base female stomackt nation's feare,
Whose sad distresse no future time shall moane,
Though vnder tyrant's yoke their spirits groane;
   Yet fame, the prize on which they ment to pray,
   In their swift barks with them they brought away.

321.

And being launcht into the sea's blacke brest,
By stormie puffe of Auster's blustring blore,
They carried were with violent storme opprest,
'Bout Bayon iles, and towards the sandie shore
With swift winde-swelling sailes their nauie bore,
   Where both the generals on the barren strand,
   Did with two thousand souldiers put to land.

322.

And as the wealthie fields of ripe-growen corne,
Which ouercharg'd with seed their heads do bow
Are by the reaper downe in handfuls borne,
Who for that meed, which th'owne doth allow,
Still plies his labour with a sweatie brow;
   So th'English did with sword and fire despoile
   The fruitfull plentie of that pleasant soile.

323.

That strong street-fenced towne, Vigo by name,
In ashie heapes on ground did groueling lie,
And on the swift wings of a golden flame,
The vaile-inriched Borsis mounting high,
With blazing shine did glase the cloudie skie,
   While eight miles compasse Vulcan's fierie fume
   Dame Ceres gifts did in the vales consume.

324.

Thus grac'd with noble conquest and rich spoile,
The valiant victors with their royall fleet,
Did passe the seas vnto their natiue soile,
Where falling prostrate at their soueraigne's feet,
With glorious prize the virgin they did greet, .
  The praise of which what they to her had giuen,
  She gaue againe vnto the King of heau'n.

325.

Vpon the deepes of Neptune's large command,
Many more high exploits were daily done,
And from the vanquisht foes by force of hand,
Many faire ships of many a hundred tunne
Full fraught with wealthie prise were daily wonne,
  For forren pens speake wonder of the fame,
  And rich spoiles gotten in *Elizae's* name.

Huighen van Linschoten and many others.

326.

That famous horse-man, launce-fam'd *Clifford* hight,
The great Heröe noble *Cumberland*,
About th'Azores in his foes despight
Did scoure the seas, and with three ships command
Each famous port vpon that slimie strand :
  For those few English, which he did assemble
  In three small ships, made all Tercera tremble.

Anno eodem 31. Taken out of the discourse written by that excellent enginer *M. Edward Wright.*

327.

Vpon the walles of Fayall, that strong towne,
Which huge mount Pyco ouerlookes from west,
He by strong hand with England's crosse did crowne,
And gainst that strand vpon the seas broad brest,
Many great hulkes with blacke rouz'd waues distrest
  Of th'Indian fleet, full fraught with prise for Spaine,
  He brought to England ore the broad-backt maine.

328.

Yet he alone braue champion euer prest,
For his faire mistresse to defend her right,
Did not triumph on Neptune's watrie brest;
But many more, all men of famous might,
The vtmost parts of earth and seas did smite
   With loud report that England's bounds did keep,
   A virgin, that was ladie of the deepe.

329.

Anno Reg. 32. Fame-winged *Drake* and *Hawkins*, that bold knight,
Vpon the coast of Spaine the foes did dare,
When at the Groyne that host lay readie dight
To passe the seas, to dispossesse Nauarre,
Gainst whom th'vnholy league did warre prepase;
   But while the royall fleet of our faire queene
   Appeer'd at sea, they durst not then be seene.

330.

Nor durst that captaine of the Spanish fleet,
Th'insulting *Don Alonso Bacan* hight,
Elizae's ships in equall battell meet;
But if by chance he found the ods in fight,
Then proudly would he vse his vtmost might:
   Yet England's blacke reuenge, alone, at length
   Did worke him shame with all his nauall strength.

331.

An. Reg. 33. For famous *Greenuile* sayling neere to Flores
Taken out of In the Reuenge of our *Elizae's* fleet,
the discourse Obscur'd from sight with th'ilands of th'Azores,
penned by Sir Spaine's great Armada did vntimely meet;
Walter
Raughley. Yet with sharpe welcome their approch did greet,
   For rich reuenge he made vpon his foes;
   Though he his life in his Reuenge did lose.

332.

Ten thousand men in three and fiftie saile,
Did in his barke alone begirt him round,
And fifteene howers space did neuer saile
With thundring shot his ship's weake wombe to wound,
Both him, and her in th'ocean to confound,
  Whom with twice fiftie men he did oppose,
  And did inferre dire slaughter mongst his foes.

333.

The great San *Philip*, that mount Etna like,
Lay spitting fierie vengeance gainst her foes,
In fight her entertaine did so dislike,
That she her sad mishap did soone disclose,
And fainting made retreate, to shun foule blowes,
  While the amaz'd Iberians stroue to saue
  Her leaking wombe from sinking in the waue.

Some say this
ship foundred.

334.

Like as a goodly hart begirted round,
With eager hounds, that thirst to see him fall,
Tir'd in the toile, turnes head and stands his ground,
And with fell blowes the dogs do so appall,
That in the end he makes his way through all :
  So noble *Greenuile* round besieg'd in fight,
  Brake through their squadrons with admired might.

335.

Saint *Michael* hight, and *Cyuil*'s great Ascension,
With th'admirall of the hulkes, three ships of fame,
Each of the which so large was in dimension,
That *Greenuil*'s ship, that bore Vindicta's name,
Did seeme a skiffe compar'd vnto the same,
  With crosse-barre shot in fight he did so wound,
  That wallowing waues their hugenesse did confound.

336.

In this fight there were fiue ships of great burthen sunke, 1000 men, and many of especiall note slaine.

Against them all she proudly did enthunder,
Vntill her masts were beaten ouerbord,
Her deckes downe raz'd, her tackle cut asunder,
Vntill her shot and powder, that were stor'd
In her maim'd bulke could scarce one charge afford;
    Yea when her sides were euened with the waue
    She would not yeeld, but still her foes did braue.

337.

And had not fate inforc'd her noble knight,
To sinke downe senselesse in her hollow wombe,
Euen he alone would haue withstood their might:
But who, alas, can contradict the doome
Of wilfull fate, when time prefix'd is come;
    From musket's mouth spit forth with vengefull breath,
    A fatall shot did wound the knight to death.

338.

And at his death, to shew his mightie mind,
Being from his ship conuei'd amongst his foes,
Feeling th'approch of his last houre assign'd,
As one not fear'd in all externall showes
To leaue this life, whose end should end his woes,
    With manly lookes amidst his enemies
    These words he spake, ere death did close his eies:

339.

This he spake in Spanish, recorded in the 99 chap. of *Iohn Huighen van Linschoten.*

" In peace of mind I bid the world adew,
For that a souldier's death I truly die,
And to my royall queene haue paid her due,
Since by my timelesse death I glorifie
My God, and her against her enemie:
    Which to my grace, since fame to her shall tell,
    With ioy I bid the world and her farewell."

340.

Thus fame's faire finger in his manly prime,
With honor'd touch in death did close his eies,
Whose glorie shall outlast the prints of time,
Caru'd in his brow, and like the sunne in skies,
In darkest times each day shall fresh arise;
 For to my verse if heauen such grace do giue,
 True noble knight, thy name shall euer liue.

341.

His ghost regardlesse did not passe away
Without reuenge: for where in haplesse fight,
Vnhappie fate did worke his liue's decay,
There *Frobisher* and *Borrough* that bold knight,
To his Iberian foes did worke despight;
 For by th'Azores on the stormie maine,
 Many a faire price they daily did obtaine.

An. Reg. 34.
Out of M. R.
Hak. in the
last part of his
second vo-
lume.

342.

The Indian barkes at th'ilands they did stop,
For which, that naked people which adore
The king of flames in steepe Olympus top,
With wicked steele their grandames ribs had tore,
To glut their spacious wombes with golden ore,
 Whom *Frobisher* did send with all their treasure,
 To be dispos'd at his *Elizae's* pleasure.

343.

Meane time, stout *Crosse* and *Borrough* valiant knight,
Against that monster of the fleet of Spaine,
The *Madre Dios*, did a noble fight
Before those ilands many houres maintaine,
Whom by plaine strength, at length they did constraine
 To stoope her pride, and hazarding the might
 Of twice three hundred, boorded her in fight.

344.

Who to inrich their noble enterprise
With a small world of treasure did abound,
Ten smaller ships fraught with her merchandise,
Which sto'd within her spacious bulke were found,
Arriued safe in Thamis siluer sound;
　For fifteene hundred tunne she did containe,
　And thirtie foot she drew within the maine.

345.

They tooke likewise the Santa Clare in fight,
Which from the Indian east for Spaine was bound,
And on the ilands in their foe-men's sight,
With flames of hungrie fire they did confound
The Santa Cruze, which did with wealth abound,
　Making each creeke and corner of the maine
　To know the rule of their *Elisae's* raigne.

346.

But should I heere assay to sing of those,
Who to eternifie their soueraigne's name,
Renown'd their swords with fall of thousand foes,
Had I a brazen trumpe to sound the same,
Which might out-sound th'eternall trumpe of fame,
　Yet not an age drawne out in length of daies,
　Would me suffice to sing their worthie praise.

347.

Huighen van
Linschoten.
The Belgian author of that large discourse
Of th'Indian trafickes, truly doth explaine
The matchlesse vertue of their natuall force,
And of their high aduentures on the maine,

Iohannes Par-
menius Bu-
daous.
That Saxons Latin muse in loftie straine
　About the world doth sing; yet cruell fate
　Vnto his life did adde too short a date.

348.

For when braue spirit did *Gilbert's* thoughts excite,
To saile the seas to search for worlds vnfound,
This worthie poet with that noble knight
In th'angrie surge, alas, was helplesse drown'd,
And swallow'd vp within the deepe's blacke sound :
   Yet life to *Gilbert* dead, his verse doth giue,
   And his owne name, in his owne verse doth liue.

Anno Dom, 1584. Sir *Humfrey Gilbert.*

349.

But leaue we heere those valiant men, that loue
To diue the deepes of Neptune's high command,
To see the wonders of the mightie Ioue,
And view meane while, with what auspicious hand,
Eliza guides her plentious peopled land,
   Whose royall raigne and bountie debonaire,
   Time's time to come shall count past all compare.

350.

While those bold martialists, that for their fame
In skill of warre affaires were so renown'd,
Did by their swords immortalize her name,
So those graue aged fathers, peeres profound,
In depth of iudgement with wit's laurell crown'd,
   In swaying th'empire's scepter all her daies,
   Did guide her steps in the true path of praise.

351.

Like gods in counsell in the state affaires,
They sate in senate skill'd in all things done,
Deeds past and future, carrying by their cares
Through broken sleepes the course of things begun
Striuing in dead of night the time t'outrun,
   By good aduice, by plots, and counsels close,
   T'oppugne, preuent, and circumuent their foes.

352.

From whom in care of state the reyall maid
Did counsell take, as from the mouth of loue,
Still rul'd with reason, as in power obey'd,
Not led with false opinions fond selfe-loue,
But by their sound aduice did ee p roue,
   How she with lawes respect might best command,
   Seeing Ioue had put the scepter in her hand.

353.

And with intent, that in her maiden brest
A deepe impression of that pregnant wit
In vse of lawes, by vse might be imprest,
Mongst the graue senate she did often sit,
And her conceit to consultation fit:
   All princes that true vertue's race do run,
   The starre-bright light of counsell will not shun.

354.

As the good shepheard with respectiue right
Of his meeke flocke, drownes not the night in sleepe,
Nor spends the compleat day in his delight;
Who distant farre vpon some mountaine steepe,
Yet nere in care them safe from spoile doth keepe:
   So her chiefe care, as carelesse how to please
   Her owne affect; was care of people's ease.

355.

Well did she know, that who would guard and keepe
The state and counsell of a realme aright,
Not vtterly dissolu'd in ease and sleepe,
Or led with loose affection of delight,
They must insist in their owne appetite;
   But their state-charged thoughts in cares begun,
   Through broken sleepes, and easelesse toiles must run.

356.

Yet if she did abstaine from graue affaires,
And found fit time to solace her delay,
With fond delight she did not ease her cares;
But with the ladie muses wont to play,
Or Pallas-like would often spend the day,
  In making wits quaint parlie her best sport,
  Amidst her virgin troope of stately port.

357.

Mongst whom, if some, yet mindfull of her worth,
With iuorie fingers touch do chance to turne
These luckie leaues, I only picke them forth
To grace Ioue's wit-bred brood, the thrice three borne
With their great worth, she dead, left now forlorne,
  That by their power, whence I this verse deriue,
  She may in them, and they in her suruiue.

358.

And yee faire nymphs, that like to angels houer
About the palace of our Britaine king,
That locke the hearts of euery gazing louer
Within your lookes, whence all delight doth spring,
Of this faire queene vouchsafe to heare me sing,
  And let her life, to whom she was vnknowne,
  A Mirrour be for them to gaze vpon.

359.

It was, alas that now it is not so,
Praise-worthie deem'd amongst diuinest dames,
In learning's lore their leasure to bestow,
For which the muses to their lasting fames,
In golden verse might eternize their names;
  But now seduc'd with each mind-pleasing toy
  In learning's liking, few do place their ioy.

360.

Yet she, that could command all ioyes on earth,
With sweets of iudgement suckt from learning, skill
In all delights, did moderate her mirth,
Nor gaue she swinge vnto her princely will
In any pleasure to affect the fill ;
    But with true temperance aduis'd aright,
    She best did loue the meane in each delight.

361.

In musike's skill mongst princes past compare
She was esteem'd ; and yet for that delight
The precious time she did not wholly square, ·
And though in daintie dance she goodly dight
Was matchlesse held for her maiestike sprite ;
    Yet not in dalliance did she go astray,
    Ne yet in dance did dallie out the day.

362.

She with the seed of Ioue, the muses nine,
So frequent was in her yeares youthfull prime,
That she of them had learned power diuine
To quell proud loue, if loue at any time
In her pure brest aloft began to clime,
    The praise of whom so chaste, and yet so faire,
    Enuie's foule selfe not iustly can impaire.

363.

In learning's better part her skill was such,
That her sweet tongue could speake distinctiuely
Greeke, Latin,.Tuscane, Spanish, French, and Dutch:
For few could come in friendly ambasie
From forren parts to greet her maiestie,
    Whom she not answer'd in their natiue tongue,
    As if all language on her lips had hung.

364.

Whereby the world did seeme to plead for right
Within her court, where in her princely chaire,
Astrea-like she sate with powerfull might
To right the wrong of those, that in despaire
Of other's helpe, to her did make repaire,
  Who after humble sute backe neuer went
  Through her court gates without true mind's content.

365.

Witnesse great *Burbon*, when that house of Guise
Did counterchecke thee in thy lawfull claime,
In thy defence what prince did then arise,
Or with strong hand, who in fight's bloodie frame
Did ioyne to wound thy rebell foes with shame?
  But England's queene, who still with fresh supplie
  Did send her forces gainst thine enemie:

366.

To beare the first brunt in those bloodie broyles,
That noble knight, the famous *Willoughby*,
Did crosse the seas, and through important toyles
Did lead a multitude, whose valiancie
Made France admire our English Britanie,
  Whom England's royall virgin did excite
  Vnto that warre t'aduance thee to thy right.

367.

And then to reinforce thy strength's decay
World-wondred *Norrice*, Mars his matchlesse sonne,
Did with three thousand souldiers passe the sea,
Who in French Britaine hauing once begunne,
Did not forsake thee, till thy warres were done,
  Whom many did in this thy cause insue,
  And in thy French dust did their bloods imbrue.

368.

An. eodem.
Earle of Es-
sex.

When noble *Deuoreux,* that heroicke knight,
To shew his loue to armes and cheualrie,
Ingag'd his person in that furious fight
Before that towne, hight Roan in Normandie,
His honor'd brother fighting valiantly;

Sir *Walter
Deuoreux.*

   Who though but yong, yet oft approu'd in fight,
   By a small shot was slaine in his owne sight.

369.

Sir *William
Sackuile.*

And thou braue *Sackuile, Buckhurst* third-borne birth,
Who in these warres didst change thy life for fame,
Although thy bones lie tomb'd in stranger earth,
Yet in thy countrie liues thy noble name
And honor'd friends, that still record the same:
   For though blacke death triumph ore humane breath,
   Yet vertue's deeds do liue in spight of death.

370.

Many more valiant men of no meane birth,
Whose names obscur'd, are yet not come to light,
Being slaine, did falling kisse their mother earth,
And with their foreheads trode the ground in fight,
Against vntruth t'aduance great *Burbon's* right,
   Who by their valour, fighting for renowne,
   Did at the length in peace enioy his crowne.

371.

Thus Albion's mistresse as an angell sent,
The sonnes of men from hel's blacke prince to saue,
The world's vsurped rule from Rome did rent,
And from her yoke sweet freedome's comfort gaue
To those her neighbours, that her helpe did craue,
   Restoring princes to their royaltie,
   Debas'd by Rome's insulting tyrannie.

372.

The which when that seuen-headed beast beheld,
Who proudly treads vpon the necks of kings
With indignation his high stomack sweld,
And of the adulterate sect forthwith he wings
Many bald priests t'enact pernicious things,
   Those close confessors, that most vse their skill
   To worke the weaker sex vnto their will.

373.

With these the bifront Iesuits, that cloake
Themselues in diuers shapes, did seeke againe,
Against their prince the people to prouoke,
And with pretence of zeale did thinke to traine
Their loyall hearts against their soueraigne:
   But these their base attempts tooke no euent,
   Seeing prudent Ioue their plots did still preuent.

An.
34.

374.

For at this time, the Irish *Oroick*,
That bloodie traytour to this kingdome's state,
That with his vtmost diligence did worke
With Rome and Spaine to execute their hate,
Being most secure of his vntimely fate,
   Preuented was, in what he did pretend
   In his foule treason by a traytor's end.

375.

For after all his plots at length he came
To proffer seruice to that roiall king,
Now monarch of this ile, and in his name,
All Ireland in subiection he would bring,
If he would shroud him with his soueraigne wing;
   But he braue prince, t'whom traitors hatefull beene,
   Did send that traitor to our noble queene.

376.

O peerelesse prince, that northerne starre so bright,
Whose shine did guide vs to the port of rest,
When our pure virgin lampe did lose her light,
If from thy sight these ruder times be blest,
But with one kingly glaunce, graunt this request,
  As liuing thou didst honour her great name,
  So shee being dead, O king, still loue the same.

377.

Persist, persist, to grace her being dead,
Who liuing did to thee all grace proclaime,
Against her name permit no scandall spread;
But quell those black-mouth'd monsters that defame
The Lord's anointed our *Elizae's* name,
  So thy great name 'gainst enuie's biting rage,
  May finde like fauour in the world's last age.

378.

After this rebel's ruine, in whose life
Rome did such hopefull confidence repose,
Hoping through him to raise some home-bred strife,
Vnable now t'auenge her on her foes,
By honour'd meanes in dealing martiall blowes;
  Being senselesse of all princely roialtie
  He sought reuenge by basest treacherie.

379.

An. Reg. 35.
Hight *Lopez* he, that was for physick's skill,
Highly respected in the prince's grace,
Corrupted was her loued life to spill,
And had the helpe of heauen not been in place,
The roiall virgin in a moment's space
  In stead of that, which should haue life protected
  Had tasted death in poison strong confected.

380.

But that great King of heau'n, whose watchfull eie
Did euer guard her maiden brest from taint
Of timelesse death, the drift did soone descrie,
And made false *Lopez* in the fact to faint,
Depicturing out his fault in feare's constraint,
  Who wretched traytor, for his blacke deed done,
  Blacke death and scandall in the world hath wonne.

He suffered death, *Anno Reg.* 36.

381.

Rome's demi-god that can at his dispose
By power from heau'n dispence with villanie,
Thus did his sanctitie of life disclose,
In plotting by inglorious treacherie,
Basely to act a virgin's tragedie;
  Whose force for fight seem'd both on seas and land,
  Too full of death for him to countermand.

382.

Yet once againe with contumelious vaunt,
Inuasion threatned was against this land,
Which did our queene's great heart so little daunt,
That to her conquering fleet she gaue command,
Which readie rig'd lay on the English strand,
  To seeke the foes for fight in their owne home,
  Thereby to ease them of their toyle to come.

383.

The royall fleet to do the dame's command,
Rig'd vp to dance on Amphitrite's greene,
With war-like musike's sound did launch from land,
To whom, in loue of Albion's honor'd queene,
Then easefull peace Spaine's warre more wisht hath beene,
  Whose bosomes twice ten thousand men did fill,
  Train'd vp to tread the paths of warre with skill.

The honorable voyage to Cadiz, *Anno Reg.* 38. Set downe in the end of the last part of the second volume of Nauigations of *R. Hakluit.*

384.

Two noble peeres stood vp to lead them out,
The one hight *Howard* he, that with renowne
Gainst Spaine's blacke fleet successefully had fought,
Who now, though honor'd age his head did crowne
With snow-white haires of siluer like soft downe;
    Yet in despight of yeares respect did goe,
    As generall of the fleet against the foe.

385.

The other peere, whose heart heauen grac'd with grace
Of goodly gifts, was *Essex* noble knight,
Whom from his youth treading the honour'd race
Of valiant men, true vertue did excite,
T'affect renowne in warre with chiefe delight,
    Who best aboue the best of high command,
    In this exploit went generall of the land.

386.

These lords, not like the foes, did put in vre,
Their high exploit, who when their blacke fleete came
Did treate of peace, to make vs more secure;
But they each where their purpose to proclaime,
Chose fame for herauld to denounce the same,
    Threatning all nations with their dames iust ire,
    That should as agents with their foe conspire.

They did pro-
claime their
intended voy-
age in Greeke,
Latin, French,
Spanish, &c.
through most
parts of Eu-
rope.

387.

Many more nobles drew their willing swords
In this exploit to trie th'Iberian might:
Braue *Sussex*, *Howard*, *Harbert*, valiant lords,
Lord *Warden*, *Burk*, stout *Veere* and *Clifford* hight,
With *Lodowicke* of Nassau that stranger knight,
    Don Christopher young prince of *Portugale*,
    And *Vanderfords* the Belgian's generall.

388.

From Plimmouth port in safe transport of these
And many gallants more, two hundred keele
Did with swift winde cut through the wauie seas,
While shee, whose heart th'effects of grace did feele,
Not giuing trust vnto the strength of steele,
   While England's sacred queene, while shee, I say,
   For her faire fleete to this effect did pray:

389.

" Thou guide of all the world, great king of heauen,
That seest all hearts with thy all-seeing eye,
Thou knowest what cause vs to this warre hath driuen,
No thirst of blood, of wealth, or dignitie,
No malice of reuenge or iniurie;
   But to defend thy truth, we lift our armes
   And to preuent our foes intended harmes.

Recorded by him that wrote this voiage, who carried it with him into Spaine, translated into Latin by D. Marbecke.

390.

Heare then, O king of heau'n, thy hand-maid's prayer,
Giue full effect vnto our iust desire,
In midst of stormes t'our fleet vouchsafe thy care,
And with thy heau'nly fortitude inspire
Our souldiers hearts, that they may not retire
   Vnto their homes without victorious fame,
   T'aduance the glorie of thy holy name."

391.

Thus pray'd *Eliza*, to whose iust request
The God of Hosts aduisefull audience gaue,
Who downe descending from his heau'nly rest,
Did safely lead her ships, as she did craue,
To Cadiz harbor ore the surging waue,
   Where to all eyes appear'd his true foresigne,
   That gainst th'Iberians they should victors shine.

392.

As that thrice happie bird, the peacefull doue,
When the old world groaning beneath the raigne
Of giants raging rule, was drown'd by Ioue,
Brought heau'nly newes of a new world againe
Vnto the Arke, then floting on the maine:
　　So now a doue did with her presence greet
　　Elizae's Arke, then admirall of the fleet.

393.

Recorded by
the Author
then present.

For loe the fleet riding at seas in sight
Of Cadiz towers, making that towne the marke
Of their desire, the doue did stay her flight
Vpon the maine yard of that stately barke,
Which long before that time was term'd the Arke,
　　Whose vnexpected presence did professe
　　Peace to the fleet; but to the foes distresse:

394.

Who from the browes of Cadiz loftie towers
With eyes amaz'd, viewing so many a keele
Floting vpon their seas, and seeing such powers
Of martiall people arm'd in brightest steele,
The cold effects of fainting feare did feele,
　　Through whose faint brests remembrance now did run
　　Of ancient wrongs to England's empresse done.

395.

The fleete descri'd, the citie high did ring
Each where with horrid sound of shrill alarmes,
In euery street Bellona loud did sing
The song of battaile, and the foes in swarmes
Did throng together in the streets to armes,
　　While fearefull noise of children's wofull cries,
　　And women's shrikes did pierce the echoing skies.

396.

The gates were open set, out rush't the boast,
Both horse and foote in armes confused sound,
Who vaunting of their power did vainely boast,
Their fainting foes in battaile to confound,
If their bold feete durst presse the sandie ground,
    Not doubting all their fleete, with fire t'inflame,
    If from their ships to fight on shore they came.

397.

And in the gulfie mouth of that faire bay,
Where the proud waues doe wash the towne's white breast,
The Spanish nauie ready anchoring lay,
All mighty ships bound for the Indian east;
But now for fight themselues they soone addrest,
    With whom twice ten stout gallies did prepare
    'Gainst th'English fleete to trie the chaunce of warre.

398.

The honour'd peeres, great *Essex*, and his mate
Renowned *Howard*, Time's swan-white hair'd sonne,
Sitting in counsell wisely did debate,
How by their fleete with best aduantage wonne,
Against the foes the fight might be begunne;
    For both the castle, forts and towne in sight,
    Did threaten danger in the nauall fight.

399.

But through the windowes of heauen's crystall bowres,
Ioue seeing the foemen's force so full of dread,
The citie so well fenc'd with loftie towres;
The sea with faire ships fill'd, the field ore spread
With men of armes, that from the towne made head,
    Did send to shield *Elizae's* fleete from harmes,
    His braine-borne childe, th'vnconquered queene of armes.

400.

Who to effect th'Olympian god's great will,
About the fleete from ship to ship did flie,
And with such courage euery heart did fill,
Inflaming their desires in fight to trie
The valour of the vaunting enemie,
    That euery one did thirst to trample downe
    The loftie pride of Cadiz towring towne.

401.

Now Earle of
Suffolk. The Norfolke noble duke's vndaunted sonne,
Sterne-visag'd like the grim-fac'd god of war,
As was decreed, the fight at first begun,
Who to the foes like some disastrous star,
Or blazing comet did appeare from far;
    Shooting forth fierie beames from his blacke ship,
    Which with the mounting waues did forward skip.

402.

Each aduerse force to fight drew forth their powers,
And in a golden morne, when Phœbus drew
From off the battlements of Cadize towers,
The ruddie cheekt Aurorae's pearlie dew,
The thundring bullets interchanged flew,
    And either side a glorious day to win,
    With deadly furie did the fight begin.

403.

The guns, astuns with sounds rebounds from shore
The souldier's eares, and death on mischiefe's back
Spit from the canon's mouth with horrid rore
Flies to and fro in clowdes of pitchie black,
And 'mongst the valiant men makes spoilefull wrack,
    While either part like lions far'd in fight,
    None feeling seruile feare of death's afright.

404.

Thus when stout *Howard* had begun the fight
With many more to quell the foemen's pride,
The noble *Deuoreux*, that vndaunted knight,
Who stood asterne his ship and wishly ei'd,
How deepe the skirmish drew on either side,
  Nere stai'd, as was decreed, to second those
  In the maine fight, but rusht amongst the foes.

405.

And as we see the sunne sometimes shine cleare
Amidst the skie, then muffle his bright face
In sable clouds, and straight againe appeare,
So famous *Essex* did applie each place,
Sometimes incircled round with foes embrace
  He stood in fight, and sometimes seene of all,
  He in the forefront did his foes appall.

406.

Which when graue *Howard* view'd from farre well dight
In noble armes, himselfe he did betake
Vnto his pinnace with lord *William* hight,
His honor'd sonne, and with their powers to make
The fight more hot, into the presse they brake,
  Where with fresh strength they labour'd to repell
  The foes stout pride, twixt whom the fight grew fell.

407.

So long as faire Aurorae's light did shine,
They equall fought and neither had the best ;
But when the feruent sunne began decline
From th'hot meridian point and day decreast,
Feare did inuade each bold Iberian's brest,
  Who through the danger of the darkesome waue
  Did flie their foes, themselues from death to saue.

408.

To shun Charybdis iawes, they helplesse fell
In Scyllae's gulfe; for after all their braues,
Being all too weake the English to repell,
Their ships they left, and leapt into the waues,
In whose soft bosome many found their graues;
 And lest ought good might to their foes redound,
 They burnt their ships and ran them on the ground.

409.

The gallies fled, the ships with secret fire
Inflam'd, did burst to shew their burning light;
Then from the shore th'Iberians did retire
Close to their walles, who boasting of their might
In equall ground before did wish for fight;
 But now beneath their walles scarce made they stand;
 For without fight the victors went on land.

410.

All from the ships did cluster to the shore,
Forth marcht the foote, whose hearts emboldned were
With their late fight, and in the front before
Great *Essex* breath'd exhorts in euery eare
To charge the foes; and not in vaine to beare
 The name of first, but first himselfe to show
 In euery deed, he first did charge the foe.

411.

With such swift force, as when wilde Neptune raues,
And ore the shore breaking his wonted bounds,
Riding in triumph on his winged waues,
Runnes vnresisted ouer lands and grounds,
And in his way all in his power confounds;
 So from the fleet at shore went th'English downe
 To charge the foes inranckt before the towne.

412.

The battels ioyn'd; but by their valour's might,
The valiant English in one hower's space
Brake through the foe-men's rankes, who turn'd to flight;
Did turne their backes and gaue the victors place,
Who to the towne pursu'd with speedie chace,
   Whose walles th'Iberians flying from the field
   Against their foes did long to make their shield.

413.

And being entred with confused cries,
The gates were shut, and in the towne each where,
A diuers noise about with horror flies;
Then in the streets thicke troopes of men appeare,
Some to the gates, some to the walles with feare
   Amazed runne, and euery hold about
   They stuffe with men, to keepe their foe-men out.

414.

Meane time to triumph in proud Cadiz fall,
Illustrate *Essex* did approch the towne,
Where scaling ladders laid vnto the wall
Were fill'd with men, who climing for renowne,
Did hazard death from off the walles cast downe:
   For from th'assault to force them to retire,
   Thicke fell downe darts, huge stones, and dreadfull fire.

415.

The fearefull cries of men on either side,
Rung through the towne, as they the walles did scale,
Not long the bold defendants did abide
Th'assailants by their prowesse did preuaile,
The foes gaue backe, their fainting hearts did faile,
   Who left the walles, and through the streets did runne,
   With ruthfull tidings how the walles were wonne.

416.

Vpon the battlements, the blood red crosse
Appear'd in sight, and from the walles downe went
The English troopes, and to the gates did passe,
Where th'iron barres in sunder they did rent,
Beate downe the posts, and all the iewses brent,
    And passage wide to them without did win,
    To whom the houses farre appear'd within.

417.

Then all the host, led by that aged lord,
The sea's chiefe admirall, rusht through the gate,
And through the towne with fierie shot and sword
Did force their way in euery street and strait,
Euen to the publike market, where of late
    The foes had purpos'd in the king's highstreet,
    To make their commons reindeuous to meet.

418.

There now the battell fresh againe begun,
For making head vnto that place, the foe
To reinforce their strength, in troopes did run,
While others downe from houses tops did throw
Ruine and death on th'English bands below,
    Where fighting gainst such ods, they haplesse lost
Sir *Iohn Wing.*   Braue *Wingfield* hight, a leader in the host.

419.

On whose dissolued life, such deepe remorse
The English tooke, that all with loud exclaime
Rusht on th'Iberians bold, and did enforce
Their speedie flight, then furie did enflame
The souldiers hearts, and in the bloodie game
    Of raging Mars, remorselesse they were all,
    To wreake reuenge for worthie *Wingfield's* fall.

420.

Like angrie lions rob'd of their deare yong,
The houses round about they now inuade,
The portals, posts and thresholds downe are flung,
The gates and walles of stone so strongly made,
And doores fast barr'd with earth are leuell made,
  And all high turrets and strong chambers shake
  With th'hot inuading, which the souldiers make.

421.

The inward roomes are fill'd with wofull sounds,
And wailing noise of folke in wretched plight,
The buildings all with larums loud rebounds,
And women with yong infants in affright,
Through chambers wide shunning the souldier's sight,
  Runne heere and there to seeke some couert place,
  To hide themselues from angrie Mars his face.

422.

About the parent's knees, the children swarmes,
Calling in vaine for helpe with pitious cries,
The spouse fast clips her husband in her armes,
In whose sad brest his cold heart fainting dies,
Seeing the armed men before his eies,
  Stand with bright swords in thicke tumultuous croud
  At th'entrie doores, crying out with clamors loud.

423.

But th'English all, that neuer vse to lift
Their hands against a yeelding enemie
By nature milde, not proud of fortune's gift,
Did not insult vpon their miserie,
But with milde hand did vse the victorie,
  And after fight they all abhorring blood,
  Did only tend the spoile of golden good.

424.

Both the braue generals, by a strict command
About the towne, this mercie did proclaime,
That none thenceforth should vse the force of hand,
Nor offer wrong to any virgin dame,
That would sweet beautie keepe from lustfull shame,
   Which vnreprou'd edict amongst all men,
   Through th'English host inuiolate hath been.

425.

Amongst the captiues not the basest mate
With any sad designe they vexed sore,
The female sex vntoucht inuiolate
Did freely passe with all that golden store
Of chaines, and gemmes which they about them bore,
   And all religious folke did find like grace,
   Free without ransome to depart the place.

426.

Thrice valiant victors, euer may my rimes
Suruiue on earth, that in their life may liue
This famous conquest to all future times,
That from the best, that for true praise do striue,
All men to you the laurell wreath may giue,
   Which that milde mercie, which you then did show,
   Doth more deserue then conquest gainst the foe.

427.

After the souldier had return'd from spoile
Loaden with riches of the ransackt towne,
To yeeld fit compensation to the toile
Of each man's paines, with fauour or renowne,
The generals did each souldier's merit crowne,
   And gaue to many a well deseruing wight
   That noble order of true martiall knight.

428.

That noble order, which in antique time
In top of fame's high tower tooke chiefest place,
To which by vertue valour's steps did clime;
Was then no base mind's meed, that nere had grace
T'ensue fame's feeting in true vertue's race;
    Though now the aged world to dotage growne,
    This noble order scarce is truly knowne.

429.

But now to sing the spoile and last decay
Of that faire towne by her owne folke forlorne,
The host all readie to depart away,
Intending first in funerall flames to burne
Her fatall pride, and all her pompe oreturne,
    Did in thicke concourse cluster to confound,
    Her high top towers and eu'n them with the ground.

430.

In number like the golden flowers in spring,
In forme like furies of the Stygian caue:
The souldiers high on houses tops do fling
Their burning brands, and round do raage and raue,
To burie that faire towne in ashie graue,
    While hungrie flames borne vp on golden wings,
    Flies through the aire, and far their splendor flings.

431.

Then the faire wals inricht with painting's grace,
And portals proud of gold are all cast downe,
Sterne Mulciber in his bright armes embrace
Doth graspe the towres, and on th'inflamed towne
Through rolling clouds of smoake doth sternely frowne:
    Whose fierce fiers climing houses far away,
    By foes are seene to worke the towne's decay.

432.

Thus burnt Spaine's Cadiz fam'd for that faire place,
Where great Alcides, when his sword did tame
The triple Gerion borne of tyrant's race,
Did fixe his pillars t'eternise his name,
With *ne plus vltra* grauen on the same;
    Thus did it burne captiu'd in English yoke,
    And all her fame lay stifled in the smoke.

433.

After the spoile, exchange of captiues made
For those, that Spaine had long captiu'd before,
Each souldier's prise aboard the fleet conuei'd,
Leauing the towne despoil'd of all her store,
All made returne vnto the ships at shore;
    At whose depart such after-signe was seene,
    As had before at their arriuall been.

434.

Recorded by
the Author
then present.

For hoysing saile at sea, loe as before
Vpon the Arke a doue her flight did stay,
With which departing from th'Iberian shore,
She from the same departed not away;
But kept her station till that happie day,
    That all the fleet did with the compleat hoast
    Arriue in triumph on the English coast.

435.

Thus when vpon *Elizae's* royall brow,
Time's honor'd age in print had set his signe,
Euen then her arme Spaine's stiffened pride did bow
And when her youthfull daies did most decline,
Then did the King of heau'n to her assigne
    The euer youthfull wreath of sacred bay,
    In signe of triumph to her line's last day.

436.

The vtmost kingdomes canopi'd of skie,
Did beare record of her triumphant fame,
The vastest ocean, that did farthest lie,
With each small creeke and hauen in the same,
Did then resound the praises of her name:
   Which to her friend's defence, her foemen feare,
   Her crosse-crown'd fleet about the world did beare.

437.

For all sea-bordering townes, that subiect were
Vnto the crowne of Rome-supporting Spaine,
Who high their breasts aboue the waues did beare,
Did tremble to behold the crookt stern'd traine
Of English ships still floating on the maine;
   For towards the sea's greene bounds they often bore,
   And many townes destroy'd vpon the shore.

438.

Renowned *Clifford* on the fruitfull deepe
Like Ioue-borne Perseus, that illustrate knight,
In his swift Pegasus, the seas did sweepe,
And after many a prize surpriz'd in fight,
To make the land record his powerfull might,
   He at that time with his triumphant host,
   Got noble conquest on the Indian coast.

Anno
38.

439.

Fortune with fame his high attempts did crowne,
And his dread name the foes with feare did fright,
Saint *Iohn de Porta Rico* that strong towne,
And her faire castle, which did seeme in sight
Impregnable gainst all assaults in fight,
   His hands to heapes of fruitlesse dust did burne,
   And with her spoile he home did safe returne.

440.

The valiant English still did worke much woe
Vnto the foemen both on seas and land,
Eliza still did triumph ore the foe,
And day by day vpon the English strand
Arriu'd rich prize surpriz'd by force of hand,
　　Whereby th'Iberian folke made poore and bare,
　　In heart did curse the canser of the warre.

441.

But leaue we heere of forren deeds to sing,
And turne we home at sound of those alarms,
Which on thy shores, O England, high did ring;
And let vs waile, alas, the wofull harmes,
Which did befall that valiant man of armes,
　　Who after all his glorie and renowne,
　　Beneath too hard a fate felt fortune's frowne.

442.

Tyrone that traytor, from whose treacherie
The first chiefe cause of his annoy did spring,
Disloyall to *Elizae's* maiestie;
Had now begun to set the war on wing
On th'Irish coast, whose townes and plaines did ring
　　With sad report of bloodie actions done,
　　By the bold rebels and the base *Tyrone*.

443.

An. Reg. 41.　Tidings whereof to England's rockie bound,
Borne ore the ocean's backe on wings of winde,
The shores with Mars his rugged voice did sound,
And noble *Essex* generall was assign'd
To crosse the fruitfull deepe, whose honor'd minde
　　Did wing him forward with desire of fame,
　　On earth to purchase an immortall name.

444.

Yet towards the coast when he this iourney tooke,
The king of flames that with delight did crowne
All that faire day before, did change his looke,
The heau'ns did thunder loud, the clouds did frowne,
And in the way Ioue cast pale lightning downe,
  Presaging sad euent of things to come,
  Which tooke effect at his returning home.

445.

At his returning home, when his deare dame
The great *Eliza*, with maiesticke frowne
Gan change milde looks, when fortune foe to fame
Did turne her wheele about, and hurring downe
His towring state, all hope of life did drowne
  In death's deepe waues, whose most vntimely end
  Both heau'n and earth lamenting did befriend.

446.

For that blacke morne, when he without appall
To lose his life vnto the blocke was led,
The sunne in heau'n, as for his Phaeton's fall,
In sable clouds did hide his golden hed,
And from so sad a sight away he fled;
  While wofull heau'n with dolefull teares sent downe,
  For his sad fall the world in woe did drowne.

447.

He being dead, being dead, alas, and gone,
That hopefull lord, hight *Mountioy*, did succeed
As generall in the warre against *Tyrone;*
To whom all-seeing Ioue tooke speciall heed,
And did direct his hand in euery deed,
  Who would not haue *Elizae's* vnstain'd praise,
  Distain'd by rebels in her aged daies.

448.

For what hath she in her affaires decreed,
Euen to her royall liue's last breathing space,
In which Ioue did not euer grace her deed,
Yea now when ripe yeares rugged prints had place
Vpon the fore-front of her princely face,
    Then did her gratious God with compleat praise,
    Perfect the vpshot of her aged daies.

449.

Anno eodem 42. Grimestone in his translation of the booke of the warres of the Netherlands.

The happie Belgians on the marine coast,
In a pight field against a prince of name,
In person fighting 'midst his royall host,
Did purchase conquest, captiues, gold and fame,
By th'only aid which from *Eliza* came :
    Without whose helpe on which their hopes did build,
    All had been lost, the foes had won the field.

450.

For when the Austrian prince on Newport Sands,
After the slaughter of the valiant Scot,
Had giuen charge vpon the aduerse bands,
When by thicke volleyes of their murdring shot,
Many stout men had drawne death's fatall lot ;
    Then many Belgians fainting fled away,
    And left their friends to win or lose the day.

451.

'Mongst whom the English chiefely did sustaine
The furious brunt of that important fight,
Where many worthie men were helplesse slaine,
Who rather chose to make that day the night
Of death's approch, then turne their backs for flight ;
    Who all had fallen by death without remorse,
    Had not the *Veres* renew'd their fainting force.

452.

For the bold brothers both the valiant *Veres*,
Deepe wounds did purchase to regaine the day,
The one breath'd comfort in the souldiers eares,
While th'other through the foes with violent sway
Of his horse troopes did force a dreadfull way,
   Through which the Belgians that before had fled,
   Might 'gainst the fainting foes againe make head.

453.

The foemen fled, the ground was stro'd with harmes
Of their mishap, their duke fled fast away,
Leauing his horse of honour and his armes
Vnto the victors to remaine for ay,
As signes of conquest and that glorious day,
   Which by *Elizae's* auxilarie traine,
   Then agents there the Belgians did obtaine.

454.

Thus to the life of our triumphant dame
Time in her reigne no yeere did multiplie,
Which fortune did not dignifie with fame,
Or praise of some illustrate victorie;
'Gainst Rome, 'gainst Spaine, or th'Austrian enemie
   'Gainst whom that houre that she expir'd her breath
   She di'd victorious in the armes of death.

455.

For when the Austrian duke with his proud hoast,
Atrides-like laid siege to little Troy,
And by a solemne vow did vainely boast,
Not to depart vntill he did destroy
That English towne; yet to his owne annoy,
   He there did lie while th'horses of the sunne,
   Their yeare's race thrice about the heauen had runne.

Anno Reg.
43, 44,

456.

For England's *Hector* and his valiant brother,
That time's young *Troylus* did the duke appall,
And his best hopes in blood and dust did smother;
Yea many a thousand at that siege did fall
In death's blacke graue before the towne's strong wall,
　　Which while the Belgian patronesse did liue,
　　Vnto the foes in fight the foile did giue.

457.

And as our queene in forraine-bred debate,
From hence to heauen victorious tooke her flight,
So here at home before her liue's last date,
Triumphant sounds of belles the starres did smite,
And bright bon-fiers the darkesome euen did light
　　With gladsome flames for worthy victorie,
　　Atchieu'd against the Irish enemie.

458.

An. eodem.　Yea, when the hand of vnremorsefull fate,
Had euen spun out the thred of her liue's clew,
Tyron, that long disturber of her state,
With shame of his offence remorsefull grew,
And on his knees did then for mercie sue:
　　That dying, she might say with vading breath,
　　I left no foes vnuanquisht at my death.

459.

But woe, alas, the dust-borne pompe of earth,
Made thrall to death, returnes to dust againe;
All vnder heauen, that haue their beeing and breath
Of nature's gift, no longer doe remaine,
Then nature doth their brittle state sustaine,
　　The prince and swaine to death are both alike,
　　No ods are found when he with dart doth strike.

460.

For I, that whilome sung with cheerefull breath
Her roiall reigne, whose like no age hath seene,
Now cannot sing; but weepe to thinke how death,
All pitilesse of what before had beene,
Did rob poore England of so rich a queene;
  And if I sing, I must in my sad song,
  Exclaime on death for doing vs such wrong.

461.

For doing vs such wrong to dim the light
Of England's virgin glorie then decaid,
Which, while heauen's light the earth's broade face shall smite,
All virgins shall admire and still vpbraid
That *Tarquin* death, with death of such a maide:
  For her, whose virgin blood no *Tarquin's* staine,
  Did euer taint, O death, thy dart hath slaine.

462.

That day shee di'd, which to her roiall sire,
To great *Plantagenet* hath fatall been;
That day, when fates did his sad death conspire:
That day when his young *Edward* dead was seene,
That day when *Mary* left to be a queene:
  That day from vs did our *Eliza* goe,
  That day, that tyrant death did worke our woe.

Thursday.

463.

But why do we 'gainst death vse such complaint,
Seeing not in youth, then short of yeares to crowne
Her head with age, she di'de by death's constraint,
But ripe in yeares, and loaden with renowne;
Made mellow for the graue, she lai'd her downe:
  And leauing earth that part, which earth had giuen,
  On faith's strong wings she tooke her flight for heauen.

Heere Clio ceast, her lute no more did sound,
But in a moment mounting from the ground,
She vanisht from my sight, and with her fled
The place of pleasure which mine eyes had fed;
With which all had been lost, if in minde,
My dreame's Idæa had not stai'd behinde.

FINIS.

END OF PART V.

VOLUME THE LAST.

CPSIA information can be obtained
at www.ICGtesting.com
Printed in the USA
LVHW081350190819
628141LV00006B/120/P